I really appreciate Robert's cle: heart in the discipline of His ch passion in how God pursues th redeemed. Robert speaks to the role of biblical community in God's redeeming of His bride through loving and redemptive discipline. It would be incredibly unloving for God to not correct His children and this work highlights the deep love of God through church discipline.

Lee Lewis
Forth Worth Campus Pastor, The Village Church, Fort Worth, TX

One of the most painful things to do as a pastor is to teach and lead out in the discipline of the church. We need need courage. This books helps encourage us as we obey the call for the purity of the gospel through the local church.

Darrin Patrick
Lead Pastor of The Journey, St. Louis, MI
Author of *Church Planter: The Man, The Message, The Mission*, and *For the City*

Books about church discipline tend to treat well one or two areas on the topic. Robert Cheong's contribution is unique, then, for its breadth: it is scripturally rich, theologically robust, narratively engaging, practically saturated, and ecclesially helpful. It is also unique because its author, a scholar pastor, has been engaged in hundreds of church discipline cases either personally or by means of counseling and training others, so his book reflects a wisdom forged through experience.

Here are three highlights that await you: the narrative opening and closing of each chapter will grip your attention so that you won't be able to put the book down, the gospel centered writing will give you a fresh perspective on the nature and purposes of church discipline, and the appendixes will treat your questions about how to engage in the actual process of redeeming the church through discipline.

Gregg R. Allison
Professor of Christian Theology, The Southern Baptist Theological Seminary, Louisville, KY

The subject of church discipline is no walk in the park. People's lives hang in the balance. My friend Robert clearly shows that church discipline is an integral part of gospel centered ministry both theologically and practically. He provides a step by step guide so that the reader understands not only what discipline is but how to go about it. In the process, he gives us a model for the body of Christ ministering to one another in the grace, compassion, and humility characteristic of the gospel. This is a must read for every pastor.

Rob Green
Pastor of Counseling and Seminary Ministries, Faith Church, Lafayette, IN

I appreciate this book for three reasons. First, it's theologically rich, anchoring church discipline in the glorious drama of God's redeeming work. Second, it's pastorally wise, written by a seasoned shepherd who knows the joy and pain of leading and protecting the flock. And third, it's practically helpful – the appendices alone are worth the price of the book. Robert's work on this important subject is a gift to every gospel-loving church leader and church member.

Bob Thune
Co-author of *The Gospel-Centered Life*
Lead Pastor, Coram Deo Church Community, Omaha, NE

Many churches are realizing that their weakness stems in part from a failure to follow what the scriptures teach about church discipline. Robert Cheong's book is a wonderfully practical and refreshingly gracious treatment of the topic. Even those who don't subscribe to everything Cheong says will find this book to be a significant help. Indeed, the appendices are a must read, for they are full of practical advice on how to carry out the process of church discipline and restoration. I suspect many pastors and church leaders will be turning regularly to Cheong's work for instruction.

Thomas R. Schreiner
James Buchanan Harrison Professor of New Testament Interpretation,
The Southern Baptist Theological Seminary, Louisville, KY

I followed a pastor and mentor who faithfully led our church to practice biblical church discipline. Of all the comments and expressions of appreciation I could make about my predecessor Bill Goode, that is by far one of the most important. His courage to be a biblical pastor made my job much easier and I am forever indebted to him. The church of Jesus Christ needs to carefully heed what my friend Robert Cheong has written. This book is wise, winsome, gospel-centered and full of grace. Some of what it teaches will require taking hard and sometimes unpopular steps. Do it for many reasons, including the respect and appreciation you will receive from the pastor who follows you.

Stephen Viars
Senior Pastor, Faith Church, Lafayette, IN

It has taken courage for Robert Cheong to write this book. He is knowingly wading into an area of much confusion and regret in churches. Church discipline is a ministry which, even if it is done well, it can be a painful experience for all involved. So it also takes the heart of a shepherd to speak to those leading through church discipline or living somewhere in it. Robert has the courage and shepherd's heart – and the Gospel clarity – to help us all in difficult times where church discipline is the redemptive way ahead.

Andy Farmer
Pastor of Community and Care, Covenant Fellowship Church, Glen Mills, PA

How we engage sin in the church reflects our view of God and His redemptive character. Robert Cheong carefully guides readers through how his local church, Sojourn Community Church, shepherds hearts back toward Jesus through restorative and instructive church discipline. *God Redeeming His Bride* is a timely addition to any pastor's – or church member for that matter – field manual for real-life ministry. I commend it to pastors who desire faithful application of God's Word in every aspect of their ministry, especially the difficult ones. This book is meant to be taken with you into the trenches of spiritual warfare.

Ed Stetzer
President, LifeWay Research, Nashville, TN

This book is a treasure-trove of grace, wisdom, and gospel truths regarding the difficult topic of church discipline, drawn from a pastor's hard-earned experience with the reality of sin and the power of the gospel. Robert Cheong shows how biblical church discipline is rooted in God's mission to bring redemption to sinners and sufferers through the work of Jesus proclaimed by the church. We see how God calls his church to participate in his relentless, loving pursuit of his people. Filled with Christ-centered theology, gracious wisdom, and practical advice, this handbook is highly recommended for pastors and ministry leaders.

Justin Holcomb
Executive Director, *The Resurgence*
Lead Pastor, Mars Hill Church U-District
Adjunct Professor of Theology, Reformed Theological Seminary, Seattle, WA

The title itself—*God Redeeming His Bride*—should alert us that this is not your typical book on "church discipline." Dr. Cheong does not disappoint as he places church discipline in its proper place as the corporate relational process of speaking God's truth in love for God's glory and the maturity and purity of God's people. Eminently practical while deeply theological, this gospel-centered approach to church discipline is a ground-breaking book that every pastor and every church leadership team should read and apply.

Robert W. Kellemen
Executive Director, Biblical Counseling Coalition, Lafayette, IN

God Redeeming His Bride is one of the best tools available to the church today that can help us recover the critical and pastoral practice of church discipline. Robert Cheong proves himself to be a modern day Richard Baxter as he has given us a thoroughly biblical, deeply theological, eminently practical, and easily accessible book I believe God will use to bring greater health to our local churches.

Joe Thorn
Author, *Note to Self: The Discipline of Preaching to Yourself*; Lead Pastor, Redeemer Fellowship
St. Charles, IL

Robert Cheong is committed to fostering gospel-centered communities that express the full range of God's love toward one another, even when it comes to correction and discipline. He expands our view of church discipline considerably by mining the riches of God's Word and grand redemptive story—beyond the handful of classic "church discipline" passages—and casting a vision for the whole church living as a patient, loving, wise, intentional, and personally engaged community. He's packed the appendices with invaluable practical guidelines to help us diligently work out the details.

Mike Wilkerson
Author of *Redemption: Freed by Jesus from the Idols We Worship and the Wounds We Carry*
Pastor and Director of Biblical Counseling, Mars Hill Church Seattle, WA

It is one thing to believe, in theory, in what God says in the Bible about the necessity of church discipline. It is another thing altogether to know how to navigate the process in the case of an unrepentant, falling church member. In this book, Robert Cheong, with biblical brilliance and pastoral compassion, provides a model for churches and leaders. Even those who hold to a different model of church government can benefit from seeing Robert Cheong trace out a path. This book is obviously the result of many years of prayer and practice. Read it not only for its helpful information, but also for its heart.

Russell D. Moore
Author, *Adopted for Life* and *Tempted and Tried*
Dean, Southern Baptist Theological Seminary, Louisville, KY

It was impossible for me to read this book without being personally convicted by my lack of faithfulness to live out the radical love of Jesus in the context of a community on mission. My failure to pursue people who have sinned and hurt the church was shown to be significant. Additionally, the book is full of sage advice on exactly HOW to walk through the rigors of church discipline. The day after I read it, I found myself quoting it several times. It's hard for me to imagine someone writing a more helpful, practical, gospel-centered book on church discipline.

Abe Meysenburg
Pastor and Elder, Soma Communities, Tacoma, WA

Robert Cheong's book has become my new favorite on the painfully glorious topic of church discipline. Our brother has given us biblical moorings, gospel implications and practical wisdom for doing the hard and heart work of discipline in the life of the local church. This book will help many Christians understand why John Calvin insisted that church discipline is one of the three essential marks of the church. But it will also make the gospel, itself, more beautiful to many, as Jesus' passionate love for his bride is explained and applied in such a profound and practical way.

Scotty Smith
Founding Pastor
Christ Community Church, Franklin, TN
Adjunct Professor of Practical Theology at Covenant Theological Seminary,
Redeemer Theological Seminary, Westminster Theological Seminary

As difficult and painful as it can be, church discipline is a crucial obligation that Jesus has given to us as his people. But how do you do it? As a pastor, how do you both care for those who are in sin and at the same time lead the church as a whole to exercise its duty to exercise discipline? And why is church discipline necessary in the first place? These are some of the questions that Robert Cheong addresses in his book *God Redeeming His Bride*. Setting the concept of church discipline in the context of the Gospel and God's work of redemption, Cheong gives highly practical advice about every step in the process – encouraging and teaching along the way. This will be a helpful book for any pastor facing the prospect of leading his church through the difficult – but ultimately redemptive – process of church discipline.

Greg Gilbert
Author, *What is the Gospel?*
Senior Pastor, Third Avenue Baptist Church, Louisville, KY

ROBERT K. CHEONG

GOD REDEEMING HIS BRIDE

A HANDBOOK FOR CHURCH DISCIPLINE

CHRISTIAN FOCUS

Robert K. Cheong serves as Pastor of Care at Sojourn Community Church in Louisville, Kentucky. Before receiving a M.Div. and Ph.D. at The Southern Baptist Theological Seminary, he served in the nuclear-powered Navy followed by almost a decade in the corporate world. Robert is married to Karen and they have three grown children. He has a passion to equip the church to engage in God's mission through gospel care in community.

Unless otherwise indicated Scripture quotations are from *The Holy Bible, English Standard Version*, copyright © 2001 by Crossway Bibles, a division of Good News Publishers. Used by permission. All rights reserved. ESV Text Edition: 2007.

Scripture quotations marked NIV are taken from the Holy Bible, *New International Version*®. NIV®. Copyright©1973, 1978, 1984 by International Bible Society. Used by permission of Zondervan. All rights reserved.

Scripture quotations marked NASB are taken from the *New American Standard Bible*®, Copyright © 1960, 1962, 1963, 1968, 1971, 1972, 1973, 1975, 1977, 1995 by The Lockman Foundation Used by Permission. (www.Lockman.org)

Scripture quotations marked NLT are taken from the Holy Bible, *New Living Translation*, copyright © 1996. Used by permission of Tyndale House Publishers, Inc., Wheaton, Illinois 60189. All rights reserved.

Copyright © Robert K. Cheong 2012

ISBN 978-1-84550-719-0

10 9 8 7 6 5 4 3 2 1

Published in 2012
by
Christian Focus Publications, Ltd
Geanies House, Fearn,
Ross-shire, IV20 1TW, Scotland
www.christianfocus.com

Cover design by Paul Lewis

Printed by Bell and Bain, Glasgow

CONTENTS

Dedication

To all of God's people who pursue and encourage one
another to fight the good fight of faith.

Foreword

I love the church. I say that without embarrassment or qualification. The bulk of my life and ministry has reflected, albeit inadequately, that passionate conviction. I am not starry-eyed in my love for the church. I know that the church we all experience is far from the church of my dreams, or more accurately the church of my theology. But that notwithstanding, 'love the church' should be every Christian's motto. Why? Because Christ does. The Bible tells us that explicitly in Ephesians 5:25. It is also implicit throughout the whole narrative of Scripture where we discover that God's purpose has always been to have a people for Himself; a people He reveals His glory to and a people He displays His glory through. If God loves the church with such passion and ruthless determination as the Bible story shows, then we as that church, should love her too.

Which is why the subject matter of this book is of such vital importance, and why my friend Robert Cheong has done us all such a huge favour in writing it. But he has not chosen an easy subject for his first book. I suspect that if church discipline were billed as a conference theme, it is unlikely the conference would attract a large, paying audience. The subject of church discipline will probably never 'go viral'. It is far too old school for that. It is not on the list of those things which satisfy our seemingly insatiable thirst for hype and the *avant-garde*. But church discipline is critical. It is not a topic of indulgence for the theology geeks among us. It is a topic for all of us who are concerned about the reputation of Christ, the health of His church and the credibility of the gospel. It really is that important.

Hebrews 12:5-11 tells us that the Lord disciplines those He loves. To *not* be disciplined is a mark of disinterest and lack of affection. It is a sign of illegitimacy (v. 8). So, given the significance and importance of discipline in the Lord's dealings with us, why is it such a neglected practice in the church?

I suspect there are a number of reasons; one is certainly image. Even the word *discipline* needs a make-over. In our world, discipline conjures images of authoritarianism, heavy-handedness, excessive control and hypocrites. I would suggest that if the average church member was asked about what came into their minds at the mention of church discipline, most would come up with words or images like ex-communication, shunning the offender, and very uncomfortable church meetings when someone was 'put out of fellowship'.

This book rectifies such prejudice. In these pages, church discipline is not given a face lift, for the simple reason that it doesn't need it. What Robert does is remove the misconceptions so it can be seen for the beautiful thing it really is. Here is his working definition of church discipline: *Church discipline is God's ongoing, redeeming work through His living Word and people as they fight the fight of faith together to exalt Christ and protect the purity of His Bride.* That surely has to go a long way in recapturing the dynamic and glory of God's instrument of maturity! What I really love about the book is the way that Robert's love for Christ, his love for the body of Christ and his understanding of the gospel of Christ shine through on every page. This is not primarily a book about strategies and procedure. It is about God's love for His people, His unfailing passion for our holiness and His unswerving commitment to His own glory. That's not to say that this is all about principles, to the extent that it neglects the practical details. There is plenty of help and direction in taking us through the necessary mechanics of implementing discipline at all levels. But the weight of the book is where it should be – on God's character and purpose as revealed in the the gospel. The book is helpful, insightful and well written. Most of all, it is deeply and consistently biblical.

Although I am neither a prophet nor the son of a prophet, I venture to suggest that this is a book whose time has come. As

I travel around, speaking with church leaders, listening to church people, I get an impression that people are becoming increasingly aware that things need to change, and increasingly dissatisfied with the status quo. A profession-based, lowest common-denominator Christianity is far from what the Lord had in mind and is never going to commend Christ to a lost world. The call of the gospel remains what it has always been: 'Be holy as I am holy'. An indispensable means to that end is the church being the church in the way we speak the gospel to each other, live the gospel out with each other and apply the gospel to each other's lives as we do life-on-life together on-mission.

I have been in Robert's home and spent time with his family. I have heard him talk about his love for Christ and His Church. I have watched him interact with colleagues and engage with those for whom he has responsibility. All this to say that there is a real connection between the author and the content of this book. This is not a theoretician writing. This is a man of integrity, who not only believes what he writes but lives it.

One of the key passages relating to church discipline is Matthew 18:15-20. It is surely significant that immediately prior to that, Matthew records Jesus speaking about the temptation to sin (vv. 7-9) and then telling the story of the lost sheep (vv. 10-14). Church discipline is God's appointed means of rescuing those of us who fall into temptation and walk away from the Lord and His people. The three teaching units together remind us of our vulnerability, our preciousness and out mutual responsibility.

This book, like no other I know on this subject, captures those truths. May the Lord use it to help us, as His church, become the beautiful bride she was purchased to be.

Enjoy grace,

Steve Timmis
Co-founder of *The Crowded House*, Co-founder of *Porterbrook Network*,
Director of *Acts 29* Europe
Sheffield, England

INTRODUCTION

THE BACK STORY

Writing a book on church discipline was never on my radar. But God had other plans. In 2009 Sojourn Community Church removed eight members from our fellowship for various scriptural violations that were embedded in months of rebellion and refusal to submit to Jesus and His church. This was the first time in the church's nine-year history in which we exercised God's redemptive steps of removal. The learning curve and heartache were immense. God was abundantly gracious as He guided us through the escalating and expanding movement of church discipline with not only the eight people we eventually removed from membership, but with the countless other situations where His people were intentionally pursued with the gospel, repented and came back to Christ.

During 2009, out of sheer desperation and necessity, I developed Sojourn's Church Discipline Guidelines which we posted on our website. As churches across the country downloaded and reviewed the guidelines, a number of church planters and pastors expressed the desire to develop such guidelines for their churches, knowing the significance of and necessity for church discipline. The overwhelming feedback was that they wanted practical help in navigating through the various aspects of church discipline.

As I took a step of faith to write about church discipline, I knew that my limited experience and perspective needed broadening. In the fall of 2010, I was blessed to interview thirty pastors across the United States and United Kingdom about their experiences with shepherding God's people through discipline. Pastors from Acts29, Sovereign Grace, Southern Baptist, Presbyterian, Anglican and various non-denominational churches participated in this rich discussion. In interviewing two to three pastors during a given conference call a dynamic and synergistic dialogue ensued that resulted in us learning from one another in encouraging and humbling ways. Another exciting aspect of this endeavor was that I was able to listen to the pastoral hearts of men who shepherded God's people with great care and conviction. I walked away from every interview encouraged by the beautiful ways in which God was growing His churches as they proclaimed and lived out His Word through church discipline.

WHY ANOTHER BOOK?

Every author battles with this daunting question. As I considered the experiences from Sojourn and other churches, along with much prayer, I began to envision how another book on church discipline could add to what has already been written. The bottom line is that another book on church discipline had to serve the church by offering both a gospel-centered perspective and practice so that it would be helpful to ministry leaders—from pastors, deacons, and small group leaders. There are four global reasons why you should read "yet another book" on church discipline:

First, you will learn how to deal with those rebelling against God primarily by understanding how God deals with you in your ongoing rebellion against Him. You cannot lead others in carrying out God's discipline if you and your people do not have a clear understanding of who God is and how He lovingly disciplines us as His bride.

Second, you will understand church discipline within God's larger story of redemption. You can easily misunderstand and distort God's design for church discipline if you carry out this important function of the church separate from His redemptive story as Jesus prepares His bride for an eternal union.

Third, you will see how God redeems His children impacted by the discipline process, from those being directly disciplined to their family members, small group members, church leaders and the entire church. God grows His people when they are forced to wrestle with the profound truths of the gospel as sin is exposed and as the church fights the fight of faith together as a community of God's people.

Fourth, you will walk away with a better understanding of the realities of the gospel life, from the continual need for faith and repentance in the midst of the struggles of life to God's ongoing work of redemption in and through His people.

God Redeeming His Bride

As the title implies, we will be spending a lot of time looking at God's redeeming work in and through His Bride, the people of God, whom He calls to engage in His gospel mission. So let's take a moment to lay some groundwork so that we can journey together with a common understanding of three major themes found throughout this book: (1) redemption, (2) the bride of Christ and (3) gospel mission.

WHAT IS REDEMPTION?

Throughout salvation history, God's redemption can be understood primarily as the deliverance of His people from the oppression of suffering and sin, whether it is from the slavery to enemy nations or from the slavery to indwelling sin.[1] But ultimate redemption in the gospel story is seen as God delivers His people from the tyranny of the devil and the condemning power of sin through the forgiving and redemptive work of Jesus Christ on the cross (Eph. 1:7; Col. 1:14). If the forgiveness of sins is not amazing enough, God goes above and beyond what we could ever ask or think as He puts a paradoxical spin on the notion of redemption. On the one hand He frees us from the bondage of sin but, on the other hand, He lovingly makes us slaves to righteousness, or slaves to Himself (Rom. 6:18, 22). In other words, we not only have been set free to live with God but set free to live for God, which is true and ultimate freedom.

This divine rescue is beautifully displayed from cover to cover in the Scriptures as God's story of redemption unfolds. The Old

---

1   See I. H. Marshall's work, "The Development of the Concept of Redemption in the New Testament;" Schreiner, *New Testament Theology*, pp. 367-369; House, *Old Testament Theology*, pp. 23, 292, 295.

Testament highlights God's redemptive work as He repeatedly delivers His undeserving people out of their plight of sin and suffering. But as the New Testament opens, we see God's redemption revealed in a way never seen before. At this moment in history, God sent the perfect Redeemer to set His people free by bearing our wickedness and enduring our affliction so that we might have life in Him. As the New Testament moves beyond the Gospel narratives, we see God advancing His gospel mission and bringing glory to Himself by raising dead people to life in Christ (Eph. 2:1-3) and redeeming His bride through the trials of life so that they conform more and more to His image.[2]

Knowing that our redemption is accomplished by Jesus' finished work on the cross, how should we think about God's ongoing redemptive work?

Redemption Accomplished and Applied

Theologian John Murray offers a helpful way to look at God's redemption not just as an historical event, but also as a continuing work of grace, commonly referred to as sanctification:

> The provision which God has made for the salvation of men is even more strikingly manifold. For this provision has in view the manifoldness of man's need and exhibits the overflowing abundance of God's goodness, wisdom, grace, and love. This superabundance appears in the eternal counsel of God respecting salvation; it appears in the historic *accomplishment of redemption* by the work of Christ once and for all; and it appears in the *application of redemption* continuously and progressively till it reaches its consummation in the liberty of the glory of the children of God. When we think of the application of redemption we must not think of it as one simple and indivisible act. It comprises a series of acts and processes. To mention some, we have calling, regeneration, justification, adoption, sanctification, glorification.... Each has its own distinct meaning, function, and purpose in the action and grace of God [emphasis mine].[3]

God not only accomplished our redemption through the death and resurrection of Jesus, but He continues His redemptive work in our

---

2   Phil. 1:6; 1 Pet. 1:6-9; James 1:2-4; Gal. 5:16-25; 1 John 1:8-10; Rom. 8:29; 1 Pet. 1:14-16.

3   John Murray, *Redemption Accomplished and Applied*, pp. 79-80.

lives through our never-ending relationship with Jesus. Pastor and theologian John Stott offers additional insights on God's ongoing redemption in the lives of His people:

> But it is a moral bondage from which Christ has ransomed us ... redemption is a synonym for the "forgiveness of sins," now as "the curse of the law" ... Yet even our release from these captives does not complete our redemption. There is more to come. For Christ "gave himself for us to redeem us from all wickedness," to liberate us from *all* the ravages of the Fall. This we have not experienced.... The New Testament people of God, though already redeemed from guilt and judgment, are yet waiting for the "day of redemption" when we shall be made perfect. This will include "the redemption of our bodies."[4]

Why is it important for us to understand God's relentless redemptive work in us as His people? Even though God has called us to holiness (Lev. 19:2; 1 Pet. 1:15-16) we still struggle with the evilness of sin as we live in a fallen world, awaiting "the day of redemption" (Eph. 4:30; cf. Rom. 8:23).

Crying Out for Redemption

Like the psalmists, we cry out for God to redeem us as we find ourselves entangled by the affliction of sin and oppressed by evil.[5] In the same way Paul saw his sinfulness with intense clarity and felt the weight of his wretchedness.[6] He cried out and groaned for deliverance, as he eagerly awaited the day of redemption, the day when all of the redeemed will no longer have any trace of sin and death. This is the sobering reality of living in the "already but not yet."

But we do not struggle and cry out like those who are without hope. Our prayers and pleas are not dispersed into the darkness of the cosmos but are directed to and gathered by our Deliverer who

---

4   John Stott, *The Cross of Christ*, p. 178.

5   Pss. 44:23-26; 55:17-19; 69:17-18; 119:133-135.

6   Rom. 7:24-25; Gal. 5:16-18. Scholars have been split whether Paul is describing his pre-Christian or post-Christian experience in the Rom. 7 passage. Schreiner states that this passage can be interpreted either way since "Paul does not intend to distinguish believers from unbelievers in this text" since the main point of this section is that the law does not have power over sin and cannot transform human beings (Schreiner, *Romans*, 390).

hears and answers our requests made according to His will (Ps. 116; 1 John 5:14-15). Like Paul, we can cry out in desperation knowing that Jesus Christ is our Redeemer.

Jesus Our Redeemer and Redemption

We can easily view our redemption either in terms of a theological concept or as a process of change. Redemption is both a real concept and about change. But redemption is much more than a concept or process. Redemption is a person. Jesus is not only our Redeemer but He also is our redemption (1 Cor. 1:30; Luke 21:27-28).

Why is this distinction important for us to understand and cling to? By understanding this truth, the gospel becomes more beautiful and intimate, the love of Christ becomes higher, deeper and wider, and His love, which is better than knowing about any concept or process, compels us to no longer live for ourselves but for Jesus (2 Cor. 5:14-15; Eph. 3:16-19). Our relationship with our Redeemer is our redemption. And it is in and through our relationship with Him that we, as the bride of Christ, experience God's gracious and ongoing redemption.

THE BRIDE OF CHRIST

In His sovereign wisdom, God showcases marriage throughout His redemptive history. In Genesis, we see the first marriage between the first man and woman in the Garden of Eden. In Revelation, we see the final and ultimate marriage that will take place at the end of time—the marriage between Jesus and His bride, the church. We can respond in a variety of ways as we seek to understand our God-given identity as the bride of Christ.

Most, if not all, women dream about marriage. They spend hours envisioning whom they will marry, their wedding dress and their wedding ceremony. Consequently, women can easily relate to being the bride of Christ. What woman wouldn't want to be in an everlasting relationship with one who offers perfect love, protection and provision?

There are some men who dream about marriage in a similar way. But no man dreams of being a bride! Men conceptually understand that the church is the bride of Christ but they can stumble when they try to make sense of this notion for themselves. Before men dismiss this biblical concept, let's consider a couple of questions.

Is it right for us as men and women to understand our God-given identity as the bride of Christ at the personal level? Absolutely! But how can men get around the difficulty regarding this gospel reality? Let's consider a line of reasoning that will explain why God's intentional metaphor does not and should not clash with any aspect of biblical manhood. We need to understand why our all-wise God chose this particular metaphor, though knowing that such imagery could serve as an obstacle for men.

To begin with, God knows that we, as finite and fallible beings, need concrete ways to understand the infinite and perfect truths of the gospel. Not only did God create marriage, but He also designed marriage to give us both a conceptual and concrete understanding of our supernatural relationship with Him in Christ. There is not a man or woman alive who does not grasp the privileged blessing of the covenant commitment associated with marriage.

Next, God knows that the "bride" metaphor has its limitations. That is why, within this overarching bride metaphor, God gives men a specific role as He compares the marriage between a husband and wife to the marriage between Christ and the church (cf. Eph. 5:22-33). In this passage, the man reflects Christ in his sacrificial love for his wife while the woman reflects the church in her submission to and respect for her husband. Interestingly, men don't struggle in seeing themselves as Christ in this metaphor, but instead struggle to love their wives in selfless and sacrificial ways. Additionally, in other passages God refers to His people as His "sheep," "the body of Christ," "the temple of the Holy Spirit" and "branches" as He speaks with vivid imagery about our spiritually intimate relationship with Jesus.[7] But we don't take offense at these metaphors because we know that we are not animals, body parts, buildings or vegetation. We don't focus on the literal meaning associated with the metaphors but on the powerful truths that the literary device is meant to convey.

God has brought us into an incomparable relationship with Christ where we experience everlasting life, peace, satisfaction, joy and pleasure.[8] Therefore, instead of focusing on being a literal bride, men should focus instead on the deep and profound truths

---

7   John 10:1-18; 1 Cor. 6:15-20; John 15:1-13

8   John 14:6, 27; Matt. 5:6; Ps. 16:11

associated with how Christ loves them, since every man, like every woman, longs to be deeply loved in an everlasting relationship.

The souls of both men and women hunger and thirst to be loved in ways described in Ephesians 5. Christ loves His bride sacrificially, dying for her so that she did not have to suffer the wrath of God for her sinfulness (v. 25). Christ cleanses His bride "by the washing of water with the word, so that he might present the church to Himself in splendor, without spot or wrinkle or any such thing, that she might be holy and without blemish" (vv. 26-27). Christ loves His bride in the same way He loves Himself, as He nourishes and cherishes her (v. 28). Christ holds fast to His bride since He is one with her (v. 29). If we take a moment to meditate on these truths found in just this one passage, we will all find ourselves drawing near to Christ in the same way a bride draws near to her ever-faithful and loving husband.

The gospel clearly reveals that Christ loves His bride perfectly. But His infinite and redeeming love has a purpose. Jesus pours out His love into our hearts so that we will be compelled by His love to live for Him and not for ourselves (Rom. 5:5; 2 Cor. 5:14-15). Jesus calls each and every one of His children to join Him as He carries out His gospel mission in an imperfect world. Let's take a look at what this gospel mission is all about.

GOSPEL MISSION

God's mission is about making His glory known as He redeems a people for His own possession, people zealous to be a part of His mission as they reflect their Redeemer in word and deed.[9] In other words, when God saves us by His grace, we not only become His people but His mission becomes our mission. But what exactly is our mission as the bride of Christ?

While carrying out His mission on earth, Jesus summed up all of the law, prophets and writings by two great commandments (Matt. 22:37-40), calling us to love God and others. God makes it clear that we love Him when we obey His commandments and love others.[10] From God's double-love command, our mission is to live by faith in obedience to our Creator and Redeemer as we love one another,

---

9   Ps. 106:8; Titus 2:14; 1 Pet. 2:9; Eph. 2:10

10   John 14:15, 21, 23-24; 13:34-35; 1 John 4:20-21

knowing that believing and doing His will gives life to us and gives glory to Him. But when we fail to trust and obey, God calls us to repent from our wicked unbelief and sinful disobedience. Such an intentional life of faith and repentance with Jesus and others describes what it means to pursue holiness. God sanctifies, or changes us by His grace, as we strive to live out the gospel with such intentionality so that we reflect our Redeemer in increasing ways (1 John 4:12, 17).

After Jesus was resurrected from the dead and before He ascended to heaven He commissioned His disciples to bear witness to His gospel message and mission.[11] Specifically, in what most would consider the preeminent passage that summarizes the church's commission, Jesus commands His followers to make disciples through His authority, by going out, baptizing those who repent and believe, and teaching them to observe all He commanded (Matt. 28:18-20). From this passage, our mission is to be disciples as we make disciples.

Combining the great commandment with the great commission results in the church's great mission. God's mission for His church focuses on both the church and the world. Therefore, the mission of the church is to glorify God by worshiping Him with our whole life, as we love one another in the church and world so that we would trust and obey God by His grace. Such a mission reflects our Redeemer, redeems us as His people and draws others to His beauty and glory through faith and repentance.

Given the topic of this book, we will look extensively at how church discipline plays an integral role in God's mission through His church.

Defining Church Discipline

Even though there is much to discuss before we can more fully understand how God disciplines us through His church, let's take a look at the definition of church discipline that will inform and guide the rest of the book:

> God's ongoing, redeeming work through His living Word and people as they fight the fight of faith together to exalt Christ and protect the purity of His Bride.

---

11   Matt. 28:16-20; Luke 24:44-49; Acts 1:8. See DeYoung and Gilbert's book, *What is the Mission of the Church?* for a robust discussion of the nature of the church's mission.

Church discipline is about God and how He disciplines us, as His children, in our ongoing struggle with sin. But it is important for us to see that God's discipline is part of His mission of redemption, not something that is separate or different. In summary, God redeems us in our rebellion through His discipline.

In what we commonly call church discipline, God uses His living Word and people to confront our evil and unbelieving thoughts and desires that lead us to fall away from Him as our living God (Heb. 4:12; 3:12-14). God calls us to pursue, encourage and warn one another[12] in the midst of our sinful struggles in ways that reflect how He mercifully deals with us.[13] The goal of such pursuit is for the wayward ones to repent of their sin and turn back to Jesus, experiencing His restoring love (Isa. 55:6-7) and seeing His incomparable glory even as they are progressively being transformed into the image of Christ (2 Cor. 3:18). Such ongoing efforts exalt Christ and protect the purity of His church. As the bride of Christ participates in God's mission by faith and obedience while serving as agents of His disciplining work, the church individually and collectively experiences and is changed by God's redeeming love.

It is important for us to understand that God's redemptive work is not only focused on the individuals who are outwardly rebellious, but also on everyone who is involved—from family members, those in the same small group, those in the same social circles to those in the entire church. We will see how God simultaneously works at both the individual and corporate levels as the book follows John and Kathy's struggles to live out the gospel in the midst of marital unfaithfulness. In John's waywardness we will also see how God accomplishes His redeeming work in Kathy, Tom and Sharon, who are their small group leaders, Pastor Greg and the entire church as they pursue and pray for John.

Not only does God wish individual believers to be holy as He is holy, He also wishes His Church to reflect His purity. We recognize

---

12   Rom. 14:19; Heb. 10:24-25; Col. 1:28

13   Ps. 23:6; Rom. 15:5; Jer. 11:7-8

that there may be some who are members of our local churches who are not truly Christ's disciples. Only God knows who are His children and who are not. We are to discern a person's confession by the fruit of their lives. This is one of the reasons why the Lord gave specific instructions to the Church to remove those who chronically refuse to submit to Christ and His church since the church is not able to affirm their profession of faith (cf. Matt. 18:17). We will see that in such cases God still does His redemptive work as God's people remove "the leaven" as they trust and obey (1 Cor. 5) and as those removed experience a foretaste of God's eternal judgment.

Now that we established a common framework for understanding redemption, the "bride" metaphor and gospel mission, along with a definition of church discipline, it's now time to see what lies ahead.

Navigating Through the Book

It is helpful to know where you are going before you start any journey. An overview helps you to navigate through the details found throughout the chapters without getting lost. A global perspective also allows you to see how the individual chapters build upon each other to provide a comprehensive understanding.

God Redeeming His Bride is divided into three parts, with every chapter ending with questions to help you to reflect and respond to the truths presented in the chapter.

Part 1 focuses on "Our Redeeming God and His Bride." Chapter 1 highlights our triune God who entered space and time to create and redeem a people for His own possession. Chapter 2 reveals the unlikely bride of Christ who has been given a radical life and mission in the kingdom of God. Chapter 3 takes a look at God's counter-intuitive ways displayed in His story of redemption as He shames the wise and the strong through the cross, as well as through church discipline.

Given the nature and mission of our redeeming God and His bride, Part 2 focuses on "The Bride's Rebellion and God's Discipline." Chapter 4 reveals our struggle to live out the gospel. As a result, we not only fail to carry out God's mission but also fail to see the need for church discipline. Chapter 5 addresses how the popular understanding of church discipline may limit and even skew how we understand God's discipline through the church, which should be consistent with His story of redemption.

Knowing that all of us will continue to struggle to live out the gospel on this side of heaven, Part 3 addresses "God's Call to Carry Out His Redemptive Discipline" for His glory and for His bride's growth. Towards the end of each chapter in Part 3, leadership points are offered to help us to consider essential elements in the everyday mission of the church, along with the escalating and expanding redemptive efforts that can come with church discipline. Chapter 6 highlights the "one another" commands as the basis for everyday gospel mission, which includes God's ongoing discipline through His living Word and people. Chapter 7 looks at the mess and mission of gospel relationships. Despite the fact that sin disrupts and divides God's people, we are still called to God's radical mission. Chapter 8 examines the essential role of community in pursuing and calling those who are in chronic rebellion back to Jesus. Community guidelines are offered to help us to see how we can get others involved in fighting the fight of faith as the family of God. Chapter 9 covers the escalating and expanding efforts of the church to call those who refuse to submit to Jesus and refuse to listen to those around them. We will see the importance of warning and waiting, withholding communion and telling the church should those warned refuse to repent. Chapter 10 guides us through what it means for the church to treat those who "refuse to listen even to the church". We will see the significance of removing those who are unrepentant from the covenant fellowship of the church and how we need to instruct the church during and after the removal. Chapter 11 discusses God's ongoing discipline after removal, the battle for repentance and God's mercy for those who repent and seek restoration. We will learn what issues need to be considered when developing a restoration plan and how we can inform the church and celebrate upon restoration, should the Lord grant repentance. Chapter 12 completes the journey by addressing the cost of gospel mission and the reality of liability as we engage in God's discipline as the church.

The story of John and Kathy, which unfolds in each chapter, serves as a concrete example of how the issues discussed in each chapter is relevant and crucial. Knowing and applying the truths and principles found throughout this book will help you shepherd the "Johns and Kathys" in your church along with those around them. Don't miss the intentional teaching points found in their story as you follow their journey. Also, be sure to learn something from each character in this realistic but fictional account.

But don't just read the chapters. You will miss an equally valuable part of the book if you do not take the time to read and utilize the practical appendix that is provided to give you a better sense of the "nuts and bolts" associated with church discipline.

PUTTING THE APPENDIX TO WORK

Appendix items tend to be overlooked. Why take the extra effort in flipping to the back of the book when you are reading through a chapter? Recognizing the tendencies of most, you need to know that you will miss an essential part of the book if you do not peruse the practical discussions, guidelines, example manuscripts and plans found in the appendix.

This handbook is designed to be a ready reference. Each appendix can be read independently but cannot be understood apart from its respective chapter. Therefore, you will do yourself a disservice if you only read the appendix to get to the "practical stuff." Remember, the truths of the gospel need to drive gospel ministry, not the other way around.

Please note that each example manuscript and plan offered in the appendix is presented for illustrative purposes. You should not use them "as is" but you should use them only as reference as you prayerfully decide how to draft your own documents. You want to make sure the wording, tone and emphasis of your documents are consistent with your own church and specific to the details of the situation being addressed.

ENJOY THE JOURNEY

May the Lord bless you as you begin your journey of understanding your redeeming God and the radical life and mission He has for you. Keep yourself open to what God has in store for you as He reveals His truths and your heart as you read and reflect on His story of redemption. Be sure to respond with faith and repentance, praising God for His abundant compassion and pardon (cf. Isa. 55:6-7).

As He draws you near, experience His redeeming love, behold His glory and enjoy His grace.

PART 1:

Our Redeeming God and His Bride

1

Our Redeeming God

AN ORDINARY COUPLE IN NEED OF AN EXTRAORDINARY GOD

John was hardly recognizable as he sat alone in his apartment, wondering how in the world he ever got to this place in his life. Never in a million years could he imagine himself with such a messed up life; in fact he had always envisioned just the opposite. All that he worked for is gone—his wife and kids, his home, his family, his job, and those closest to him. Why did God abandon him at this time in his life? Yes, he had wrestled continuously with doubt and fear of being a man, a husband, and even a father, but God always came through for him, giving him grace to manage each step of the way.

Kathy was numb. She sat dazed, reeling from the deep hurt inflicted by her husband, the man who was to protect and cherish her. What happened? Where did all of this come from? What became of the man she fell in love with thirteen years earlier? She doesn't believe John will ever change. She trusts God one minute, then wonders if He even hears her cries the next. Overwhelmed and plagued by pain she resolves never to let herself get hurt again. She is too weary of fighting for her husband and marriage. It's time to move on and start over. Surely God has something better for her, because God doesn't want her to live a miserable life, right?

As a church, what do you do? Do you help a couple like John and Kathy? If so, how? It is a pressing question because situations like theirs are being lived out in churches all over the world.

Such questions demand thoughtful responses, not quick fixes. Such struggles require gospel truths and intentional, redemptive efforts, not pat Bible answers, subjective opinions or careless interactions. Such chaos calls for a Redeemer God who works through His bride, the church. Such suffering must be seen through God's redemptive lens, not through the lens of an individualistic and pain-free life. Why begin a book on church discipline with a marriage crisis? As I talked with pastors across the country, I found that, by far, marriage issues are at the top of the list for reasons that lead to church discipline. Not only that, I want to show that the gospel addresses the concrete realities we face day in and day out. We have to see church discipline, not merely as a doctrine of the church to be understood and obeyed, but as an outflow of God's story of redemption working in the lives of real people in a real world.

Instead of jumping directly into the nuts and bolts of church discipline, we will first seek to understand how God deals with His wayward people throughout His redemptive story.

John and Kathy's messy situation is not merely a case for marriage counseling or a case for swift church discipline but is a scene in God's larger story where Jesus Christ redeems ordinary people with an extraordinary gospel in a world marked by pain and brokenness.

GOD'S STORY OF REDEMPTION

We live every day thinking that reality is what we see, hear, taste, touch, and smell. We also place ourselves in the center of a universe where all that matters is our image, pleasure, health, relationships, work, hobbies, and comfort. In other words, we think we live in a very limited world where we expect everything to revolve around us. But in actuality, we live in a much bigger world where God reigns and where everything centers on Him, our majestic King. His kingdom takes priority over our kingdoms. His story defines ours.

When viewed rightly, life is all about God. We live in His world where we are living out His story. God's dynamic story of redemption is a four-part movement:

1. **Creation**—when God created the first man and woman in His own image, which established the first relationship between God and humanity;

2. **Fall**—when Adam and Eve questioned and rebelled against God, breaking their relationship with God and marring every aspect of creation with sin and suffering;

3. **Redemption**—when Jesus Christ came to ransom a helpless people from the slavery of sin as He died on the cross. He also overcame death and ascended to heaven, restoring the relationship between God and His people. As part of Christ's ongoing redemption the Spirit is sent to reorder/renovate the lives of the redeemed; and

4. **Consummation**—when Jesus Christ returns, dwells with His people forever, and makes all things new, which completes the marriage between Christ and His Bride, the church.

God's cosmic drama of redemption is played out against the kingdom of evil in the gritty details of our lives, including John and Kathy's individual and marital chaos. But even extending beyond John and Kathy's lives, God's story of redemption also involves you, whether you are part of their extended family, church family, neighborhood, or workplace.

Regardless of how you intersect John and Kathy's lives, you will miss the big picture of God's redemption and mishandle the situation if you get lost in either the conceptual realm of theology or the concrete details of John and Kathy's struggles. You need both since the gospel interprets, directs and changes our lives. In other words, you need to understand and minister to their hearts and marriage with the gospel (conceptual) applied in practical ways (concrete). So, in order for us to understand and live our lives in light of the gospel, we must first understand our redeeming God who is accomplishing His purposes and fulfilling His promises through our joys, sufferings and struggles.

OUR REDEEMING GOD

The unfolding of God's eternal plan of redemption began the moment He established time and space as He spoke creation into being in the midst of a dark and formless world. God's crowning jewel of creation was the first man and woman made in His image and He declared, "It is very good."

Our God is not a God who keeps Himself at a distance but chose to reveal Himself and His glory through a personal relationship with people like you and me. He knows each of us intimately. He knows every day of our lives before we are even born. He knows every word in our hearts before a syllable is spoken and He knows the heights of our faith and the depths of our unbelief far better than we do ourselves.

Not only does God know us intimately, He designed us purposefully. God designed us ultimately for His glory. And He graciously designed us to see and know His glory through our thoughts, affections, and will as we relate to Him and others in His world. He gave us the ability to think and reason so that we can know Him and get a glimpse of His infinite and perfect ways; affections so that we can experience His love that surpasses knowledge; and desires so that we might long for Him and be satisfied in Him. In all things and every way, God desires to be glorified and He desires for us to experience His glory.

But sadly, we infrequently experience God's glory. This has nothing to do with any deficiency on God's part, and everything to do with our inability to see, believe and even desire God's glory. Our deficiency can be traced back to Adam and Eve and their eating the forbidden fruit in the Garden of Eden. They listened to the evil counsel of the serpent and rejected the wise counsel of God. They willfully chose their glory over God's glory, followed their own will rather than God's, and were compelled by self-love over God's love, believing their thoughts and ways were better than God's thoughts and ways. What treason! How could they rebel against the God who created them and brought them into the most intimate relationship they could ever experience?!

Despite expelling Adam and Eve from the Garden of Eden and putting an armed angel at the entrance to keep the sinful man and woman from returning to the holy dwelling place, God covered their shame and nakedness with the skins of animals sacrificed on their behalf. God's redeeming action points to the ultimate sacrifice of the spotless Lamb of God on the cross.

As we follow God's story throughout the Old Testament, and see Him deal repeatedly with the wayward and adulterous hearts of His people, we learn more and more about our redeeming God. Again and again God reveals His character as He declares His faithfulness and righteousness in the midst of His people's unfaithfulness and wickedness:

"The LORD, the LORD, the compassionate and gracious God, slow to anger, abounding in love and faithfulness, maintaining love to thousands, and forgiving wickedness, rebellion and sin. Yet he does not leave the guilty unpunished; he punishes the children and their children for the sin of the parents to the third and fourth generation." (Exod. 34:6-7, NIV)

I will punish their sin with the rod, their iniquity with flogging; but I will not take my love from him, nor will I ever betray my faithfulness. I will not violate my covenant or alter what my lips have uttered. (Ps. 89:32-34, NIV)

Throughout His redemptive story God continually calls His people back to Himself, reminding them of their intimate relationship with Him, their Redeemer:

O Israel, hope in the LORD; for with the LORD there is lovingkindness and with Him is abundant redemption. And He will redeem Israel from all his iniquities. (Ps. 130:7-8, NASB)

But now, thus says the LORD, your Creator, O Jacob, and He who formed you, O Israel, "Do not fear, for I have redeemed you; I have called you by name; you are Mine! ... I have wiped out your transgressions like a thick cloud and your sins like a heavy mist. Return to me, for I have redeemed you." .... Thus says the LORD, your Redeemer, and the one who formed you from the womb, "I, the LORD, am the maker of all things, Stretching out the heavens by myself and spreading out the earth all alone." (Isa. 43:1; 44:22, 24, NASB)

God's redemption is abundant and personal as His forgiving love prevails over all of our sins.

THE REDEEMING SON OF GOD

God, the all-wise Creator, who chose to reveal His glory through His intimate relationship with His people, knew that we could not rescue ourselves from our incurable sin condition. Out of His mercy God the Father sent His own Son from heaven to earth, to dwell with us in the likeness of humanity while serving as an exact representation of the invisible God.

Jesus Christ, being fully man and fully God, lived a sinless life to fulfill the righteous requirements of the law. Jesus offered Himself as a perfect sacrifice to satisfy the wrath of God and died in our place, bringing us back into a right relationship with our

Holy God and enabling us to live a new life in Him. Through the cross of Christ God demonstrated His supreme love and forgiveness for His wayward people. He vindicated His holiness in an unimaginable way by punishing, not His sinful people, but His sinless Son. By taking extraordinary measures to redeem a people for His own possession He displayed His relentless faithfulness and mercy.

> For the grace of God has appeared that offers salvation to all people...the appearing of the glory of our great God and Savior, Jesus Christ, who gave himself for us to redeem us from all wickedness and to purify for himself a people that are his very own, eager to do what is good. (Titus 2:11-14, NIV)

God's extraordinary relationship with us is so intimate that He describes it in terms of marriage, with Jesus Christ as the bridegroom and we as His bride. God mercifully establishes an everlasting covenant with us despite our unfaithfulness to Him.

> Instead of your shame you will receive a double portion, and instead of disgrace you will rejoice in your inheritance. And so you will inherit a double portion in your land, and everlasting joy will be yours. "For I, the LORD, love justice; I hate robbery and wrongdoing. In my faithfulness I will reward my people and make an everlasting covenant with them.... I delight greatly in the LORD; my soul rejoices in my God. For he has clothed me with garments of salvation and arrayed me in a robe of his righteousness, as a bridegroom adorns his head like a priest, and as a bride adorns herself with her jewels." (Isa. 61:7-8, 10, NIV)

We deserve shame and disgrace but He lavishes His grace upon us by bringing us into an everlasting covenant with Himself. We deserve rags but He clothes us with the glorious wedding attire of Christ.

THE REDEEMING SPIRIT OF GOD

Before Christ went to the cross He promised that after His return to the Father He would send a Helper, His Holy Spirit, so that He might complete His work of redemption that He began in each of us who believe (Phil. 1:6). Christ knows that, because of our ongoing struggle with indwelling sin and unbelief, we are totally incapable of living a life that brings Him glory apart from His abiding presence. Even though we have been freed from the power of sin by the finished work of Christ on the cross, we still do the evil we don't want to do and we don't do the good we want to do (cf. Rom. 7:14ff). So how will God continue to redeem us in the midst of our ongoing disobedience against Him?

The promised Spirit reminds us about Christ (John 14:26; 15:26) and prays for us according to the will of God (Rom. 8:26-27). The Spirit of Christ dwells in those who have been saved by grace so that we might know His love (Rom. 5:5; 8:9-10) and experience His power (Eph. 1:17-20; 2 Cor. 12:7-10). The Spirit of God produces gospel fruit in us (Col. 1:9-12; Gal. 5:22-23; 1 Pet. 1:2) as He continually works in us, conforming us to the likeness of Christ (Rom. 8:29). The grace of Christ is always with us through His Spirit until either He returns or we die and go home to live with Him forever (cf. Rev. 22:21).

THE REDEEMER'S CONSUMMATED MARRIAGE

In Revelation, when we get a glimpse of the new heaven and earth, our redeeming God once again describes His relationship with His people as a marriage. When Jesus returns and makes all things new, He will consummate His marriage with His Holy Bride and they will dwell together in the Holy City for all eternity. God uses the metaphors of *Holy City* and *bride/wife of the Lamb* to express the complete union and continual fellowship between Christ and His people.

> Then I saw "a new heaven and a new earth," for the first heaven and the first earth had passed away, and there was no longer any sea. I saw the Holy City, the new Jerusalem, coming down out of heaven from God, prepared as a bride beautifully dressed for her husband. And I heard a loud voice from the throne saying, "Look! God's dwelling place is now among the people, and he will dwell with them. They will be his people, and God himself will be with them and be their God." (Rev. 21:1-3, NIV)

> One of the seven angels who had the seven bowls full of the seven last plagues came and said to me, "Come, I will show you the bride, the wife of the Lamb." And he carried me away in the Spirit to a mountain great and high, and showed me the Holy City, Jerusalem, coming down out of heaven from God. It shone with the glory of God, and its brilliance was like that of a very precious jewel, like a jasper, clear as crystal. (Rev. 21:9-11, NIV)

Because of the Bride's absolute purity, God will dwell with His people in a manner never before experienced in history, "they will see his face..." (Rev. 22:4). After the Fall, God never allowed this level of intimacy with His people. In fact, God told Moses, "You cannot see My face, for no man can see Me and live!" (Exod. 33:20, ɴᴀsʙ)

Besides Moses, only the high priest was allowed to enter the Holy of Holies, the innermost room where God symbolically lived with His people, whether it was in the tabernacle in the wilderness, or later in the temple in Jerusalem. The high priest could only enter this most sacred place once a year on the Day of Atonement to offer a sacrifice for the sins of God's people. But even with this arrangement, God still required the high priest to go through a strict ritual of preparation which included bathing before putting on his holy garments and then atoning for his sins and for the sins of his fellow priests through specific offerings (cf. Lev. 16:1-11). He also had to wait to enter the sacred space until the room was filled with incense so that he would not see clearly the presence of the Lord (cf. Lev. 16:12-13).

In reading this, you might think that God is some recluse who keeps people at a distance. But the reason for His limited contact has everything to do with Him and us—a holy God cannot be in the presence of sinful people. The sheer weight of His glory and the piercing light of His holiness would crush and blind us. God limits His presence not as punishment, but out of His great mercy. It is God's holy patience that makes Him wait for the full redemption of humanity before offering His full presence.

But, as we've seen, Christ came to bring about both the full redemption of humanity and the presence of God among His people. God ends His redemptive story by declaring once again His enduring and mutual covenant relationship with His people. Because of the intimacy and oneness between them, God's glory will permeate His Holy Bride in such a way that God's glory will be His Bride's glory and His Bride's glory will be His glory. Therefore, God's mindblowing approach in revealing His glory through His relationship with His people will burst forth in everlasting brilliance in the new heaven and earth.

Tʜᴇ Gᴏsᴘᴇʟ's Rᴇᴅᴇᴇᴍɪɴɢ Rᴇʟᴀᴛɪᴏɴsʜɪᴘs

The redeeming work of the Father, Son, and Holy Spirit provides a beautiful and comprehensive portrait of our redeeming God. The story of God's redemption of rebellious, hopeless, self-exalting, idolatrous, and unbelieving humans reveals:

1. God the Father's patience, mercy, sovereignty, justice, wrath, forgiveness, and love towards us;

2. God the Son's humble, sinless, sacrificial, self-giving, and redeeming life, death, and resurrection; and

3. God the Spirit's abiding, comforting, interceding and sanctifying work in us.

God brings about progressive gospel change in His people through the relationship and work of each person of the Trinity so that we might live as a family in the kingdom of God by faith in Christ and conform more and more to His image.

You might be wondering, why do we need to know about our redeeming God before we dive into the issue of church discipline? The answer is simple. We need to first understand how God relates to us in our sinfulness so that we can best reflect Him as we relate to others in their sin.

But there is another important reason for starting with God. John Calvin stated, "Without knowledge of self, there is no knowledge of God ... and without knowledge of God, there is no knowledge of self."[1] In other words, knowing God is linked inextricably with knowing ourselves, and knowing ourselves is fully accomplished only through knowing God.

So what does this relational dynamic between knowing God and self have to do with church discipline? As we more intimately know our redeeming God, we will more intimately know the wickedness in our hearts and the weakness of our flesh. Such knowledge about ourselves will make us more humble, less judgmental, and more merciful as we deal with those who are straying from God. This growing knowledge of our sinfulness will compel us to pursue and depend on Christ more fervently, and as a result we will more deeply know the power, beauty and love of our holy God. Such knowledge enables us to pursue others struggling with sin with more confidence, intentionality, and perseverance, for we have personally experienced God changing our hearts and pursuing the completion of His work of redemption begun in us.

---

1   John Calvin, *Institutes*, Book 1, pp. 35-39.

A Story Within a Story

So, how will you help John and Kathy as the church? How do their marital struggles intersect with God's story of redemption? Is the redemption of their marriage possibly a part of this grand story? Is their marriage the only, or even the most important focus in God's overall redemptive story? The answer to this question may surprise you, but it's *No*. Then what is? We will address this in the coming chapter.

But we will also need to address what John, Kathy, and their marriage have to do with you and your church. Should the church get involved in their lives even though our tendency is to keep things like this behind closed doors? If you and your church do decide to step into their lives, will you be stepping in over your heads? The answers to these questions may surprise you. But to get to the answers, we'll need to turn our gaze to the bride of our redeeming God, the church.

REFLECT AND RESPOND:

1. How do you see your life differently knowing that you are part of God's story of redemption? How will knowing this change the way you see and live your life?

2. Reflect on the truth that God chose to reveal Himself and His glory through a personal relationship with people like you and me. What does this truth help you to see about your redeeming God? What does this truth help you to see about your relationship with Him?

3. Consider how Jesus, the redeeming Son of God, has brought you into an intimate relationship with Himself and how you will dwell with Him perfectly and permanently in His holy city as His holy bride. How do these present and future realities make a difference in how you live with God and others right now?

4. Have you ever considered getting involved with those in your church who are struggling with life? How do the life struggles of those in your church impact the health of the entire body of Christ?

2

The Bride of
Our Redeeming God

A COMMON UNDERSTANDING OF A SUPERNATURAL REALITY
John and Kathy have attended church ever since they became
Christians in their mid-twenties. Like most of us who profess Jesus Christ as Savior, John and Kathy understand they should go to
church every week but they miss the crucial point that they are the
church. They have learned much about what goes on at the church
but have learned little about how to be the church. John and Kathy
see church as an event to help them re-focus and renew before starting another week, as well as a place to gather with other people
who believe in the same God and who share the same values. Even
though they associate themselves with the church, they do not see
themselves as the church.

John and Kathy, like most of us, have a limit to what they're
willing to share with their friends at church. Even though they freely
ask others to pray for their practical needs, they rarely ask others to
help them with their personal decisions or struggles. They don't feel
comfortable sharing with those in their class or small group what is
really going on behind closed doors. What would their friends think
if they knew about their constant arguments and the relentless
struggles within each of their hearts? John and Kathy already feel
insecure about their "spiritual maturity" as they consider everyone
else in their circle of friends as having it "all together" and knowing
more about the Bible than they do. Still, they enjoy the times that
the church gathers and find the practical tips for living helpful.

But beyond the weekly services and the do's and don'ts of a moral lifestyle, John and Kathy do not really understand the purpose of Christianity. They think that the Christian life is simply about getting right and staying right with God. They view pastors, deacons, and missionaries as special, more-gifted people who are the only ones good enough to do God's work. They readily acknowledge they are like "dumb sheep" that need help, and they certainly will never be able to help others.

Again, you might ask. "What does this discussion about the church have to do with church discipline?" Everything! It is not because "church" is itself a type of discipline, but because God has ordained the church to be a primary means for accomplishing His redemptive work. We must have a clear grasp of how God sees the church, how He relates to the church, what He expects from the church, and how He does His transforming work in the church as we participate in His redemptive mission. Part of this redeeming work is known as church discipline. That is the connection.

An Unlikely Bride

Marriage is something most dream about. Deep down inside we all desire to be in a relationship where we can enjoy the intimate experience and deep joy associated with enduring love. For you who are married, take a moment and think about how you met your spouse, what attracted you to each other, the love you felt, and how you decided to marry that person. More than likely, the person who won your affections expressed and demonstrated love for you in a variety of ways.

The gospel story includes a marriage as well but the details of the relationship are shocking from every angle. First, the bride and groom are radically different. The bride is completely human, while the groom is God the Son, Jesus, who is fully human, fully God. Despite the immeasurable differences between Christ and His bride, there are several important implications that we must know and believe:

1. *Christ fully delights in His bride,* since He chose her for Himself, dying for her so that she might have life (Zeph. 3:17; Eph. 1:4; John 1:3).

2. *Christ fully knows His bride*, since He created her and knows everyday of her life before she was even born (Ps. 139:16; Luke 16:15). Moreover, their intimate knowledge of one another reflects the intimate knowledge between the Father and the Son (cf. John 17:21-23).

3. *Christ is fully one with His bride*, since Christ dwells in her and is one with her, just as He is the vine and she is the branch (Rom. 8:10; cf. John 15:1-11) and she serves as His body (cf. 1 Cor. 12:12ff).

4. *Christ is fully committed to His bride*, since He established an everlasting covenant with her and promised that nothing will ever separate her from His love (Jer. 32:40; Rom. 8:35-39).

Second, the bride is not worthy of the groom's love since she is impure and unfaithful. God describes His bride, apart from His redeeming grace, as full of shame and disgrace (cf. Isa. 61:7), an adulterous wife who prefers strangers to her own husband (Ezek. 16:32; Hosea), whose love is like the morning mist that disappears (Hosea 6:4; Rev. 2:4).

This is not the type of woman you want to bring home to your parents. You and I would never enter into a life-long marriage covenant with someone we knew would cheat on us time after time. But Christ chose us anyway as His bride, knowing that His love would cleanse and change us for His glorious wedding.

Third, the relationship between Christ and His bride makes no sense from a worldly perspective. Christ possesses all the beauty and glory. Christ offers all the love and grace. Christ produces all of the fruit. Christ gives everything; His bride will never be able to offer anything to Christ that He doesn't first give to her. But Christ gives Himself fully to His bride so that everything He has belongs to her. Christ is the most incredible husband imaginable. Despite their radical differences, Christ delights in His bride as He sees her through His own beauty, righteousness, and glory.

If we fail to see ourselves as this bride of Christ, we will neither understand nor experience the most profound, beautiful, intimate and glorious relationship we can ever and will ever have. If we do not see ourselves as this unlikely bride of Christ, we will miss the humility of Christ, remaining stuck in our pride and self-righteousness; we will miss the faithfulness of Christ, remaining blind to our unfaithfulness; and we will miss the provision of Christ, and continually crave other things more than Him.

God brings each of His children into a relationship with Himself. He created us so that we would personally and individually experience intimacy with Him. Take a moment to listen, look, and imagine the intimate and confident relationship between David and His God:

> For God alone, O my soul, wait in silence, for my hope is from him. He only is my rock and my salvation, my fortress; I shall not be shaken. On God rests my salvation and my glory; my mighty rock, my refuge is God. (Ps. 62:5-7)

As you read this passage, you can almost see and feel David's hope, refuge, salvation, and glory seamlessly connected to His sovereign God. You desperately want to mouth the words of David for yourself—my soul waits in silence for God alone, my trust is in Him at all times, I pour out my heart before Him.

We yearn for this kind of personal and individual relationship with our redeeming God and we struggle to comprehend the greatness of our own unlikely union with Jesus Christ. But we need to understand one more thing.

You Are Not the Only Bride

Christ's bride does not consist of just one person, but of all who have been saved by God's grace. David reminds us in the next verse that we are not the only ones in this intimate relationship:

> Trust in him at all times, O people; pour out your heart before him; God is a refuge for us. (Ps. 62:8)

We are saved individually to live collectively with others as the bride of Christ. God is not only a refuge for each of us distinctly, but for all of His people. God is the only God, but each of us are one of many. We are many members in one body. Collectively, we are the body of Christ, the bride of Christ.

Now you can begin to understand the importance of seeing yourself and others, whom you see week after week during Sunday gatherings and perhaps in your weekly small group, in this way.

Why is it important to understand this concept called the church? The answer is simple: When we fail to see ourselves as the church we will get everything wrong. We will not understand or live out our radical life and mission as the bride of our redeeming God.

The Bride's Radical Life

Christ calls us, as His bride, to live a radical life on this side of heaven so that we can prepare for our marriage to our Redeemer and give testimony to His powerful redeeming love. In Matthew 18,[1] Jesus describes the radical life He wants for His bride. He calls us to live out the gospel with individual and mutual responsibility in a way that reflects His life with us and results in unity and peace within the family of God. As with all of His commands, Jesus calls us to live in ways that confront our sinful tendencies and which will give Him glory as we imitate Him and reflect Him.

First, Christ knows His bride's continuous desire for self-glory, so He calls us to live a *radical life of humility*, where there are no "great ones" (v. 1), but only "little ones" (vv. 6, 10, 14), where the humblest are the greatest (v. 4), and where Christ is the only great and exalted One. Our struggle with pride causes us to reject and rebel against Christ as we live according to our own will instead of His will. This same struggle also causes us to judge and condemn those around us, resulting in disharmony and division with one another. Fundamentally, our pride damages our relationship with God and others since we do not want anyone to get in the way of the glory we desire.

Second, Christ knows His bride's on-going struggle with sin, so He calls us to live with a *radical life of intentionality*, where sin is fought with vigor and where we deal seriously with those who cause others to stumble in gospel community (vv. 6-9). Sin is serious to God, but sadly, we do not understand or experience the full weight of our sins. We see our sins as merely "mess-ups" or as justified responses to our circumstances. We are often blind to our sinful ways. Moreover, we neither grasp how our sin impacts others around us nor how our individual sins weaken the overall health of the church. Worst of all, we do not see how we in our unbelief

---

1   My friend Andy Farmer, Family Pastor at Covenant Fellowship Church—Sovereign Grace Network—directed me to this holistic approach to Matt. 18 presented in France's Commentary.

accuse God of being a liar. When we obsess with fearful thoughts ("God, you are not with me"), or don't desire God ("God, you can't satisfy me"), or follow our own wills ("God, your ways aren't the best") our lives scream that we don't believe God is who He says He is or that He will keep His promises. We are more sinful than we could ever imagine. When we treat sin lightly or fail to go after it with intentional effort, we are declaring that we do not care about our "engagement" with God and that we are better off with other lovers.

Third, Christ knows our legalistic hearts so He calls us to live a *radical life of joy*, where we can rejoice always, even when things go wrong, since Christ is our source of hope and joy. Remarkably, God not only calls us to rejoice in Him, but He rejoices in us, especially after He pursues us when we go astray and we repent and come back to Him (Matt. 18:10-14). Even more incredibly, our Heavenly Father celebrates the redemption of the wayward one more than the obedience of the rest. Such rejoicing flies in the face of our law-driven, performance-oriented mentality. Like the older brother in Jesus' parable (Luke 15:11-32), we draw more attention to our own obedience than to God's powerful work of grace that calls the wayward younger brother to repentance and back to God. We can also be ruled by a sin-seeking perspective that fails to rejoice when someone repents since we focus more on their failure to observe the do's and don'ts of the law rather than on God's ongoing work of redemption in the lives of His people. When we fail to find joy in Christ—for who He is, what He has done, and what He is doing—we fail to love God because we seek the glory that rightfully and solely belongs to Him. We also fail to love others when we do not rejoice in God's redemptive work in them because of our envy, selfish ambition or judgmental attitude. How can we, as the bride who is "unequally yoked"—in sinfulness, worth, and contribution—question God's mercy, which we have freely received, and fail to rejoice in His beautiful and powerful redeeming love, through which we have been changed?

Fourth, Christ knows our tendency towards autonomy, so He calls us to a *radical life of community* where we encourage and challenge one another to live out the gospel as a scattered and gathered body (vv. 15-17). Because we all tend to be blind to our own sin, God gives us guidelines for pursuing those who refuse to submit to Christ and His ways. Further, we tend to think we don't need anyone else's help to live rightly and therefore withdraw from others who may "get into our business." God knows that a mutual life of accountability with others opposes our autonomous, self-seeking ways. When we need help, we want community. When we rebel, we pull away from community, because we want our way. This is the opposite of what we actually need. We have so much to learn about the benefits and blessings of living an open life with others in a dependent, sacrificial, and loving way. When we live together in such a way, we demonstrate a practical knowledge of the gospel and of our identity as the bride of Christ, since God made us to live and grow in community as His body.

Fifth, Christ knows our struggle with bitterness and forgiving, so He calls us to a *radical life of forgiveness* where each of us is called to reflect the gospel by continually forgiving one another just as our Christ continually forgives us (vv. 21-35). Because of our ongoing struggle with sin, we will sin against others and others will sin against us. This is where our identity as the bride of Christ helps us to put everything in perspective. Christ desires the relationship with His bride to reflect the oneness experienced between Him and His Father—unified and at peace. How can Christ be one with His bride when her body is full of division and bitterness? At the micro level, such internal strife can be compared to a cancer, where the white blood cells are destroying their ally red blood cells; the result is a body that is literally destroying itself. In other words, how can the bride, with any sincerity and purity, say she loves Christ when she is filled with anger, bitterness, malice, and slander towards others? Even more serious, when we as the bride refuse to forgive and love others as Christ has forgiven and loved us, we not only refuse to show our gratitude for what He has done for us, but also refuse to trust and obey Him. How can we as the bride love our God with all of our heart, soul, mind, and strength when our hatred distracts and divides us?

As you can see, Christ calls His bride to live a radical life of faith that enables us to deny ourselves, take up our cross and follow Him with our entire life so that we reflect Him and experience the power of His grace in increasing ways. But in the gospel, God does not separate life from mission. As seen in God's story of redemption, He uses everything in life to sanctify us. Likewise, He calls every one of

His people to live in such a way that others might be changed by the love of God. This is our life. This is our mission.

The Bride's Radical Mission

We all struggle with our identity and purpose in life. By His grace, God doesn't let us just "find ourselves" or allow us to define our own identity. God knows we get confused and get things wrong if left to our own wisdom. So throughout His story, God declares His identity and then declares our identity—not merely through statements of fact, but through His relationship with us. Not only does God want us to know our identity, but He also wants us to experience our identity as He dwells with us:

> I will take you to be my people, and I will be your God, and you shall know that I am the LORD your God ... I will dwell among the people of Israel and will be their God. (Exod. 6:7; 29:45)

> My dwelling place shall be with them, and I will be their God, and they shall be my people. Then the nations will know that I am the LORD who sanctifies Israel, when my sanctuary is in their midst forevermore. (Ezek. 37:27-28)

> And I heard a loud voice from the throne saying, "Behold, the dwelling place of God is with man. He will dwell with them, and they will be his people, and God himself will be with them as their God." (Rev. 21:3)

God repeatedly places His identity alongside our identity, as He places Himself with us. We cannot separate our identity from God's since we are made in His image, remade by His grace, and renewed to see, reflect, and share in His glory through Christ. Neither can we separate our identity from our purpose in life. In fact, God designed our purpose to flow from our identity. As the bride of our redeeming God (identity), we were made for Him, made to reflect Him, and made to live for Him according to His will and ways (purpose).

So how does God define our purpose in life? To answer that question, let's see what Christ says when the Jewish leaders asked Him what was the greatest commandment of all the law. Jesus replied:

> "You shall love the Lord your God with all your heart and with all your soul and with all your mind. This is the great and first commandment. And a second is like it: You shall love your neighbor as

yourself. On these two commandments depend all the Law and the Prophets." (Matt. 22:37-40)

Jesus summed up the Scriptures and defined our mission, or purpose, for living in His two-fold command to love—we are called to love God first, then love others. God made us so that we would love and glorify Him through everything we do in life, and particularly as we love others in ways that reflect Him and His love for us. Just like Jesus, who did only what the Father did (cf. John 5:19), we, who are the bride of Christ, are called to follow Jesus and join Him in His ongoing mission of redemption. Jesus sacrificed His life so we might have life through knowing and loving God; therefore, we must live submissive and sacrificial lives so that others might have life through knowing and loving God. God's mission is now our mission.

So, how does this mission impact us as the church? In His wisdom, God's mission of redemption is dynamic and multi-faceted. God brings about change in us as we join Him in His work of redemption. Christ prepares us, as His bride, for our eternal marriage as we help others to love God and others in ways that reflect the gospel. Not only does God do His redemptive work in us as we love one another in the church, He also grows us as we lovingly engage those outside the church. God builds up His church and advances His kingdom every time we cry out to Him for hope and help (cf. Rom. 5:5; Ps. 121); every time we love and forgive others like Christ (cf. Eph. 4:31-5:2; 1 John 4:12); every time we overcome evil with good (Rom. 12:17-21); every time we restore one another from sin with a spirit of gentleness and bear another's burden (Gal. 6:1-2); and every time we are compelled by the love of Christ to engage others with the mercy of God (2 Cor. 5:14-15), all by the grace and power of His Spirit.

WHO CAN HELP?

How are John and Kathy's identity and purpose in Christ relevant to their marital mess? They see their biggest problem being the flesh and blood person they sleep next to every night. God's radical life and mission for them not only seems irrelevant, but also unattainable, perhaps even undesirable. What would you do if John and Kathy asked for your help at this point? When you consider the training and "wisdom" of professional counselors, you may feel foolish and think you don't have anything to offer them. You may wonder if you, as a friend and ministry leader, should "interfere" in their marriage, or try to help, since you are not a trained counselor and you don't have it all together in your own marriage. Well, God thinks otherwise.

REFLECT AND RESPOND:

1. What difference does it make knowing you don't go to church but you are the church?

2. What was your reaction when you, as a child of God, were described as "an unlikely bride" and were reminded you are not the only bride?

3. Read and meditate through Matthew 18. God has called us to a radical life of humility, intentionality, joy, community, and forgiveness. Which aspects of this life seem to be the most challenging for you and why?

4. God has called us to a radical mission of redemption as understood in His two-fold command to love. Consider how your mission, or purpose, flows out of your identity. Give a "mission update"—rate first how you are doing in knowing and loving God, then how you are helping others to know and love God.

3

God's Redeeming Thoughts and Ways

COMMON STRUGGLES AND CONFUSION

The skirmish between John and Kathy seems all too familiar. John expends all of his energy pursuing success in the workplace but allows complacency to settle in his home. He fails to be present with Kathy when he is home and does not pursue her with either love or intentionality. John often defaults to Kathy's initiative and willingness to "carry the ball" with household issues, the children, finances, and social engagements.

Over time, after countless attempts to talk and address these ongoing issues, Kathy grows bitter and resentful towards John. She finds herself respecting him less. When they argue, they hurt each other deeply as they blame and accuse each other, not to mention the wounds they bring up from the past. Kathy makes any excuse to avoid physical intimacy since the only time John seems to pay her any attention is when he wants to make love. It's not that she is withholding to punish him, but their relationship has gotten so tense and disconnected that John seems like a stranger.

John and Kathy each have their own idea of what needs to happen, what they want for themselves, and what they want from each other. John has talked to a number of his buddies at work about his struggles at home and how he never imagined marriage would be so hard. Kathy has spent many hours over coffee talking with her girlfriends about her continual frustration and growing disrespect towards John. Each of them is surprised that their friends seem to experience similar struggles and they find themselves confused as they try to sort through it all.

Neither John nor Kathy sees how the gospel relates to their messed-up lives. They get more depressed when they read the Biblical passages on marriage or how to live the Christian life, since God's thoughts and ways seem so different from their own. Plus, everything within them recoils when they consider God's call for them to "follow Jesus," to consider others more important than themselves, not to return evil for evil, and to pursue peace with one another. In their own way, John and Kathy are ready to give up, for they have come to believe that nothing can change their spouse or their situation.

GOD IS NOT LIKE YOU AND ME

God created the heavens and earth and He created us in His image, so that we might reflect Him through our thoughts and ways. But because God is God and we are not, and because He is perfect and we are not, God's ways and thoughts are not like ours. But by His grace, we can know God and His moral will through His written Word and by His Spirit, who knows the thoughts of God and makes them known to us (cf. 1 Cor. 2:11-13). However, we can only know God partially not only because He is infinite and we are finite, but also because of our ongoing struggle with sin—our indwelling sin blinds us to the truth and defiles our thoughts, affections, and will. Nevertheless, God calls us to think His thoughts since we have been given the mind of Christ (cf. 1 Cor. 2:16), and to walk in His ways since the Spirit of Christ dwells in us (cf. Deut. 10:12; Rom. 8:9-10).

As we have seen through God's story of redemption, God pursues His wayward people and calls them to return to Him time after time. God not only uses His living Word, the Bible, but He also uses His bride, the church, to call His people back to Himself. Isaiah 55 helps us to see the radical nature of God in the face of Israel's repeated rebellion against Him. God opens the passage by calling all who are thirsty to come to Him, to eat and drink what is good without cost, and to delight in His abundant and faithful mercies (Isa. 55:1-3). Then God, who remembers His everlasting covenant with His people, announces:

"Seek the LORD while he may be found; call upon him while he is near; let the wicked forsake his way, and the unrighteous man his thoughts; let him return to the LORD, that he may have compassion on him, and to our God, for he will abundantly pardon. For my thoughts are not your thoughts, neither are your ways my ways, declares the LORD. For as the heavens are higher than the earth, so are my ways higher than your ways and my thoughts than your thoughts. For as the rain and the snow come down from heaven and do not return there but water the earth, making it bring forth and sprout, giving seed to the sower and bread to the eater, so shall my word be that goes out from my mouth; it shall not return to me empty, but it shall accomplish that which I purpose, and shall succeed in the thing for which I sent it. For you shall go out in joy and be led forth in peace; the mountains and the hills before you shall break forth into singing, and all the trees of the field shall clap their hands. Instead of the thorn shall come up the cypress; instead of the brier shall come up the myrtle; and it shall make a name for the LORD, an everlasting sign that shall not be cut off." (Isa. 55:6-13)

God dealt with Israel not only by pointing out their sinful ways and thoughts, but also by reminding them that He is not like them. Yes, they needed to repent, but embedded in His call for them to repent was His desire for them to seek Him, to call upon Him while He is near, and to experience His merciful and forgiving love.

God's Gracious Call—Return to Receive (vv. 6-7)

Often, when we wrongly assume God thinks and acts like us, we avoid Him out of shame, we flee from Him as an enemy and as a result, we remain in chaos and unrest.[1] But God tells us, "I don't think like you and I don't act like you." This is good news! The radical message of the gospel resounds as God called Israel to repent, to forsake their ways and thoughts and *return* to Him so that they might *receive* His compassion and forgiveness. God's promise of kindness and mercy stirs our souls and compels us to forsake our sinful stance, so that as we *return* to Christ, we humbly *receive* our Lord's mercy and pardon. God declares and demonstrates this gospel dynamic of "return to receive" all throughout His story of redemption. We are blown away by such grace and mercy in light of our rebellion

---

1   cf. Calvin, 1996, p. 169

against our redeeming God, since we tend to do just the opposite to those who reject and abandon us.

God's Infinitely Different and Superior Ways (vv. 8-9)

God humbles us as He calls, challenges and changes us with His gracious love. God's redeeming love is radically different and superior to our love in at least three beautiful ways. First, *God loves us relentlessly*. In the midst of the spiritual battle raging in and around us as we rebel against our Savior King, God Himself pursues us even when we go astray (cf. Matt. 18:12; Ps. 23:6). Because God is preparing us for His eternal union with us, He pursues and redeems us through every circumstance, every relationship, and every life situation. He will never let us go and will never allow anything to snatch us from His hands (Rom. 8:35-39; John 10:27-30).

God doesn't grumble as He pursues us relentlessly, but rather *God loves us joyfully*. He demonstrates His radical love through His response when we return. Not only does God lavish us with compassion and forgiveness through Christ when we return to Him, but He rejoices as He and the heavenly hosts celebrate the effective work of His Word through the power of His grace and Spirit.[2]

In addition to pursuing us relentlessly with joy, God also *loves us generously*. He deals with our unfaithfulness with abundant grace and patience as He calls us to come back to Him over and over again. He covers us with infinite mercy and pardon when we return to Him, and then rejoices with over-the-top celebration and feasting. God's lavishes His perfect and infinite love upon us. He pours His love into our hearts through His Spirit so that we can have a hope that will never disappoint. What mercy! What love!

God's thoughts and ways do not resemble those of men and women, especially where suffering and sin are involved. When someone sins against us, we tend to respond with self-justifying *thoughts* of hatred, bitterness and judgment, coupled with the self-protecting *ways* of avoidance, slander, and revenge, all targeted against the one who offended us and others who get in our way. However, despite being rejected and forgotten, God's thoughts and ways are all about His mission and glory. God responds by calling us back to seek Him, to cry out to Him, to put aside our self-serving ways and thoughts, to return to Him so that we might receive infinite compassion and

---

2   Isa. 55:12-13; cf. Luke 15:22-24; Matt. 18:13-14

forgiveness. God's thoughts and ways are infinitely superior and radically different from ours since He cannot be swayed to give up His mission of redemption and His quest for glory.

God's Effective and Successful Word (vv. 10-11)

God not only declares that His thoughts and ways are far greater than those of men and women, but He declares that His Word is effective and successful. God gives us a concrete example from nature to illustrate this point. In a manner similar to God sending the rain from heaven to water the ground, which produces the crop planted by the farmer, which then feeds the people, God sends forth His Word, which will not return empty, but will accomplish the very purpose for which His thoughts and ways were expressed. God's Word is living and active and is able to judge the thoughts and intentions of the heart (Heb. 4:12). Ultimately, God's Word is effective because His Word points to and is fulfilled in Jesus Christ, our Redeemer:

> In the beginning was the Word, and the Word was with God, and the Word was God. He was in the beginning with God. All things were made through him, and without him was not anything made that was made. In him was life, and the life was the light of men. (John 1:1-4)

God creates all things through His living Word, Jesus Christ. God reveals who He is and what He will do through His Word (cf. Col. 1:15). God fulfills all His promises through His Word (cf. 2 Cor. 1:20). God accomplishes His mission through His Word.

God's Redemptive Glory (vv. 12-13)

All of God's creation bows to His will and celebrates His redemption, as Christ makes all things new. Instead of the thorns, God will bring forth the cypress and instead of the brier, God will produce the myrtle. Metaphorically, God can transform anything useless and hurtful by making it an instrument for His righteousness and redemption. Practically, God accomplishes His purpose of redemption in a way that defies the dynamics of a fallen world, as He brings about beauty from ashes, turns mourning into joy and despair into praise (Isa. 61:3). As God redeems our broken and sinful lives, He makes a name for Himself and receives glory.

But again, God is not like you and me. Even though God will not give His glory to another (cf. Isa. 42:8; 48:11), He graciously enables us to stand in the presence of His glory (cf. Jude 1:24). He goes above and beyond what we could ever ask or imagine. Even though we are undeserving, unfaithful, and unrighteous, our Redeemer grants us the privilege of sitting with Him on the throne of glory, in a way that reflects Him sitting down with His Father on His throne after overcoming evil on the cross (cf. Rev. 3:20-21). As His holy bride, we will forever delight and dwell in His infinite and incomparable glory, eternally safe and secure.

THE FOOLISHNESS OF THE CROSS

God's ways and thoughts seem radical to us because of our ongoing battle with sin. Like an inner-ear infection that messes with our equilibrium, sin makes us think we are right-side up when we are really upside down. Thankfully, God sees right through our foolish and arrogant condition. With sovereign wisdom and power, God presses on with His mission of redemption with a message and method that seems foolish and weak to us. The message is the gospel—the Word of the cross. The method is the gospel proclaimed—the Word spoken, the Word read.

The way of the cross seems foolish because of the paradoxes that challenge our reason and how we think life should be. Christ did not reveal Himself as a king but as a suffering servant. He came not to be served but to serve. He ushered in His kingdom not with a bloody revolution but by shedding His own blood. Jesus did not demand immediate justice but loved and forgave His enemies. He came to earth not to live but to die so that we might live. Christ did not seek comfort and safety but He suffered so that He would conquer death and receive glory.

> For the word of the cross is folly to those who are perishing, but to us who are being saved it is the power of God. For it is written, "I will destroy the wisdom of the wise, and the discernment of the discerning I will thwart..." For since, in the wisdom of God, the world did not know God through wisdom, it pleased God through the folly of what we preach to save those who believe...but we preach Christ crucified, a stumbling block to Jews and folly to Gentiles, but to those who are called, both Jews and Greeks, Christ the power of God and the wisdom of God. For the foolishness of

God is wiser than men, and the weakness of God is stronger than men...But God chose what is foolish in the world to shame the wise; God chose what is weak in the world to shame the strong; God chose what is low and despised in the world, even things that are not, to bring to nothing things that are, so that no human being might boast in the presence of God. And because of him you are in Christ Jesus, who became to us wisdom from God, righteousness and sanctification and redemption so that, as it is written, "Let the one who boasts, boast in the Lord." (1 Cor. 1:18-31)

God battles against our so-called wisdom and strength so that we might see our foolishness and weakness apart from Him and His grace. God shames us in our sin and humbles us so that we boast only in Jesus Christ our Lord, who alone is our wisdom, our righteousness, our sanctification, and our redemption.

As we step back and consider God's radical ways and thoughts displayed throughout His story of redemption, with Christ carrying out the ultimate paradox of the cross, we need to summarize some important implications for our life with our redeeming God. Beginning with the obvious, we need to remember that God is God and we are not. He knows what is best for us because He made us and saved us. Next, we need to trust God's thoughts and ways even when we don't want to or when the world says we are foolish and weak. Because of our ongoing battle with sin, we struggle to believe God is all good, wise, powerful and loving. Third, we need to believe that God redeems us through every life situation and He grows and changes us as we step out by faith to follow Him. We will experience His love and grace in deeper and more personal ways as we depend upon Him through every blessing and struggle in life. Last, we should remember God is always with us. He enables us to walk in His ways through His Spirit and He uses our life on earth to prepare us for eternity, where we will dwell with Him and feast on His glory forever and ever.

The Foolishness of Church Discipline

If the gospel seems foolish to the world, then church discipline will definitely seem foolish. In reality, church discipline even seems foolish to many members of the church. There is much confusion and a multitude of questions surrounding what seems to be either a barbaric and insensitive practice or an unknown entity. Some people are conflicted about the "aura and stereotype" of church discipline and do not want any part of it. Others might have a sense of the "whys and hows" of church discipline but have never been a part of a church that carried it out. There are some who are a part of a church that practices church discipline but they are still not sure about some of the approaches or outcomes they have witnessed. Still others have been involved in carrying out church discipline. To this day, they remember the anguish and anxiety that accompanied the relentless pursuit, the loving confrontation and the disheartening rebellion against God that preceded removing the unrepentant person from the church. They also remember the numbness, pain and brokenness in the aftermath of not only the one(s) offended, but the church as a whole.

But in spite of the tumultuous waves of confusion and concern, we can boldly enter the waters of church discipline. We have the proper course and bearings for engaging the issues of church discipline now that we understand our redeeming God in and through His story of redemption. God relentlessly pursues us as He continuously changes us more and more into the image of Christ. We have a proper vessel and crew for engaging the issues of church discipline now that we understand Christ has claimed us as His unlikely bride. He calls us to a radical life and mission of redemption, not only individually, but as a family who live in covenant community. We have the proper navigation instruments for engaging the issues of church discipline now that we understand God's radical and counter-intuitive ways and thoughts. We need to stay alert and sail by our instruments, because even as Christians, we can be tempted to think that the message of the cross is foolish and weak.

God has graciously and providentially set us on this voyage of redemption where we have to depend on Him for perspective, provision, perseverance, and protection. We will reflect our redeeming God through every nautical mile of this journey, as we love one another through intentional and redemptive relationships. We will be changed through this trip of faith as we navigate through the treacherous sea of suffering and sin while feeling the constant wind of His steadfast love and presence. We will have a deeper ballast of faith and experience His grace and power in more personal and profound ways as we sail through the dark storms of life. We will survive this journey if we do not rely on our own intuition or become pulled off course through the undercurrents of worldly philosophies and practices. Essentially we will complete this voyage if we steer by the timeless and powerful message of God and by His redeeming ways seen throughout the Scriptures.

DESPERATELY STEPPING OUT BY FAITH

Tom and Sharon Davis have noticed the increasing tension between John and Kathy over the past several weeks in their small group gatherings. After praying about if and how they might approach the Smiths, Tom and Sharon decided to invite John and Kathy over for dinner. Reluctant at first, the Smiths accepted the dinner invitation but were a bit anxious as they wondered if the Davises suspected anything about their failing marriage. Both couples were stepping out by faith to do what they had never done before.

LOOKING AHEAD

As we head into Part 2 we will take a closer look at how our sinful disobedience hinders us in living out our radical life and mission. We will also look at why and how God disciplines us, address some common ways of understanding church discipline, then come back to the definition of church discipline.

REFLECT AND RESPOND:

1. What are some personal examples that illustrate how God's ways and thoughts are better and more effective than your ways and thoughts?

2. How does God's consistent call to "return to receive" change your understanding of repentance? As God calls us to reflect Him in all we do, how does this gospel dynamic inform how you should relate to others, especially those who sin against you and those who are running from God?

3. The message of the cross is foolish to many and church discipline seems foolish to some. How has your view of church discipline changed as a result of seeing (1) how our redeeming God deals with our sinfulness, (2) how we are called to a radical life and mission as the bride of Christ, and

(3) how God glorifies Himself and shames the world with what seems weak and foolish?

4. How do you understand and accept God's purposes for your life? What do you need to change about your attitude, your approach to life, and your relationships so that you can be more faithful in God's mission of redemption?

PART 2:

The Bride's Rebellion and God's Discipline

4

Where the Gospel
Meets Real Life

BEGINNING THE JOURNEY

John and Kathy felt loved as they enjoyed a delicious meal with Tom and Sharon and chatted about the kids, movies and vacations. It seemed like such a long time since they had fun together with another couple. Tom discovered that both he and John enjoyed the same sports and the women shared a common love for cooking. During dessert and coffee, Tom transitioned the conversation by saying that he and Sharon looked forward to the evening because they desired to grow deep with other couples in their small group. Tom and Sharon shared some of their past and current marital struggles with John and Kathy and explained how the gospel enabled them to love, forgive, and grow in the grace of Christ.

John and Kathy felt confused and curious at the same time. Why did the Davises share what they shared? How did the gospel help them in their marriage? John didn't quite know how to respond to Tom's candor as a husband. Kathy started crying as she listened to Sharon share about her struggles and hope. Sharon asked Kathy about her tears. Kathy replied that it was so good to hear that other couples struggle and that the past several years have become increasingly difficult in their marriage. John felt uneasy as his wife shared about their less-than-perfect marriage. But by the end of the conversation, John accepted Tom's invitation to join him with one other man to encourage and challenge one another on Tuesday mornings before work. Sharon and Kathy were also looking forward to getting together weekly over coffee while the kids were in school.

REMEMBERING TO CONNECT THE DOTS

In the exact same way we need to see John and Kathy's lives within God's larger story, we need to see every aspect of church discipline from God's perspective. First, we need to remember that the context for pursuing and ministering to John and Kathy emerges out of God's larger story of redemption rather than seeing their suffering and sin simply within the context of their failing marriage. Second, we need to remember that the message and manner in which we minister to John and Kathy must reflect the gospel in every way, rather than offer mere pragmatic solutions as if this couple were a special project to be fixed or a unique problem to be addressed. Third, we need to remember that the motive and goal of our efforts to help John and Kathy need to correspond to the mission of the gospel through which God redeems His bride rather than to a personal mission to save every marriage or to prove our ministry effectiveness.

When we fail to keep John and Kathy's very real marital crisis within the framework of God's work of redemption, we will not get any closer to understanding church discipline from God's holistic perspective. Neither will we grasp the broader implications of church discipline unless we remember that it's not just about the one who is refusing to repent but it's also about the entire body of Christ in general, and about you and me in particular.

GOD'S DISCIPLINE BEGINS WITH YOU AND ME

As we have already seen, each one of us as God's children rebels against Him continually in spite of being called to live a radical life with Jesus. But in God's sovereign wisdom, church discipline has as much to do with our redemption as it does with John and Kathy's. A crucial point we need to remember is that regardless of our level of involvement with John and Kathy, our ability to participate in God's discipline of His people requires that we live with gospel intentionality so that we can experience God's redemptive work in our own lives and in our relationships with others.

Sadly, because of our ongoing battle with sin, along with the relentless schemes of the enemy, we struggle to live for the glory of Christ in our own lives. Not only does this make us ineffective servants in God's mission of redemption, but it can also lead to even worse consequences. Because of our own blind and hardened hearts, we can become the ones who turn away from the living God and need others to pursue us with the gospel and call us back to Christ.

BATTLING TO LIVE FOR THE GLORY OF CHRIST

Our Struggles to Live for God's Glory

Based on knowing our redeeming God and His bride, God calls His church to live for the glory of Christ, particularly in living with gospel intentionality while participating in God's mission. Satan and his evil kingdom continually battle against God's kingdom and His redeeming work. The kingdom of evil attempts to thwart and push back God's ongoing work of redemption day in and day out in the heart and mind of His bride, and in every one of her relationships. Therefore, in the midst of this continual struggle, all of creation groans and longs for God's final redemption and glory (cf. Rom. 8:18-23).

When we remember that God's radical mission of redemption involves relentless warfare, we will be more careful to live with a wartime mentality. God calls us to be watchful, to have minds prepared for action, to stand firm in the faith, to cling to our steadfast hope and to do everything in love (cf. 1 Pet. 1:13; 1 Cor. 16:13-14), all for the glory of God. We also need to be reminded that our struggle is not *"against flesh and blood, but against the rulers, against the authorities, against the cosmic powers over this present darkness, against the spiritual forces of evil in the heavenly places"* (Eph. 6:12). However, the reality is that we forget about this relentless spiritual warfare and live with a vacation mentality in which we live merely for ourselves and seek God only when we want Him to bail us out of trouble.

God not only calls us to take up arms in this very real and present mission, but He also calls us to share in the sufferings of Christ for the redemption of others. Each of us needs to remember that we are not the only bride but God has called us to live collectively as His family. It is so easy to forget that when one member is struggling with suffering and sin, we are all affected, since we are all part of Christ's body (cf. 1 Cor. 12:25-27). Such sacrifice for others is costly in terms of time, energy, and self-denial but such intentional ministry builds up the church in love and is at the core of God's vision of church discipline.

51

Our Struggles in Proclaiming His Gospel Message

Living for the glory of God also includes proclaiming and preserv-ing His gospel message. We bring glory to Christ when we preach the gospel not only to ourselves but also to those around us. The message of the cross cuts across gender, personality, and cultural backgrounds and offers a hope that never disappoints. Because this timeless message applies to both believers and unbelievers, we don't need to know two different messages. If we have truly tasted the kindness of God and experienced the transforming nature of His love, we will be compelled to proclaim this incredible and radical news to everyone around us. Unfortunately, the enemy does every-thing he can to undermine and minimize our efforts to proclaim the gospel message.

The message of the cross reveals the power of God, but Satan uses false teachers to twist and distort the gospel so that people walk away confused, disinterested, or believing in a false gospel that leads its hearers astray. The enemy does all he can to deform the message and distract people from it so that the bride becomes useless in God's mission and those who don't know Christ are drawn into hell. We must help one another see how false gospels undermine God and His gospel message and mission. Church leaders and members must identify, rebuke and remove such enemies of the gospel.[1] The church should take disciplinary measures to protect and preserve the gospel message and community.

When we fail to proclaim the gospel message, we also fail in our mission to those all around us. The world will not see the glory of Christ when we don't live out the glory of the gospel in our homes, neighborhoods, and workplaces. If the gospel is not a priority for us, we will not only keep the message hidden from others, but we will keep the gospel from having a redemptive effect in our relation-ships. Even if we strive to live out the gospel within our own homes, we may avoid taking our discussions and relationships into gospel territories for fear we may be rejected, ridiculed, or do damage to the people we care about. How will people hear the gospel unless we share the good news with our mouths and our lives? How will people see their need for Christ if we do not help them see how His gospel speaks to the struggles in their lives? How can we help

---

1   2 John 10-11; Rom. 16:17; Gal. 1:8-9; 2 Pet. 2:1-2

people see the relevancy of the gospel unless we step into their world, understand their hearts and proclaim the gospel in personal and life-giving ways? Proclaiming the gospel in our relationships in these and other ways is central to God's intent for disciplining His church.

Our Struggles in Participating in His Gospel Mission

The church should also live for the glory of Christ by participating in His gospel mission of redemption. Christ prepares His bride for an eternal life with Him as she labors alongside Him in building up His church in love and advancing His kingdom in this world. But we, as gospel ministers, are often sidelined in our God-given mission because of our ongoing battle with sin's deceptive and divisive ways.

Sin deceives us in many ways, but its ultimate deception is to tempt us through our thoughts, affections, and actions to reject Christ. We reject Christ whenever we believe the thoughts that swirl in our heads rather than what He declares to us through His Word. We reject Christ whenever we are swayed by our ever-present and persuasive feelings rather than the powerful and hope-filled faith that He enables by His Spirit. We reject Christ whenever we choose to pursue anything and everything other than Jesus Himself. We declare with our mouths and with our lives that Christ is not enough when we continually seek after other "lovers" and allow our hearts to be drawn away from Him as we find joy, refuge and satisfaction in ourselves and in the things of this world. We reject Christ in these and other ways every time we sin. That is why we need each other to help us see and call us back to what is true, honorable, right, pure, lovely, admirable, excellent and worthy of praise (cf. Phil. 4:8; Eph. 5:16). We will fail to see the depth, breadth and ongoing need for church discipline if we do not grasp the depth and breadth of our ongoing struggle with sin and how it impacts our ability to engage in the life and mission God has called us to live.

But as sin deceives individual hearts, it also divides the church in subtle and significant ways. Sin deceives and divides when we know that we have something against someone else, or when someone else has something against us, and we make no attempt at reconciliation. Sin deceives and divides when we believe we have forgiven someone yet decide we will have nothing to do with him or her again. Sin deceives and divides when we gossip and slander others who have wronged us or let us down. When we do not reconcile with one another as a result of real or perceived sin, Christ's body becomes divided and her health becomes impaired. How can the body of Christ live as one when she is divided against herself? How can the bride of Christ fulfill her mission when she is sidelined by her own sin? Pursuing peace, loving and forgiving like Christ, and reconciling are all essential and ongoing relational gospel practices that are essential for the unity and health of the church. Such a life requires intentionality and discipline in the spiritual battle between the kingdom of God and the kingdom of evil.

In addition to sin destroying lives and relationships, there is another real and serious consequence of our failure to repent and live by faith. In our struggle with sin, we can distort the gospel message through the way we live. What a travesty when the bride of Christ rejects her identity and lives as if she is not in a covenant relationship with her redeeming God. The church and the world will not see and experience the gospel when we fail to love, forgive, pursue peace, reconcile, and serve others. The church and the world will be confused when we say we know God but live in unfaithfulness, addictions, fears, anger, bitterness, divisions, and fantasies. Given that we often fail to see our need to live in ways consistent with the gospel, it's no wonder that even the church is confused over the issues of church discipline.

Bottom line, when we don't intentionally live out the gospel, we will waste our lives and become ineffective in God's mission as the bride of Christ. Moreover, we will not experience the fullness, beauty, and power of God's love in our lives and in those around us. Even worse, when we fail to labor hard with Christ in His gospel mission, the enemy's relentless efforts will re-establish strongholds in our hearts, minds, and relationships. We will also miss very real and present opportunities for redemption in the church and in the world. As a result, we will not see the relevancy or sense urgency for church discipline.

TURNING AWAY FROM THE LIVING GOD
There are times when we can become so hardened by the deceitfulness of sin that we turn away from the living God. During these times of deep and lasting rebellion, not only can we refuse to submit to God's

will and ways, but we can also refuse to turn back to Christ and reject any form of rescue from God and His people. We think that we are right and everyone else is wrong. We step into this arrogant and foolish posture after we reject God and decide to live as if He no longer exists or we think that He needs to take a back seat while we take control of our own lives. When we get to this point, we can see ourselves as all-knowing and all-powerful, as we live in our own fantasy world. We can imagine ourselves to be martyrs, willing to risk everything we care about to get what we want.

However, we just don't wake up one day with this kind of resolute rebellion. Such hardness typically emerges from deep disappointment and unfulfilled longings over a period of time. Our deep disappointment with God, self, others and life itself leads to doing whatever will give us some form of relief or distraction. Our unfulfilled longing for love, pleasure, and power leads us to do whatever it takes to get whatever we want so that we can satisfy our desires or change the way we feel or see ourselves.

Because Christ knows our ongoing struggle with sin, He calls us to *"exhort one another every day ... that none of you may be hardened by the deceitfulness of sin ... leading you to fall away from the living God"* (Heb. 3:13, 12). Christ calls us to pursue one another when we wander like sheep away from Him so that we might return to receive God's abundant compassion and forgiveness. This is part of the over-arching strategy of church discipline.

God Disciplines His Wayward Bride

God is fully aware of our struggle to live for Him. Because of His enduring love for us, God doesn't watch and wait passively as we stray from Him. What kind of father would do nothing if one of his children is actively rebelling against him as well as jeopardizing his own life and others? To do nothing would further allow and engrain sinful patterns of living and risk the health, mission and honor of everyone involved. This is why God disciplines His children.

The Big Picture of God's Discipline

The Scriptures use the explicit term "discipline" to describe how the Lord deals with His people in their rebellion. God disciplines us because He loves us,[2] which compares with the way a father

---

2   Deut. 4:36; 11:2; Job 5:17; 1 Cor. 11:32; Rev. 3:19

disciplines his son.[3] God clearly addresses the blessings of accepting or the foolishness of rejecting His discipline, which can also lead others astray.[4] The Lord describes His discipline as severe (Ps. 118:18) so that He might remove our foolishness (Prov. 22:15). The Lord's discipline is also described as a way of life (Prov. 6:23) due to our enduring struggle with sin, but such godly discipline produces the fruit of righteousness (Heb. 12:4-13). God's discipline reflects His merciful love since such intervention prepares us for our eternal life with Christ by helping us not to live for ourselves. Further, it conforms us more and more in the image of Christ by renewing our hearts and minds so that our thoughts, affections, and will are compelled by Christ and His love.

Whom Does God Discipline?

God disciplines those He loves, those He has adopted into His family as children, bringing them into His unshakeable kingdom (Heb. 12:6, 28). Does God discipline those who have not been redeemed by the blood of Christ? According to the Scriptures God does not discipline those who never come to faith in Christ. Rather, God punishes and pours out His wrath upon the wicked, resulting in eternal punishment.

What Motivates God's Discipline?

God's discipline is driven both by His glory and love. Everything God does is consistent with His character; therefore, everything He does is motivated by and results in His glory[5] since there is no other like Him.[6] Additionally, God explicitly declares that His discipline is motivated by His love for His children (Heb. 12:6; Rev. 3:19).

When Does God Discipline Us?

God disciplines us when we refuse to live for Him and His glory. He made us in His image, for His purposes, and for His glory. When we live in ways that do not reflect God or His ways, we end up reflecting Satan and experiencing disordered, deceived, and destructive lives.

---

3   Deut. 8:5; Eph. 6:4; Heb. 12:6-11
4   Ps. 50:17; Prov. 3:11; 12:1; 13:1, 18; 15:5, 32; 19:27; Heb. 12:5; Prov. 10:17
5   Pss. 23:3; 79:9; 106:8; Isa. 43:7; Ezek. 36:22
6   Exod. 8:10; Deut. 4:39; Isa. 42:8; 45:5; 46:9; 48:11

When we live in ways that do not result in gospel mission, we end up expending our gifts and talents on temporal matters and fail to be a part of God's redemptive work both in the church and world. When we live for our own glory and not for the glory of God, we end up disillusioned, disappointed, and depressed. In the end, when we live contrary to God's design, we not only fail to experience the fullness of our humanity and creation, but we fail to experience God Himself, who is perfect love, peace, comfort, strength, wisdom, joy, and pleasure. Therefore, God disciplines us as His bride so that we will experience the fullness of His glory and the life He purposed for us, which glorifies Him and conforms us to Christ.

How Does God Discipline Us?

God primarily uses His living Word and His living church to accomplish His redemptive work of discipline. Nothing cuts the heart deeper and exposes its sinfulness more accurately than God's living Word worked in by the Spirit of God. How many times has the Lord brought about undeniable conviction to you through a passage read or passage remembered? Moreover, not only does God discipline in the privacy of our hearts but He also uses His people to engage us when we are blind to our own sinfulness and struggle with unbelief and lies. How many times has the Lord used the words of others to bring about conviction of sin?

Given the importance of the Word and the people of God in carrying out His discipline, you can now see how the gospel message and mission of redemption is not only our calling, but it is also the means through which He disciplines His wayward bride. In other words, the radical life and mission of the church accomplishes God's purposes for His church, including the ongoing discipline of His bride.

WHY DOES GOD DISCIPLINE US?

God is intentional in everything He does. So what are God's purposes in His discipline? As we step back and remember that God is carrying out His redeeming work in every possible realm of life—in our individual lives and relationships, in every member of His body and also in the world—we will understand the purposes of church discipline knowing that our Redeemer calls us to follow Him in His radical mission. God accomplishes four major purposes through the discipline of His children: (1) restores relationship, (2) removes wickedness, (3) renews His people and (4) reveals His love and glory.

Restores Relationship. When we as God's children rebel against Him, He seeks to restore His relationship with us. Despite our foolish attempts to doubt and even "destroy" our relationship with Him through our sinfulness, God continually calls us back to Himself since He promised that nothing will ever separate us from His love and that He will never leave or forsake us. God pursues us by His Spirit as He works through His living Word and people to open our deceived eyes and soften our hardened hearts so that we might return to Him in the midst of our rebellion. What a tragedy when we choose to dwell in the evil of darkness instead of the light of God's merciful love and life-giving glory seen in the face of Christ.

Removes Wickedness. God will not be mocked. God does not allow sin to detract from His glory and deceive His people. Out of His love, God removes His children from His covenant community when they cling to wickedness rather than to Christ, whether it is through false teaching or false living, so that they might come to their senses. God also removes those from His covenant community who do not belong to His family, children of wrath who have not been redeemed by the blood of Christ. God wants His people to be sobered by the wickedness of sin and not to be confused about the way, truth and life (cf. John 14:6). What a tragedy when we refuse to see our sin as adultery against God and withdraw from the only One who can rescue us.

Renews His People. God is relentless in completing the work that He has begun in each of His people. God uses our waywardness for His redemptive purposes as He afflicts us and humbles us through His discipline,[7] knowing that He wants us to share in His holiness, individually and collectively as a church. God is renewing everything in our souls that has been marred by sin. He renews our identity so that we will reflect His Son and He renews our calling so that we will serve in His kingdom as ministers of reconciliation. What a tragedy that we live in ways that reflect our former lives associated with the kingdom of evil and refuse to join with our Redeemer in His mission of redemption.

---

7   Pss. 25:16-18; 32:1-5; 38; Isa. 30:20-22

Reveals His Love and Glory. God never reveals our deep wickedness without also revealing His powerful and merciful love. We must never forget God's declaration and demonstration of ultimate love through the cross where Christ suffered to take our shame from sins and absorb God's wrath for us. In revealing His love, God reveals His glory so that we might be reminded of who He is, what He has done and what He has promised to do through our incomparable relationship with Jesus. As God reveals His love, the lost and dying world will also get a glimpse of His glory so that ultimately, every knee will bow and every tongue confess that Jesus is Lord. What a tragedy when we settle for the imperfect and failing love and glory of our world rather than the perfect and everlasting love and glory of God.

God's purposes for discipline must drive the church's purposes for discipline, since we are ambassadors for Christ and ministers of His gospel. God's discipline is meant to have a ripple effect on the entire church so that we can all be reminded of God's call to live out His will, to reflect Christ in our lives, to live a radical life of mission, to see more deeply our sinful hearts so that we can more clearly see the glory of Christ through the cross, and to love one another in a way that reflects the gospel.

THE UPS AND DOWNS OF LIFE

Tom and John have been meeting weekly on Tuesday mornings before work for the past two months. Not only are they memorizing and working through Romans 8, but they are also sharing how they are struggling to live out the gospel. Tom has noticed that John seems to be growing increasingly agitated and angry, even though there are moments of grace when he simultaneously sees his wicked heart and the love of God. Despite these glimpses of redemption, John seems to be falling back into the trap of blaming Kathy for the difficulties in his life and has even confessed that he has turned to internet pornography as a way of finding relief from all the stress of work and family.

Sharon and Kathy have experienced some sweet and deeply redemptive conversations during their coffee chats. Kathy feels like a new woman as Sharon has encouraged and challenged her with the gospel. Kathy has never experienced such intimacy with her Redeemer, and the Scriptures are coming alive to her like never before. Even though John has withdrawn and become more aggressive in his language towards Kathy, she is able to respond with a patient grace, which is totally opposite to her emotional outbursts whenever John was rude to her in the past.

In one sense, John and Kathy are taking different paths even though they are both meeting with Tom and Sharon on a regular basis. The tension between them is evident to their children, who have even asked their parents if they are getting a divorce. Both John and Kathy reassure their children that nothing like that will ever happen.

REFLECT AND RESPOND:

1. Where are you on the spectrum of understanding church discipline: Opposed—Confused—Unsure of Certain Aspects—Supportive? Explain how and why you have developed your stated position about church discipline.

2. What are some specific and concrete ways you struggle to live out the gospel in your everyday life? Explain how you tend to live with a "wartime" or "vacation" mentality.

3. What are some specific ways your life and relationships run contrary to God's mission of redemption?

4. How might your view of church discipline change as you consider God's purposes for His discipline?

5

Looking at Church Discipline from God's Perspective

GROWING REALITY AND FANTASY

In spite of spending consistent time with Tom, John is growing more distant from Kathy and more hopeless about their life together. John can find nothing in their marriage worth fighting for, except the kids. John realizes both of his children will be devastated if he were to leave their mom but he sees no alternative. Life is too hard the way it is and he doesn't see any hope for change.

What complicates matters is that John has fallen for a co-worker who seems to be everything Kathy is not. Meredith is young and vivacious. She seems to appreciate him for who he is. She laughs at all of his jokes and seems to respect him more than Kathy did. In fact, Meredith mentioned to John over lunch one day that she has always dreamed of marrying an older, wiser man like him. She knows about Kathy and she is not bothered by the fact that John is married. By the way John has described his marriage, Meredith can see why John feels the way he does towards Kathy and she is convinced she can offer him a better life.

John doesn't dare tell Tom about Meredith because he knows what Tom would tell him. John makes one excuse after another to miss his weekly times with Tom. Consequently, Tom has grown increasingly frustrated with John, thinking that John could at least be considerate enough to tell him what is going on.

Before long, John finds himself lying to Kathy about work so he can slip away to spend time with Meredith. It doesn't take long for their relationship to turn sexual. John obsesses over this woman who makes life so exciting and makes him feel so much like a man, in ways Kathy never did.

Kathy rationalizes John's increasing time at work by telling herself he is withdrawing because of their marriage. John justifies his adulterous affair by telling himself it is something he deserves, something he needs to survive, and something that enables him to envision his life after Kathy and the kids.

Clearly this marital situation has turned for the worse. What would you do if and when you discover a married man in your church is involved in an adulterous relationship? If you have been meeting with him regularly, when would you need to shift away from the more informal meetings over coffee to the more formal meetings in an office setting with a church leader? At what point would the church need to carry out formal church discipline. As we consider these and other questions, we need to take a step back to better understand church discipline. Remember, the goal is to seek to understand church discipline from God's point-of-view, consistent with His story of redemption.

We will start by looking at some of the categories used by pastors when discussing church discipline. Then we will look at some of the general and particular Biblical passages associated with church discipline so that we can develop a Scriptural understanding of this important aspect of the church. Finally, we will work toward a definition of church discipline so that we can understand this aspect of the church from God's perspective and as a result, live and function as the bride of Christ according to God's design.

Understanding Aspects of Church Discipline

When you bring up the topic of church discipline, you may hear terms that describe certain aspects of the process. For instance, you may hear a distinction made between instructive and corrective church discipline. Moreover, you may hear a distinction between the informal church discipline that takes place in everyday life and the formal church discipline that takes place when church elders get involved in pursuing and dealing with an unrepentant church member.

Are these distinctions helpful? Yes, to the extent in which they describe *different aspects* of the ministry of the Word in helping a member grow in Christ (instructive and corrective) and *different degrees* of the church's redemptive efforts in calling a wayward member back to Christ (informal and formal). Let's take a closer look at each of these categories of thinking so that we can better understand church discipline.

"Instructive" and "Corrective" Church Discipline

In a broad sense, church discipline is a term used to describe the means through which the church helps one another to conform to Christ, as described by Paul:

> Him we proclaim, warning everyone and teaching everyone with all wisdom, that we may present everyone mature in Christ. For this I toil, struggling with all his energy that he powerfully works within me. (Col. 1:28-29)

From this passage and others (Eph. 6:4; 1 Thess. 5:12, 14; Col. 3:16), we see that Paul proclaims Christ as the means for maturing others in the gospel. But notice Paul describes two aspects of the ministry of the Word—warning *and* teaching. *Warning*, or admonishing, involves correcting attitudes and actions so that we might live for God. Such corrective efforts include activities like confronting, rebuking, and encouraging with the Word of God. *Teaching* involves instructing with the purpose of helping others to know and live for God. Such instructive efforts include activities like preaching, teaching, and studying the Scriptures. We need to *correct* and *instruct* others with the gospel so that we might grow in Christ and equip others to do the same. Paul gave his life to this task while depending on the power and energy of Christ to accomplish God's mission of redemption.

Why should we be careful to include both the corrective and instructive aspects whenever we minister the Word to one another? If we correct without offering instruction, we will focus on the commands and can become people concerned more about the rules than relationships. If we instruct without correcting, we will focus on concepts without consequences and can become people who fail to connect truth with life, *hearers* and not *doers* of the Word.

We can see that the distinction between instructive and corrective discipline is helpful when it serves as a reminder of the dual nature of the ministry of the Word. But don't become confused, thinking that the ministry of the Word is *only* instructive or *only* corrective. Rather, it is *both* instructive *and* corrective. When we understand that we need instruction *and* correction all the time, we will seek *both* aspects, knowing that God designed this dual approach for our growth.

Furthermore, if you take an either/or perspective, you can miss the deeper overall message and mission of the gospel. Have you been in churches where they focus solely on either sound teaching or correction, and as a result, you experience more law than gospel? You might feel on edge, fearful that you don't know enough and thinking you just need more teaching rather than engaging others with the gospel by faith. Or you might feel on edge, fearful of revealing any sin because you have received dutiful correction and judgment rather than rejoicing with one another over confessed sin, which is evidence of Christ's ongoing work of redemption in your lives.

When we take a look at the interaction and dialogue between a husband and wife working through a recent conflict, the lines between instructive and corrective discipline are blurred and seem somewhat artificial. How would you classify the interaction when a husband confesses that his anger towards his wife emerged from his discontent with what God has given him in life and he asks the Lord and his wife for forgiveness? Was this corrective or instructive discipline, or both? The husband was clearly the recipient of discipline but in this case, he confessed and asked for forgiveness without his wife saying a word. The Lord clearly disciplined the husband through the conviction of the Holy Spirit. At the same time, as the wife listened and watched her husband approach her with love and humility, she was convicted of her own sinfulness while rejoicing in seeing God's redeeming grace at work in her and her husband. So should we say she experienced instructive or corrective discipline, or did she experience both? Do you begin to see how the categories of *instructive* and *corrective* discipline overlap per God's wisdom as it relates to the ministry of the Word? Again the two distinct aspects of the Word of God are biblical and necessary but such distinctions may become reductionistic and misleading when it comes to thinking about church discipline.

Given our discussion about "instructive" and "corrective" discipline, let's now take a look at the categories of "informal" and "formal" discipline.

"Informal" and "Formal" Church Discipline

In order for us to think through this issue of "informal" and "formal" church discipline, we need to begin by looking at these categories from two different perspectives—context and severity.

The distinction between informal and formal discipline can be understood first from the basis of context. We might call teaching that takes place during some form of church *gathering* as "formal instructive discipline." However, when parents talk about the gospel over dinner with the kids, we might classify that as "informal instructive discipline." We might classify a conversation where a friend confronts another friend in a coffee shop about his sexual sin as "informal corrective church discipline." However, we will describe a church meeting where the name of an unrepentant member is brought before the members for prayer and pursuit as "formal corrective church discipline." But as we consider the radical life and mission that God calls us to live, we begin to see a more fluid picture of how God calls His bride to minister the Word to one another as we *gather* and *scatter* as the church.

The distinction between informal and formal discipline can also be understood from the basis of the severity and progression of a given situation. For those who have participated in pursuing and confronting someone blinded by sin within the church, you may have experienced the shift from the informal to more formal efforts that results in:

1. An increasing involvement of church leadership.

2. An increasing number of hours invested and attempts made in redemptive effort.

3. An increasing formality and intensity of the warnings.

4. An increasing portion of the church body being informed and called to pray for and pursue the unrepentant person.

5. An increasing hardness and deceitfulness of the unrepentant person's heart.

6. An increasing withdrawal of covenant fellowship as final warnings are ignored.

Even though the redemptive purpose and goal of the discipline never changes in the shift from the informal to the formal pursuit, the seriousness of the situation intensifies.

In describing church discipline as *informal* and *formal*, even though the content and the intended purpose are the same in both descriptions, the main differences seem to be the context as well as the severity of the situation. Is this particular distinction in church discipline helpful or does it serve to create more confusion? Does it distort and restrict the church's understanding of God's redemptive mission that He purposed to take place in and through His church in general and through redemptive relationships in particular?

Could it be that such distinctions between informal and formal church discipline emerge from our desire to be precise in our systematic, and perhaps, reductionist understanding of church discipline? To look at this issue in a different way, we might ask if there is such a thing as *informal* ministry of the Word, *informal* gospel mission, or even *informal* redemption? Most of us would respond, "Absolutely not!" So why do we make a distinction between informal and formal church discipline?

A church leader who leads in discipline matters knows the visceral sense when a pastoral issue turns for the worse and the husband he has been counseling becomes hardened and wants out of the marriage. In one sense, since most of us have been shaped by these distinctions, we ask ourselves, "Okay, when do I need to shift this marriage counseling to formal church discipline?"

A group of pastors from the Sovereign Grace network explained that such a question seems artificial and shifts them from a pastoral orientation to more of a process orientation that typifies a "check-list" approach to church discipline. We need to guard against any systematic approach to church discipline that comes across detached and wooden. The truth is that you are shepherding the husband and wife from the time you begin the marriage counseling, if not before, until you may be forced to remove the husband from membership due to his hardened and unrepentant heart. All of your efforts are meant to reflect God's redemptive pursuit, including your exhortations and encouragements.

So at the end of the day, should we make a distinction between *informal* and *formal* church discipline? In order to answer this question, we will now survey the Scripture passages that define how we are to live with one another and some key passages typically associated with "church discipline."

LOOKING AT THE "ONE ANOTHER" PASSAGES
Most Christians might agree that instructive and corrective discipline should be happening in everyday gospel community, whether

it is through the intentional interactions between a husband and wife over dinner or when men or women challenge and encourage one another in their weekly accountability group. In everyday life we don't describe such interactions as informal instructive and corrective church discipline. By God's design we should view and experience such redemptive relationships as helping one another to live out the gospel together in community. However, when we shift to using language like "informal church discipline," we suggest we are doing something beyond God's purposeful and on-going ministry of the Word as the means for redemption. In other words, the term "church discipline" implies more of the exception rather than the norm when considering our radical life of gospel mission.

Through the "one another" passages, Jesus and the authors of the New Testament provide a beautiful picture of how we should live out the gospel as the bride of Christ. Our prevailing call is to love one another so we can reflect Christ in His love for us and that we might fulfill His royal law (cf. James 2:8). God provides a rich and specific array of "one another" commands to help us to better understand ways we are called to love one another:

Highlights of the "One Another" Passages

Love and be kind to one another John 13:34-35; Rom.12:10; 13:8-9; 1 Cor. 13:4-7; Gal. 5:14; Eph. 4:15; 32; 5:1-2; Heb. 10:24; James 2:8; 1 Peter 1:22; 4:7; 1 John 3:11, 23; 4:7,11-12, 19-21	Forgive and reconcile with one another Matt. 5:9-15; Mark 11:20-25; Eph. 4:32; Col. 3:13; Matt. 5:21-28	Encourage, build up and bless one another Rom. 14:19; 15:2; Eph. 4:16, 29; Heb. 3:13; 10:25; 1 Thess. 4:18; 5:11
Give thanks and glorify the Lord with one another Rom. 15:6; Eph. 5:19-20	Honor, respect, be humble and patient, submit to one another Rom. 12:10; Eph. 5:21; Col. 3:12; 1 Thess. 5:12-13; 1 Pet. 5:5	Pursue peace and maintain unity with one another Rom. 15:5; 1 Cor. 12:25; 2 Cor. 13:11; Eph. 4:3; Col. 3:14

Rejoice, confess, pray and give thanks always Rom. 12:12, 15; 1 Cor. 12:26; 1 Thess. 5:16-18; James 5:16	Hold fast and draw near to Christ with one another Rom. 12:9; 1 Thess. 5:21; Heb. 4:14-16; 10:22-23	Comfort, weep and suffer with one another Rom. 12:15; 1 Cor. 12:26; 2 Cor. 1:3-5
Teach, admonish, rebuke and exhort one another Col. 1:28; 3:16; 1 Thess. 5:14; 2 Tim. 3:16; Heb. 2:13	Restore one another who is in sin 2 Cor. 13:11; Gal. 6:1; James 5:19-20; Jude 23	Help and bear the burdens of one another Rom. 14:19; Col. 3:13; Gal. 6:2; Eph. 4:2
Do not repay evil for evil but do good to one another Col. 3:9; 1 Thess. 5:15, 22;	Do not lie and grumble or speak evil against one another Eph. 4:15; James 4:11; 5:9	Serve, contribute to the needs and show hospitality to one another John 13:14; Gal. 5:13; 1 Pet. 4:9-10; Rom. 12:13

What a beautiful and expansive portrait of life together in the gospel, all for the glory of Christ. Our Redeeming God designed every "one another" expression of love between members of the body of Christ to serve as a means of preparing His bride for eternal glory:

> He makes the whole body fit together perfectly. As each part does its own special work, it helps the other parts grow, so that the whole body is healthy and growing and full of love. (Eph. 4:16, NLT)

We might agree that such "one anothering" includes most aspects of what we might associate with both *informal* and *formal* church discipline. But if we try to divide these passages between *informal* and *formal* discipline, not only will we create artificial distinctions, but we can shift the intent of these passages from a fluid and relational orientation to a more rigid and dutiful orientation of the gospel life.

LOOKING AT THE "CHURCH DISCIPLINE" PASSAGES

However, when Jesus and Paul instruct the church on how to deal with those deceived and hardened by sin, even though they do not use the term "church discipline,"[1] they call the church to address the unrepentant person in ways that seem to go beyond the everyday "one another" passages. What we see in these passages is an expanding and escalating effort to call the unrepentant one back to Christ.

Jesus offers a progression of actions to be taken towards one who refuses to repent after being caught in sin (cf. Matt. 18). The offended person is directed to go to the offender in private to address the sin (v. 15). If the offender refuses to listen, then the offended person is to invite one or two other people to serve as witnesses to the alleged offense (v. 16). We might agree that these first two steps should reflect the "one another" interaction that should take place in gospel community. However, Jesus takes the scenario further. If the offender refuses to listen to this group of two to three people, then the offended person should tell the church (v. 17a). If the person still refuses to listen even to the church, the church should then treat the unrepentant person as an unbeliever (v. 17b).

In confronting a difficult situation, Paul rebukes the church in Corinth for not dealing with the serious sexual sin of a man in their church (1 Cor. 5). Paul pronounces judgment on the man and directs the church, when they assemble, to remove the man from their midst (vv. 2-3) and to turn him over to Satan for the destruction of his flesh so that he might ultimately be redeemed (v. 4-5). Paul continues to instruct the church that they are called not only to judge those in the church who fail to repent from their life of sin, but they are also called not to associate or even eat with them (vv. 9-12). He ends the chapter by exhorting the church to purge the evil person from among them (v. 13).

As a possible follow up to the situation addressed in 1 Corinthians 5, or possibly another situation involving Paul himself, Paul acknowledges the "punishment by the majority" as being sufficient towards the offender (2 Cor. 2:6). It can be understood that the church, as the body of Christ, took disciplinary actions towards the offender. Paul then calls the church to forgive, comfort, and reaffirm their love for the offender so the person would not be overwhelmed

---

1   Matt. 18:15-20; 1 Cor. 5; 2 Cor. 2:5-11; 1 Thess. 5:14-15; 2 Thess. 3:14-15; Titus 3:9-11

by excessive sorrow and that Satan would not outwit the church (vv. 7-11). Such a call gives us a picture of reconciliation made possible only in the gospel, where redemption is the goal of any and all discipline and where the church can freely forgive and love since they, too, have received abundant mercy and pardon.

In two other passages, Paul addresses one who fails to reflect the gospel life through his idleness (2 Thess. 3:6-15) and one who causes division through foolish and worthless talk (Titus 3:9-11). In both cases, Paul exhorts the church to avoid such people (2 Thess. 3:6; Titus 3:9) after warning them (Titus 3:10), but also have nothing to do with them so that they might experience shame, or godly sorrow, that leads to repentance (2 Thess. 3:14; 2 Cor. 7:10). But Paul offers a final word to not treat the person as an enemy but warn him as a brother (2 Thess. 3:15).

As we step back and consider the drastic actions commanded by Scripture in situations associated with an unrepentant believer, we must view such actions as redemptive and as a means to preserve the glory of Christ while protecting the purity of the church. Such significant action seems to take place when a person turns away from the living God in spite of repeated attempts to rescue the unrepentant person from the destructive and deceptive nature of sin.

BRINGING IT ALL TOGETHER

Now that we surveyed a number of passages that help us to better understand church discipline, let's summarize what we have seen. In one sense, the "one another" passages not only cover the essence of what is called *informal* church discipline, but also cover most of what takes place in *formal* church discipline. Whether we are referring to informal or formal church discipline, it involves battling *for* the souls of those blinded and hardened by the schemes of the evil one (cf. 2 Tim. 2:25-26). God calls us to fight for one another in every day community with divinely powerful weapons that destroy everything that rises up against the knowledge of God (cf. 2 Cor. 10:3-5). However, we find two major concepts in the passages associated with formal discipline that are not clearly articulated in the "one another" texts—the mobilization of the entire church gathering and the removal of the unrepentant person from the covenant fellowship should a person fail to repent after repeated redemptive efforts.

Why is it essential that we understand the importance and intentionality of these "one another" and "church discipline" passages? The gospel message can be compromised not only through false teaching but also through false living. The church and the world become confused when the gospel is mixed with falsehoods and when the gospel doesn't seem to make any difference in who we are and how we live. The gospel mission can be jeopardized when the church fails to address the very thing the mission is all about—God's redeeming work in the midst of our struggle with suffering and sin. If the church fails to pursue and help those who are hurting, as well as those who are hurting themselves and others, the church and the world will not understand and believe that the gospel is relevant, let alone effective, on this side of heaven. God calls the church to take decisive action when the gospel message or mission is at risk. Why? Ultimately, in the cosmic clash between the kingdoms of God and evil, the glory of Christ and the redemption of His bride hang in the balance.

Towards Defining "Church Discipline"

By His wisdom, God brought us into His family so that we can experience His grace and love as we encourage and challenge one another in the gospel so that we might live by faith in Jesus Christ. God uses such intentional and redemptive gospel-driven interactions to discipline us in tangible ways through our church family whenever we turn our backs on Him. Such discipline addresses struggles ranging from our daily fear, anger, and escapism to abandoning our families through adultery or addictions, while rejecting God through our actions and attitudes. Understanding these real struggles, we can offer a definition of church discipline:

> God's ongoing, redeeming work through His living Word and people as they fight the fight of faith together to exalt Christ and protect the purity of His Bride.

This definition of church discipline focuses on how God disciplines us through His church for the purposes of restoring relationships, removing wickedness, renewing His people and revealing His love and glory.

This definition does not differentiate between *informal* and *formal* church discipline since such a distinction may not exist from God's perspective as He accomplishes His redemptive work.

In fact, this definition helps us to view church discipline not from our perspective, but from God's perspective. Such a definition also helps us to see God's discipline through His church more as His *ongoing* work through His living Word and people. Inherent in this definition is an understanding that church discipline involves a continuum that includes *expanding* (involving an increasing number of people) and *escalating* (involving elders and more formal warnings) efforts over time to fight for those who relentlessly refuse to turn back to their living God.

This definition also recognizes that God disciplines us in everyday gospel community as we struggle with unbelief associated with who He is or what He has done through Christ, perhaps as a result of our intense suffering or fears. With this point, it is also helpful to remember that the ministry of the Word both instructs and corrects. God is in the business of always encouraging and challenging us in the gospel. Regardless of the reason for the discipline, from the first redemptive engagement to the last efforts taken with an unrepentant person, the gospel message serves as the means, redemption is the goal, and Christ and His Spirit are the ones who make all things possible.

By using the terms *informal* and *formal*, we place the focus more on the *process* rather than on God's ongoing work of redemption and on the *person* who has turned His back on the living God. If we focus on the changes in the process, we do see an increase in church leadership involvement, in redemptive efforts and warnings, and in the church's involvement, which we equate with *formal* church discipline. However, when we consider the heart struggles of those being pursued, God views their unbelief and lack of repentance as a personal rebellion from the very start. Even though the consequences associated with chronic waywardness can increase in severity over time, never once does God view such hardness of heart as shifting from an *informal* realm to a more *formal* realm.

Every confused heart that questions whether God is good or faithful in the midst of suffering offends their Redeemer. Every rebellious heart, regardless of the immensity or intensity of the sin, offends their God. But here is where God's ways and thoughts are not like ours. No measure of rebellion disrupts or blinds God's redemptive gaze of His people. God will complete the redemption He started in each of His children and He uses His church to pursue, call back, and even remove the unrepentant person to not only redeem the wayward person, but also to redeem His bride as a whole. God always transforms what is meant for evil and redeems it for His glory. Such is the nature of His gospel mission. Such is the nature of church discipline.

Where Do We Go From Here?

One of the most important things that I do as a pastor is to help God's people connect the dots between the gospel truths they hear and agree with on Sundays and the details and difficulties of their everyday lives. We all struggle to connect the gospel with life. Take for instance the struggle with anger. People know when their anger is sinful, but they need help seeing what fuels their anger and how their anger is ultimately sin against God. How so? James 4:1-4 reveals that when our anger flows from hearts warring with sinful desires, we not only commit adultery against God but we actually declare our hostility towards Him.

Both John and Kathy will tell you that their constant arguments and the resultant pain have destroyed their marriage. What desires are raging in each of their hearts? How can they reconcile this great divide in their marriage? Where do they begin? How is their bitterness towards each other sin against God? What do they not believe about the gospel in the midst of their hopelessness regarding their marriage? What does repentance look like in their situation? What would look different if they live by faith day by day? Who should they go to for help?

God has called and equipped the church to sort through the chaos of John and Kathy's hearts and marriage. As we peel back the layers, we see that we all face similar struggles but with different contexts and past details. God appoints His bride to step into the messiness of each other's lives by faith with His gospel so that the body of Christ will be built up in love. This is gospel ministry. This is the ministry of the Word at the battlefield level.

Because God's call to a radical life and mission of redemption includes situations like John and Kathy's, if we fail to get involved and pursue them as God pursues us, we fail to fulfill God's purpose for our lives. But you must know that such a life requires intentionality, involves suffering, but results in eternal rewards. Are you up for this everyday gospel mission? Are you ready to step out of your comfort zone and be stretched like never before? If so, let's move towards John and Kathy in love.

LOOKING AHEAD

In Chapters 1-3, we highlighted the crucial context for understanding church discipline from God's story of redemption. In Chapters 4–5 we normalized what is commonly referred to as church discipline and looked at church discipline from God's perspective. As we head into Part 3, which is intended to address the practical issues related to God's discipline through His church, we will unpack the "one another" passages in a way that will give additional breadth and depth to how God calls us to engage in everyday gospel mission.

REFLECT AND RESPOND:

1. Given the dual aspects of the ministry of the Word—both instructive and corrective—can you share why it may be necessary, or not necessary, to describe church discipline as either instructive or corrective?

2. Reflect on the rich and broad array of the "one another" commands found throughout Scripture. How are these redemptive commands understood and being put into practice in your church?

3. Given the discussion on informal and formal church discipline, how might you find such distinctions helpful, not helpful?

4. Review the definition of church discipline offered in this chapter. How does this definition compare and contrast to your present understanding of church discipline? What aspects would you add or remove from this proposed definition?

PART 3:

God's Call to Carry Out His Redemptive Discipline

6

Everyday Gospel Mission

A new commandment I give to you, that you love one another: just as I have loved you, you also are to love one another. By this all people will know that you are my disciples, if you have love for one another (John 13:34-35).

Exposed and Overwhelmed

Tom was very aware of the growing disconnection between him and John. In fact, Tom emailed or texted John frequently only to receive cursory responses stating that he was thankful for their friendship but he was extremely busy and barely had time for his family, let alone time to meet with Tom.

Then one afternoon when Tom was on the outskirts of town waiting for a business client at a restaurant, an uneasy feeling stirred within as he heard a familiar laugh and saw the back of a man who resembled John, but who was sitting with a woman who clearly was not Kathy. Tom debated for several minutes about whether or not he should approach the table to get a better look and if he did, what would he say. Tom said a quick prayer for wisdom and grace then got up and walked over to the table. When Tom was within arm's reach of the table, the woman looked up at Tom and then quickly looked nervously at John. At the same time, John turned to look over his shoulder and saw Tom. Both men were speechless. Meredith knew this was an awkward yet significant moment.

After some quick exchanges, the men agreed to call each other later that night. Tom's heart was beating wildly as he tried to keep himself composed on his way back to his table and during the course of his business meeting that followed. His mind was flooded with thoughts and emotions.

By the time Tom got into his car to head home, his cell phone rang. It was John, who was at first apologetic about Tom seeing him with Meredith, but then he accused Tom of spying on him. Tom let John ramble, then after a long silence, Tom tore into John for lying to him and for cheating on Kathy. John didn't want to hear anything Tom had to say and hung up on Tom. By this time, Tom had to pull over to the side of the road because he was so shaken. After a few minutes, Tom was able to compose himself and he headed back home, all the while wondering what he would share with Sharon, how he would confront John again, if and when he and Sharon should tell Kathy, and if he should inform any of the pastors at church about this situation.

Let's join Tom and Sharon as they prayerfully step into a situation in which they never dreamed they would be involved. Given their understanding of God's call to follow Christ in His gospel mission, watch as they step into this mess of life trusting in Jesus and not in their own abilities.

EVERYDAY OPPORTUNITIES

Life is full of hurt, disappointment, and sorrow. You cannot go a single day or even a single moment in the day without experiencing your own sin and the sins of others. The wickedness in our hearts, the godlessness and debauchery lived out in the world, and the evil that Satan stirs up wreaks havoc in our minds, destroys relationships, and distorts what God created for good. You learn that a friend from church is slandering you. You are out to dinner with a couple and they spend the entire time hurting one another with disrespectful and condemning jabs. A wife shares with you over coffee that she is growing weary of being married to a man who doesn't understand her and doesn't lead them spiritually as a family despite her constant pleas. You noticed that a fellow small group member has not only developed a pattern of kicking back a few beers every night after work to take the edge off but is also getting drunk every weekend. A friend shares that she is really struggling to believe that God loves her as she is battling despair in her loneliness. As in Tom's situation, you discover a close friend is having an affair. What do you do? What do you say? Should you tell anyone?

It is in these, and hundreds of other scenarios that are played out every day, that we can step into God's mission of redemption by faith as we connect the gospel to real life. God designed every detail of life on this side of eternity to provide opportunities where everyone involved will not only experience God in a more personal and powerful way, but also, can experience His transforming grace both individually and collectively.

CONNECTING COMMUNITY TO MISSION

Regardless of your family, workplace or season of life, God calls you to live out the gospel in authentic community and engage in His mission. But what does this look like? Well, let's take a moment to review and re-connect some dots so that we can better understand what gospel mission through community is all about.

We need to remember that God's call for us to join Him in mission originates with His greatest command to love Him with our entire being (Matt. 22:37-40; Rom. 12:1-2), which means He wants us to live for Him and for His glory through the power and grace of His Spirit (1 Cor. 10:31; Heb. 11:6). We are called, individually and collectively as a community of believers, to follow our Redeemer who did nothing apart from His Father's will (John 5:19-21; 30; 14:10, 31). Therefore, since God is still working out His grand story of redemption, we too must be about His mission. We were ransomed and redeemed for His purposes (Eph. 2:10) so that we can co-labor with Him as His bride and not become sidelined by our own self-absorbed agendas. God is glorified when we no longer live for ourselves but for our Redeemer, as ministers of reconciliation and ambassadors of Christ (2 Cor. 5:14-21) in His radical mission.

We also need to remember that the ministry of the Word has two aspects that always go hand in hand—being both instructive and corrective. From God's perspective we should encourage and challenge one another in our daily conversations, as we minister the Word for the purpose of helping one another live out the gospel. In other words, we should be comforting and confronting one another on a regular basis as opposed to only when a situation is extremely good or bad. Sadly, such intentional and heart-probing gospel conversations are more the exceptions than the norm; therefore, such encounters often are received with surprise, defensiveness, and over-reaction.

EVERYDAY GOSPEL MISSION

God calls us to engage in this face-to-face gospel mission whether we have been directly sinned against, or we learn about a friend's unbelief during intense suffering or we learn about a brother or sister's struggle through the fruits of their sin-driven life. This is why God provides biblical principles and specific gospel truths through the myriad of "one another" passages. He knows we need help in navigating the messiness of life and relationships in light of the gospel. Even more, when we bear each other's burdens, we fulfill the law of Christ (Gal. 6:1-2). Why? Because God redeems His bride and receives glory when we care for one another through community in the everyday realities of life by:[1]

1. Loving God and one another.

2. Engaging one another with the gospel.

3. Fighting for one another in suffering and sin.

4. Forgiving and reconciling with one another.

Such intentional, redemptive, inter-dependent body life serves as a picture of the gospel in action, protects the purity and unity of the church and provides the foundation for church discipline.

LOVING GOD AND ONE ANOTHER

The best starting point for understanding gospel mission through community is the Trinity. The perfect community of Father, Son, and Holy Spirit exists, functions, and is held together in perfect love as each work together to accomplish God's redemptive mission. God calls us to join in His Trinitarian mission as we serve as His ambassadors.

In order for us to be best equipped and mobilized to serve Him, God wants us first to experience His love so that we might be rooted in His infinite and powerful love (Eph. 1:17-18). His love

---

1   Appendix 6 shows how these four broad categories of one another commands can serve as a practical guide for everyday gospel mission.

serves as the motive and means through which we carry out His mission. This is why Jesus states that all of Scripture is summarized by God's two-fold call to love (Matt. 22:37-40). But God knows that we can misunderstand love and make it all about us. So He leaves no room for confusion by defining love by the cross of Jesus Christ. Love comes from God. Love is personified and defined by God (1 John 4:9-10, 19). By His design, we experience the fullness of our humanity and we best reflect our Redeemer by loving God first and foremost, and by loving one another in the way Christ loves us.

Why is loving God and others mission critical? Without love, we are nothing and we will accomplish nothing of God's agenda (1 Cor. 13:1-3). By His nature and wisdom, God redeems and sustains us as we abide in His love (John 15:1-17). In Christ, nothing else counts except faith working through love (Gal. 5:6). All of the "one another" commands can only be understood and applied within the realm of God's double love command.

ENGAGING ONE ANOTHER WITH THE GOSPEL

We all struggle with relationships, whether it's because of time constraints, differences of opinions, clashing personalities, fear of being known by others, apathy in caring about others, or a lack of experience in sharing lives in a transparent way. We have to fight to develop lasting and meaningful friendships that help us to grow in the grace of Christ. God calls us to engage one another with the gospel by:

1. Building one another up in the gospel.

2. Speaking truth in love.

3. Stirring one another up to love and good works.

4. Staying away from gossip, slander or complaining about others.

How else can we love one another unless we spend intentional time talking and listening to each other and journeying with one another in ways that go deeper than superficial niceties and self-protective maneuvers? All of us need help in connecting the gospel truths to the realities of our lives.

Richard Baxter, a pastor in England during the seventeenth century known for his faithful service in the ministry of the Word, makes a shocking statement regarding gospel ministry:

I have found by experience, that some ignorant persons, who have been so long unprofitable hearers, have got more knowledge and remorse in half an hour's close discourse, than they did from ten years' public preaching. I know that preaching the gospel publicly is the most excellent means, because we speak to so many at once. But it is usually far more effectual to preach it privately to a particular sinner ...[2]

J. I. Packer, a theologian, comments on Baxter's assertion:

Therefore personal catechizing and counseling, over and above preaching, is every minister's duty: for this is the most rational course, the best means to the desired end. So it was in Baxter's day. Is it so now?[3]

These thoughts offered by Baxter and Packer highlight the importance of engaging one another with the gospel in personal and particular ways. Paul gives us a crucial reminder of our mission to those in and out of the church:

We proclaim him, admonishing and teaching everyone with all wisdom, so that we may present everyone perfect in Christ. To this end I labor, struggling with all his energy, which so powerfully works in me. (Col. 1:28-29, NIV)

Paul understood the challenge and goal of gospel mission. We must examine ourselves and ask, "To what end do I labor and give my whole life to God for the sake of the gospel?"

FIGHTING FOR ONE ANOTHER IN SUFFERING AND SIN

As the body of Christ, we are in a relentless spiritual battle, both individually and collectively because of our own indwelling sin, the world, and Satan. God grows and matures us in the gospel as we enter the fray with our brothers and sisters in Christ, as well as when we allow others to enter into our lives with the gospel. We fight for one another in our suffering and sin by:

1. Bearing one another's burdens.

2. Pursuing for the sake of redemption.

---

2   Richard Baxter, *The Reformed Pastor*, p. 18

3   J.I. Packer, introduction—*The Reformed Pastor*, p. 18

3. Approaching one another privately and personally.

4. Confessing sin to one another.

We need others to fight for us when we are blinded by the deceitfulness of sin, distracted by the allure of the world and enslaved by the lies of the enemy. We need to believe that the struggles of a brother or sister in Christ impact the whole body. Apathy and self-centeredness does not advance the mission of God. We need to cling to and follow our victorious Redeemer with a wartime mentality, focused on His mission and glory. To do anything less makes us ineffective and we will fail in reflecting and glorifying our King.

FORGIVING AND RECONCILING WITH ONE ANOTHER

Gospel community is messy because of our ongoing sin against one another. Knowing this gospel reality, God makes it clear that we are to forgive and reconcile with one another so that our relationships in community reflect His relationship with us. God calls us to forgive and reconcile with one another by:

1. Putting off bitterness, anger, and vengeance.

2. Pursuing peace and unity.

3. Loving and forgiving as Christ loves and forgives us.

4. Reconciling with one another.

When we fail to forgive and reconcile with those who sinned against us or we have sinned against, we not only fail to reflect our God but our lives are antithetical to the gospel. When we fail to encourage and challenge others to forgive and reconcile, perhaps out of fear, oversight or apathy, we fail to love them. Not only should we fight for each other's souls, but we must also fight for unity and peace. To do anything less divides and weakens Christ's body and undermines gospel mission.

To gain a broader and deeper understanding of each category of the one another commands, see Appendix 6.1—"Understanding and Applying the One Another Commands." You will find an explanation of "why" God calls us to live out each command, "how" we might follow through by faith and "evaluate" how well you are doing in each area.

But you must know that understanding the one another commands is the first step in carrying out everyday gospel mission as a community. The next thing we must do is to understand our struggles to live out the gospel in a more in-depth way.

THE BATTLE WITHIN THE HEART

God knows the deep dark recesses of our sinfulness yet He not only claimed and redeemed us as His bride, but He patiently continues His work of redemption in our persistent disobedience against Him. James reminds us that the battle within reflects our demand for sovereignty, pleasure, and glory.

> What causes quarrels and what causes fights among you? Is it not this, that your passions are at war within you? You desire and do not have, so you murder. You covet and cannot obtain, so you fight and quarrel. You do not have, because you do not ask. You ask and do not receive, because you ask wrongly, to spend it on your passions. You adulterous people! Do you not know that friendship with the world is enmity with God? Therefore whoever wishes to be a friend of the world makes himself an enemy of God. (James 4:1-4)

This very real and relentless turmoil rages in our "hearts." The biblical term, "heart," describes the essence of our inner being, the immortal soul that God created and integrated with our bodies. Jesus said:

> For from within, out of the heart of man, come evil thoughts, sexual immorality, theft, murder, adultery, coveting, wickedness, deceit, sensuality, envy, slander, pride, foolishness. All these evil things come from within, and they defile a person. (Mark 7:21-23)

The apostle Paul described this constant battle in the heart with striking clarity before he declared "there is now no condemnation for those who are in Christ Jesus" (Rom. 8:1):

> For I do not understand my own actions. For I do not do what I want, but I do the very thing I hate... For I have the desire to do what is right, but not the ability to carry it out. For I do not do the good I want, but the evil I do not want is what I keep on doing. (Rom. 7:15-19)

How does God deal with all of this wicked chaos in our soul? Well, all throughout God's story, God brings order out of disorder through His spoken Word (cf. Gen. 1, John 1, Rev. 21-22). The gospel provides the interpretive lens for understanding the chaos of life and serves as the authoritative truth that must be believed, obeyed and proclaimed to bring order out of the disorder in our lives. God's living Word exposes the thoughts, affections and desires of our hearts through His Spirit, who reveals our sinfulness, convicts us of our rebellious hearts, and leads us to repentance. God's living Word also points us to the horror and the beauty of the cross while our Redeemer calls our doubting and wayward hearts back to Him. But why should we understand the struggles of the heart in order to care for one another with the gospel?

CARING FOR ONE ANOTHER WITH THE GOSPEL

In the everyday mission of the gospel, God works *in* each of His people but He also works *through* His people so that He accomplishes His redemptive plan. God calls us to join with our Redeemer, who is the wonderful counselor, in bringing order out of disorder by ministering the Word to one another through the power of His Spirit. This is the essence of gospel care. In short, gospel care describes what we do when we minister the gospel to one another. Gospel care is the up close and personal ministry of the Word where we speak the gospel into the realities and difficulties of each other's lives as a community of brothers and sisters in Christ.

Gospel care has two major components—understanding and proclaiming—each comprised of two elements. In order to *understand* those struggling in the midst of suffering and sin, you need to listen to and explore their hearts. As you begin to understand their heart struggles in relationship to God and others within the details of their lives, you can more effectively and personally *proclaim* gospel truths. You can minister the gospel by helping them to envision how God is calling them to trust and draw near to Him while speaking truths in love that will encourage and challenge them to live out the gospel in community by the power and grace of the Holy Spirit.

Gospel Care			
Understanding		**Proclaiming**	
Listening	Exploring	Envisioning	Speaking
for opportunities for faith & repentance as well as evidences of God's grace	the heart (thoughts, emotions, actions, desires & affections) struggling with faith, hope and love	Jesus our Redeemer in compelling ways for rescue & refuge in the midst of suffering & sin	gospel truths in love to encourage & challenge one another to live out the gospel
In Relationship with God & Others			

Here are some over-arching guidelines to keep in mind as you begin your adventure in caring for one another with the gospel in community:

1. Remember God is the one who accomplishes His redemptive work in spite of your inadequacies and ongoing struggles with sin.

2. Remember that God calls you to be faithful ambassadors, journeying with others in intentional and redemptive ways.

3. Remember that God calls you to rest in your weakness through the power of Christ. Gospel ministry is beyond your abilities, but you have the Spirit of Christ. The Spirit of Christ convicts, not you. The Spirit of Christ redeems, not you. The Spirit of Christ is all wise, not you.

LEADERSHIP POINTS—LIVING OUT EVERYDAY GOSPEL MISSION
As a church leader, the most important thing to consider at this point is how to help your people understand and embrace God's call on their life for this everyday mission of redemption. Here are some guidelines to consider as you look to equip your people to do the work of the ministry:

Start With Yourself

1. You need to live out the gospel in every aspect of life. If you don't know how to apply the gospel first in your own life and

relationships, how do you expect to develop and equip others in your church to do the same?

2. Are you encouraging and challenging your friends and family with the gospel in your everyday life? Unfortunately, the vast majority of individuals and couples struggle to connect the gospel with the routine and rigors of life. Those in your church need your leadership and example.

Evaluate Your Relationships

1. Whom have you invited to explore your heart and life so that they might comfort and confront you with the gospel? Have these people given you permission to do the same? It is not uncommon for men and women to have such intentional redemptive relationships with their peers but fail to develop such intentionality in their own home.

2. When was the last time one of your friends called you out because of your blindness to your own sin? How did you receive it? Did you get defensive, try to justify yourself, or point out a fault in your friend?

These leadership points are in the form of questions for reflection because it is important for you to look first at yourself with the gospel mirror.

DISGUSTED AND KICKED OUT

Tom hasn't been able to sleep since seeing John with Meredith and having the disturbing phone call afterward. Just days after that incident, John broke the news to Kathy about his affair and told her he had no intentions of breaking off his relationship with Meredith. Kathy broke down upon hearing what she had feared even before marriage. John inflicted additional wounds by telling her he had never loved her, that she ruined his life by making him feel that he never measured up as a man, and that he could never please her. Kathy immediately called Sharon in hysterics, asking over and over, "How could he do this to me?!" while also screaming "I am going to kill him!"

Kathy demanded that John leave the house and never come back. Tom and Sharon found themselves in a dilemma because to their surprise, John asked if he could stay in their basement because he had no place else to go. John had just learned from Meredith that she too was married and her husband was not aware of the affair since he spent several nights away every week for his medical sales job. She told John so that she would eventually marry him but she never thought they would be found out before she had the chance to get out of her present marriage. John was confused and kept rambling that he didn't know what he would do without Meredith but he ranted in anger that she never told him she was married.

With your expanded understanding of church discipline along with the guidelines for gospel community and care, how would you guide and direct Tom and Sharon in this very present and pressing dilemma? Knowledge of the Scripture turns to wisdom when you are able to apply gospel truths to real life drama. What should Tom and Sharon, along with John and Kathy, do next in this journey of redemption?

REFLECT AND RESPOND:

1. Do those in your church understand and step into the gospel's everyday mission? If so, how was such a culture developed? If no, what are some steps that you can take to help develop such a culture?

2. How did you fare as you evaluated yourself in understanding and applying the one another commands as unpacked in Appendix 6.1?

3. Have you considered the battles within your heart in light of the gospel? What has God been showing you about your sinful thoughts, affections, desires and will? How do Christ and His gospel truths offer comfort and challenge to your heart struggles?

4. How does the overview of gospel care encourage and challenge you in your own relationships and community? Can you see how such care is the foundation of how we love one another by engaging with, fighting for, forgiving and reconciling with one another?

7

The Mess and Mission of Gospel Relationships

If your brother sins against you, go and tell him his fault, between you and him alone. If he listens to you, you have gained your brother. (Matt. 18:15)

Brothers, if anyone is caught in any transgression, you who are spiritual should restore him in a spirit of gentleness. Keep watch on yourself, lest you too be tempted. Bear one another's burdens, and so fulfill the law of Christ. (Gal. 6:1-2)

My brothers, if anyone among you wanders from the truth and someone brings him back, let him know that whoever brings back a sinner from his wandering will save his soul from death and will cover a multitude of sins. (James 5:19-20)

"One of the tests of true spirituality is a readiness to set those who stumble by the wayside on the right road again in a sympathetic ... spirit." – F. F. Bruce

BRUISED AND BATTERED

Tom and Sharon knew they were in over their heads, but they also believed that God had providentially placed them in John and Kathy's lives. Despite their disgust with John's choices and situation, they agreed to let him stay in their basement, thinking they would have more opportunity to talk some sense into him if he was under their roof.

John arrived at the house around midnight with a suitcase and a duffel bag stuffed with his belongings. Tom and Sharon could see the weariness in John's eyes as soon as he walked through their door. Tom showed him where he would be staying in the basement and had towels laid out for him along with a fresh set of sheets on their sofa bed and a key to the house so he could come and go on his own. Very little was said between the men. Tom told John he was welcome to stay as long as it would take to work through this ordeal and that they would talk the next evening.

Tom had a hard time sleeping, knowing that his good friend was in the basement because of the mess created by his sinful choices. Tom cried out to God for wisdom and words to confront John the next day, but the more he thought about the situation, the more he felt anger towards him. How stupid and selfish could John be! How dare he hurt Kathy and the kids in this way! Out of sheer exhaustion Tom finally drifted off to sleep before his alarm went off.

By the time Tom got ready for work and went downstairs to grab a quick bite to eat, John's car was gone. Tom quickly checked the basement and saw that John had already gotten up, fixed his bedding, and left the house. After quickly eating a bagel and drinking his usual cup of black coffee, Tom kissed Sharon goodbye and told her that John was already gone.

Later that night, as Tom and Sharon finished their last bite of dinner, they heard John pull up to the house. Tom got up from the table and greeted John at the door, and asked him if he wanted some dinner. John politely thanked Tom and Sharon for the offer but said that he had grabbed dinner after work. Tom quickly asked John if they could chat after he had a chance to change and unwind a bit. John agreed and asked if they could wait until 8:00.

Tom's heart began racing as he anticipated his conversation with John. He was thinking through where he would start, what he would say, and how he would respond if John started getting defensive. Finally at 8:00, Tom walked downstairs to the basement and found John dozing in a chair.

As Tom approached, John stirred and quickly sat up. John thanked Tom again for letting him stay at his house. He then started by telling Tom that he knows that he placed him and Sharon in an awkward spot and he doesn't want to take advantage of their friendship but that he is also very confused because he loves Meredith.

In that instant, Tom went from appreciating his friend's gratitude to being angry as John expressed his love for Meredith. Everything that Tom had planned to say was jettisoned when John said that he loved another woman. Tom shouted at him that he needed to get his head screwed on right because if he didn't watch it, he would lose both Kathy and the kids. John immediately got defensive and accused Tom for not understanding him and how tough it was to live in a house with a nagging wife.

One thing led to another as each man bruised and battered the other with hurtful judgments and accusations. Finally, Sharon came down and told both of them that they needed to stop. As soon as they heard Sharon, they both shut up and agreed to part ways for the evening.

THE MESSINESS OF RELATIONSHIPS

What do you call a group of sinful Christians with different personalities, family backgrounds, life experiences, passions and preferences and who are also at different points in their growth in maturity and wisdom? The church! Everywhere you turn you see evidence of sin taking a toll on relationships: between friends, husbands and wives, co-workers, neighbors and fellow members within the same church. A man is offended by the careless and cynical talk of his friend. A woman is deeply hurt by a jealous friend's slander. A young man offends others by his demanding and inflexible ways. An older woman pulls away from mentoring a younger woman who seems ungrateful and disrespectful.

How does the gospel deal with these and similar situations that occur in every relationship? We need to remember how God deals with us (vertical relationship) so that we know how to deal with others (horizontal relationships).

God meets our sinfulness with His redeeming mercy, through the radical love of the cross and through His kindness that brings us to repentance. He deals with us personally and intimately in Christ and through the indwelling and sanctifying work of His Spirit. God pursues us and invites us with welcome arms to come back to Him. His approach is creative and timely, consistent with His nature and written Word. He never loses sight that he created us in His image and causes all things to work together for His redemptive good. Ultimately, God takes what was meant for evil and uses it for His glory.

Often we look for the "Red Sea" dilemmas, where we are trapped between an advancing army and a mass of water, to shine for God. But God wants us to see the cynicism, slander, demands and disrespect found in every relationship as opportunities for growth in the gospel.

GOSPEL OPPORTUNITIES LEAD TO GROWTH

Both Tom and Sharon are confronted with significant gospel opportunities in their relationships with John and Kathy. But why is this situation not just about John since, after all, he is the wayward person? For Kathy, in the midst of her troubled marriage and her husband's adultery, God is calling her to trust primarily in Jesus and not in her husband. God will also use this time of suffering and pain to wean her from milk as an infant to the meat of the gospel as a woman of God. In her growth, she will experience the incomparable peace that comes only from the Prince of Peace and she will know the love of Christ in deeper and more profound ways as she learns to live by faith in Christ. Tom will grow as a man of God as he learns to follow the lead of the Spirit of God rather than the fury of His flesh and he will grow in wisdom as he spends countless hours seeking the Lord in Word and prayer so that he can lead in this difficult situation. Sharon will grow as she keeps from growing bitter as she sees her husband being mistreated and verbally attacked while she also learns how to minister Christ to Kathy during her time of need.

Regardless of the situation—whether someone sins against us (Matt. 18:15), we catch someone in sin (Gal. 6:1-2) or someone wanders from the truth (James 5:19-20)—we need to respond in ways that reflect the gospel message and align with gospel mission. We need to keep in mind the over-arching commands and principles associated with "one another" passages since it is far too easy for us to approach situations in an overly simplistic manner, guided by a few specific commands mixed with our own sinful motives. That is why we need to consider some important guidelines before, during and after confronting[1] someone with the gospel, knowing

---

1   The term "confront" can be understood in a negative light based on our personal experience or because of the bad connotation within our culture. Biblically speaking, confronting one another with the gospel can be understood as speaking the truth in love, or encouraging and challenging with the gospel, so that we can help one another to live a life of faith and repentance, knowing that we are prone to sin and unbelief.

that our approach should emerge from the breadth, width and depth of God's story of redemption.

BEFORE CONFRONTING WITH THE GOSPEL

Whether you need to confront someone who personally offended you or someone who has been living a life contrary to the gospel, you need to check your own heart before you approach the person privately while remembering the gospel realities that hold true regardless of the situation.

Check Your Heart

Identify the sin involved. Ensure that you are confronting someone for a clear Scriptural violation, as opposed to a preference or difference of opinion. Write down the Scripture passage(s) that apply to this situation. If you fail to do so, you might end up confronting someone with your own self-righteous agenda and worldly wisdom. Moreover, if you merely select and use passages out of context without careful study and prayerful reflection to see if they truly speak to the situation at hand, not only will you dishonor God but you will also distort the gospel.

Take the log out of your own eye. Consider how you may have contributed to the situation through your own sin (cf. Matt. 7:1-5). Write down the Scripture passage(s) that may apply to you in this situation. You may be blinded to your own sinful contribution to any given situation. You may also be driven by your emotions, looking for someone or something to blame to protect your reputation or self-image.

Run to God first, then to others. Remember that going to others to get "advice" can lead to gossip and/or slander. Don't fall into the trap of relying more on the counsel of others than on God. Seek the Lord's wisdom through dependent prayer, submissive obedience to God's Word and the redemptive counsel of others.

Pray. Ask for wisdom, grace, discernment and love since your motives, like those of the offender, can be distorted by your own sin. Ultimately, this issue between you and the other person is not about your agenda but about God's agenda and His mission of redemption in the midst of the spiritual warfare. Put on the armor of God so you can fight *for* the other rather than *against* the one who sinned against you (cf. Eph. 6:12-13).

You should be aware that feelings of anger, bitterness, hatred, and a desire for vengeance can be cloaked in motives and purposes that look righteous. Your response and attitude toward those who sinned against you should not be based primarily on their sinful offense against you or their response and attitude. Rather your posture should be based on God's redemptive pursuit and work in each of you as His bride.

Assess your hesitation. Ensure you don't avoid approaching the one who offended you because you might be denying or minimizing the sin and hurt or because you fear the person's rejection or disapproval more than obeying and pleasing God. However, your hesitation may be the Spirit prompting you to slow down and reassess so you can best determine if the most loving thing is not to address this particular situation now but to wait and see if there is a pattern for the behavior or attitude of concern.

Arrange a time to meet. You will need to determine a time and place to meet. Make sure you talk soon after arranging the meeting. Long delays cause undue tension and anxiety. Avoid addressing the issues via phone or e-mail. Eye contact and non-verbal communication are essential elements to gospel confrontation. Make sure you allow enough time so both of you can share and ask necessary clarifying and exploratory questions.[2]

Remember Gospel Realties

Remember that Christ is your Redeemer. As believers, the blood of Christ redeems each of you and He promises each of you the same inheritance that will never fade and is reserved in heaven for all of His church (cf. 1 Pet. 1:4, 18-19). You can easily think that Christ is only "your Redeemer."

Remember and believe that everyone needs the gospel. Everyone struggles with sin. Everyone needs to grow in grace. No one has arrived. There is no one righteous except Jesus; therefore no one is able to boast in the presence of God or others. Everyone needs Jesus and His gospel every moment of every day.

Remember God designed the church to grow together. You can experience God's grace as you encourage and challenge one another with the gospel. Again, you should see this situation as an opportunity that can lead to growth in the gospel.

---

2   Adapted from Lauterbach, *Transforming Community*, pp. 108-109.

Remember that love covers a multitude of sin (Prov. 10:12, 1 Pet. 4:8). You should be careful not to develop a spirit of judgment, where every sin is addressed every time. Otherwise, you will struggle to grow in patience, or long-suffering, and love.

Remember that gospel confrontation is about the gospel, not you. Even if you were the one sinned against, Christ bore the penalty for your sins and the sins of others. God gives you opportunities to trust, grow in, and reflect the gospel as you help others to turn to Christ so that they might believe, grow in, and reflect the gospel.

Private Approach and "Public" Address

Confront in private. Privately approach the person who sinned against you. No others need to know about the offense if the person listens and repents.

Consider the person's spouse. There are times in a marriage when one spouse commits a sin that also affects the other, given their one flesh relationship: adultery, pornography, financial fraud, or any criminal activity. Approach the offending spouse first in private, then ask him to confess to his wife in private, then provide care for them as a couple.

In the case of adultery, where you are not directly involved, you may also have to approach the other person with whom the adultery was committed.

You do not need to approach both spouses if the issue at hand does not affect their one-flesh union: relational conflict with another person, issue of greed or laziness, or disrespect to another; however, you need to encourage the person to share the situation with her spouse so that he will hear how the Lord revealed sins and enabled growth through His grace and gospel community.

In matters of criminal offense (such as abuse in any form), do not approach the person in private but select a person to go with you under the oversight of the legal system.[3]

Address public sins in public. Once the offense has been addressed and resolved in private, the process of gospel confrontation and reconciliation needs to be addressed to others who might be directly involved. Here are some examples of when sins need to be addressed with appropriate others:

---

3   Sande, *The Peacemaker*, p. 147.

a. When an offense was experienced in a small group setting, the person offended needs to approach in private the person who caused the offense. Once they reconcile, the person who caused the offense needs to share with the rest of the group about their gospel confrontation, how they resolved the issue, and how they reconciled. The one who was offended should also share about their redemptive efforts so that everyone in the group not only sees how conflict should be handled but also know that the reconciliation was genuine and mutual.

b. When an elder is involved with a life struggle that requires him to step down for a season or has committed sins which call for his resignation, the church needs to be informed as the situation demands (cf. 1 Tim. 5:20).

WHEN CONFRONTING WITH THE GOSPEL

Take time to understand the person and situation. You need to clearly understand the context and the details of the situation before launching into what you believe is their sin. What seemed like an offense may have been a miscommunication or something wrongly perceived. Ask, listen, and learn. Based on what you heard, you may need to change your approach or what you originally planned to say.

Confront with a spirit of gentleness, humility, and love. Share in ways that build up and share only what is needed in the moment to give grace (cf. Gal. 6:1-2; Eph. 4:15, 29).

Confess your sin(s). You may have contributed to the conflict so you need to confess and ask for forgiveness. Do not demand that the one who sinned against you confess as well since the Holy Spirit is the one who convicts us of our sinfulness.

Forgive if the other person repents and asks for forgiveness. Avoid expectations of what their repentance should look like and keep yourself from judging their repentance. Jesus taught that if someone sins against you seven times in a day, you must forgive (cf. Luke 17:3-4). Ideally both you and the offender should not only understand the deeper struggles within your own hearts underneath the expressed and experienced sinfulness, but also understand what ongoing faith and repentance look like.

Make every effort to reconcile. God calls us to pursue peace and unity so do so before the end of your time together. Affirm your care and love for them.

IF THERE IS NO REPENTANCE OR RECONCILIATION

Do not threaten the person with church discipline. God's discipline should not be used as a club to manipulate or threaten someone into repentance and submission.

Prayerfully consider the next steps. What happened and did not happen? What was said and not said? What could be done differently next time?

Ask the Lord for another opportunity. God pursues and engages us repeatedly, never giving up on us. We must do the same knowing that such intentionality expresses love and reaches for redemption.

Confronting a brother or sister in Christ requires prayerful preparation and interaction. But as we discussed earlier, effective ministry requires us to listen to and explore the heart with gospel intentionality and purpose so that we can proclaim the gospel in personal and compelling ways. Appendix 7.1 highlights some key elements for you to consider when you sit and work through real struggles with real people with the real gospel.

LEADERSHIP POINTS—CULTIVATING GOSPEL RELATIONSHIPS IN THE CHURCH

As a church leader, you are responsible to lead, teach, and care for your flock. But the beauty of God's design is that He has appointed you not to do all of the work, but to equip His people to do the work of gospel ministry (cf. Eph. 4:11-12). You best equip them when you help them understand not only the gospel message, but also how the gospel applies to real life. You most effectively equip them when you, and those leaders you have trained, personally guide them in dealing with the messiness of relationships by following Jesus and His living Word. You should also take the time to assess the situation, lead them when they are unsure of what to do and follow-up with them to see if matters were addressed appropriately.

1. Equip your people.

You need to help your people understand how God's call to a radical life of mission can be lived out in general through knowing and doing the "one another" commands and specifically in various difficult situations, or gospel opportunities. Also, the more you can equip the deacons and other ministry leaders with the basics in gospel relationships, the more they can equip others to do the same.

Your people need to know they can talk to you about difficult situations but you should also encourage them to seek the Lord for wisdom through Word and prayer before coming to you. Here are some general guidelines to let your people know when they can inform church leadership of a given situation:

Situations that Demand Immediate Contact (Table 1)

Emergency hospitalizations – miscarriages, illness, surgeries	Abuse of child – neglect, abandonment, physical, sexual
Suicide threat or attempt	Any reported illegal action
Death of a member or a member's immediate family	Adultery, marital separation or abandonment
Abuse of adult – physical or sexual	Drug or alcohol abuse

Note—Call 911 first as appropriate

Situations that Require Contact after Prayerful Effort (Table 2)

Disagreement between ministry leaders in dealing with a situation	Unresolved division within a small group
When ministry efforts are not effective – no redemptive movement after a period of time, increasingly hardened heart(s), the need to ask others to step in to help	Unsure how to handle a situation – where to start, how to work towards forgiveness and reconciliation, a counseling struggle, etc.

2. Enforce God's Word.

Encourage those who talk to you about a relational conflict they have with another person, despite the apparent urgency, to approach the person in private. Ask them to follow up with you for accountability and further supervision as needed. Your people need to know you will not tolerate any gossip or slander and that they need to live out God's "one another" commands for the sake of unity and health of the church.

3. Assess the situation.

You need to understand the big picture along with the associated details about the situation so that you can provide relevant and helpful leadership. Here are some of the issues you should evaluate:

a. What are the particulars of the situation? Would you assess this situation as mild, moderate, or severe in terms of threat to life, abuse, marital infidelity, drug or alcohol abuse, or medical emergency?

b. Who is directly involved and who is aware of the situation? You may need to limit those directly involved to minimize conflicting counsel.

c. Who has been providing guidance and counsel up to this point?

d. Does the small group leader know about the situation? If so, what steps have been taken?

e. Is the man or woman involved in an accountability group and do they know what is going on?

f. Who is the person most connected with in his or her small group?

g. Does a threat of suicide exist? (This may or may not be a relevant question.)

4. Provide leadership.

You need to provide the necessary guidance to those who approach you and ask for help about a situation. You should take the time to:

a. Give them a redemptive perspective.

b. Discuss the possible redemptive pathways that can be taken.

c. Help them to think through who needs to be involved.

d. Help them to see evidences of God's grace.

e. Explain the possible sin dynamics that might be involved.

5. Follow up.

Especially with moderate to severe issues you need to follow up sooner rather than later to minimize unnecessary relational pain between those in need and to avoid deterioration in the situation. Following up with those you oversee allows you to:

a. See whether or not your people understand the gospel and are striving to live it out in the midst of their specific struggles.

b. Assess if you need to step in with more involvement or provide additional care.

c. Identify emerging leaders and less mature members as you listen to their perspective of the given situation, understand their knowledge of the Scripture, observe ways in which they interact with others and assess their level of initiative and engagement.

HUMBLED AND AWARE

Tom was reeling from his intense confrontation with John. What in the world happened? Everything was a blur. Things did not go as planned. Tom was expecting John to be more broken. And when John stated that he was confused because of his love for the other woman, Tom lost it because he was hoping that John would repent.

After spending some time on the front porch talking to God while gazing upon the moonlit sky, Tom was deeply convicted of his self-righteous attitude and judgmental heart. He recognized that he lashed out at John more out of the sin in his own heart than from anything John did or said. He also realized that the most redemptive thing that came out of their conversation was how God was exposing his own sin and seeing his ongoing need for Jesus.

Later that evening Tom went down to the basement to check up on John who was still up watching television. There was an awkward silence as the men made eye contact but Tom took a deep breath and began to explain what the Lord was teaching him in all of this mess. Tom confessed his sin against John and asked him for forgiveness. This took John by surprise. He thought for sure that Tom returned to launch another round of attacks. John was also taken off guard because he couldn't remember the last time someone took the initiative to deal with his own sin and ask for forgiveness even though he knew he contributed to the argument as well. He forgave Tom but shared that he needed more time to process all that happened because he was still confused.

The next morning, Tom was convinced he was in over his head and needed more guidance, so he called Pastor Greg, the elder overseeing Tom and Sharon's small group. They scheduled a time to meet the next day over lunch to discuss this situation. During dinner, Tom shared with John that he called Pastor Greg for help but that he didn't share any names with him. Tom invited John to join them for lunch so they could talk things out with someone who had more experience in handling this important and pressing situation. As soon as he heard that Tom called Pastor Greg, John dropped his fork in shock, pushed away from the table in anger, and walked away screaming, "I can't believe you called him!" Tom and Sharon looked at each in shock as well. In that moment, they both knew that they had a very tough road ahead of them.

REFLECT AND RESPOND:

1. There are many aspects to consider as you deal with conflict with others. What aspect(s) of gospel confrontation do you find the most challenging?

2. Think about a recent conflict in which you were involved.[4]

    a. As you reflect on your thoughts, desires, emotions, and actions during and after the encounter, how can you view the situation, yourself and the other person differently as you take the various aspects of your experience back to the cross?

    b. How did you listen and explore the other person's heart so that you could better understand his or her struggles?

    c. How did you speak and envision gospel truths in love so that both of you saw your need for Christ and the need for redemptive "next steps"?

---

4   Review then refer to Appendix 7: Gospel Care in Redemptive Relationships as you answer these questions.

8

Redemption in Gospel Community

But if he does not listen, take one or two others along with you, that every charge may be established by the evidence of two or three witnesses. (Matt. 18:16; cf. Deut. 19:15)

And let us consider how to stir up one another to love and good works, not neglecting to meet together, as is the habit of some, but encouraging one another, and all the more as you see the Day drawing near. (Heb. 10:24-25)

LEARNING AND SERVING TOGETHER

Tom sat defeated in Pastor Greg's office as he shared the story about his and Sharon's time with John and Kathy, from their first meal together to the blowup the night before after hearing about Tom's meeting with the pastor. Greg listened carefully and compassionately as he saw how Tom stepped out in faith to engage his friend with the gospel, opening his heart and home during John's time of need. Tom kept berating himself regarding all of the missteps on his part, but he shared that God used his failures to reveal his deep need for Christ. He also kept apologizing to Greg because he was not able to make a difference in his friend's life and marriage.

Greg stopped Tom as he started into another round of despairing regrets. Greg looked at Tom straight in his eyes and told him how proud he was of both him and Sharon. He expressed how

God's grace was very evident not only in this situation but also in how the Spirit of God is working in beautiful ways in both of their lives. Greg continued by sharing that he prayed God would raise up more individuals and couples who understand and submit to Christ's mission of redemption. Greg acknowledged the missteps but assured Tom that God would give everyone involved the wisdom for the difficult journey ahead.

Given the adultery and separation, Greg thanked Tom for coming to him as soon as he did. He also mentioned that he would now take the lead in this situation but that he needed both Tom and Sharon to maintain their important relationship with John and Kathy. Greg asked who else had been involved in this couple's lives from the small group, and others whom they trust and respect. Unfortunately, John and Kathy opened themselves up to no one, even though others in their small group reached out to them. At that moment, Tom realized that he and Sharon were their closest friends who knew anything about them, mainly because they pursued them after being prompted by God.

Pastor Greg attempted several times by phone to set up a meeting with John to talk about matters, but John never picked up nor did he return any calls. In the meantime, Greg met with Kathy several times, together with Tom and Sharon. He explained to Kathy that it was important for Tom and Sharon to be with her in these meetings not only to keep abreast of all of the details of the situation but also to be equipped to know how to care for her and minister the gospel to her as she battles with doubts, fears, weariness and bitterness. He also asked Kathy to prayerfully consider asking other women from her small group to join her in this journey so that she would have a broader and deeper network of support, knowing that Tom and Sharon could not always be there for her based on the demands in their own lives, nor could they help bear her burdens alone. Kathy sat in disbelief—she had never imagined she would have to face such an ordeal but also never imagined people like Tom and Sharon, and even Pastor Greg, would actually care for her, giving their time and energy to help fight for her and John. Oddly enough, she felt scared and loved simultaneously.

EXPERIENCING COMMUNITY

In this particular situation, Tom and Pastor Greg tried to appeal to John face-to-face but he avoided any contact with them. But many times, the opportunity to confront a brother or sister in Christ with one or two others more easily presents itself in community where there are ongoing and natural encounters. Such organic communities emerge in a number of different venues—Sunday school classes, fellowship groups that meet either on the church campus or in homes, friendships with co-workers and neighbors or in other groups based on mutual interests and activities.

You might already see the wisdom of having one-on-one gospel relationships, but can you also see the value of a community of men and women where the common denominator is Christ and the goal is to encourage and bear the burdens of one another in every aspect of life? The sad reality for most of us is that we have not experienced such intentional and redemptive relationships even though we long for them.

We struggle to experience gospel community because of the busyness of life as well as the fear of others knowing our deep heart struggles. Regarding the busyness, we are convinced we barely have time to care for our own family members let alone someone else. The needs of others never seem to coincide with our availability or rise above our own needs. Regarding the fear of being known, we are convinced that others will judge and pull away from us when they hear what is really going on in our hearts and home. But also we don't want others getting in our way when we want something so bad that we are willing to lie, cheat, and steal to get it.

In one sense, each of us can be our own main hindrance for experiencing community. You can easily see that when each of us collectively takes this same sinful and self-centered approach to community, the net result is that very few of us experience the gospel community in which we were created to live.

FIGHTING FOR ONE ANOTHER

The radical life and mission we have in Christ calls us to fight for, not against, one another as we struggle to live out the gospel. Even when fellow brothers and sisters refuse to see how their ongoing decisions and responses to life are contrary to the gospel and refuse to listen to our pleas to come back and submit to Christ, we do not have the option to give up. You can use the following gospel community guidelines to help you work through the necessary "next steps" if the private gospel confrontation did not result in repentance and reconciliation.

GOSPEL COMMUNITY GUIDELINES

Allow time for the Holy Spirit.
You can easily forget that the Holy Spirit is the one who opens blind eyes, brings conviction to hearts, and compels His people to turn back to Christ.

Be patient. God uses you as means of redemption, but you need to make sure you don't get impatient and rush God's timing. Don't try to orchestrate God's providential ways so that you can get the response you are expecting from the person who is struggling with sin.

Reflect Christ. One of the major themes in God's radical kingdom life is for His people to love and forgive like Christ. Remember how God pursues you in a variety of ways, more often with subtle and gentle reminders than with firm rebukes. Again, the key in journeying alongside a brother or sister who is struggling to walk in the path of righteousness is to remember how God deals with you as a rebellious and prideful bride.

Look and listen with expectancy. Whenever you minister in the flesh, apart from the Spirit, you end up restricting your field of vision, which hinders you from seeing evidences of God's grace. As you deal with others in the flesh you can tend to look only at the immediate situation and forget to assess the long-term movement of God's grace over a period of time and to foresee how God will continue to work in the days, weeks and months to come. Moreover, when you operate in the flesh, you tend to hear what you want or expect to hear. Listening without judgment requires faith and grace from God. But if those who are struggling profess faith in Christ, then listen for how they might resonate with gospel truths, wrestle to believe, and express their need for Christ. Use all that you see and hear to better understand their hearts so that you can more personally and relevantly proclaim the gospel in compelling and persuasive ways through the power of the Holy Spirit.

Remember God's ways. Even though God is holy and just, He doesn't discipline His children in a rigid step-by-step process. God brings about redemption in creative and unexpected ways. God uses all things to accomplish His good purposes. God is not anxious about whether He will complete the work of redemption in each of His people. He promised that He would complete His work at the day of Christ, when Christ reigns in the new heaven and earth (Phil. 1:6; Rev. 21-22). So in one way or another, God will accomplish His redemptive plans in His bride.

Know when to involve others.

You will need to discern if a person is refusing to listen because of outright rebellion or due to a difference of opinion or simple misunderstanding. The issue boils down to whether the person is willing or unwilling to discuss the matter in light of the gospel.[1] If a person either doesn't see his sin or refuses to repent after repeated and varied attempts through patient and loving confrontation, then invite others into the situation.

If you are part of the same community, then identify one or two others whom you both respect. Those you bring in should have the following character and ministry traits:

1. Understand and intentionally live out the gospel in their own relationships and community.

2. Know how to minister the gospel to others with humility, love, and courage in Christ.

3. Can maintain neutrality and confidentiality.

4. Submit to and support the elders' philosophy and vision of gospel ministry.

5. Can provide ongoing support and leadership as the situation necessitates.

If you are not part of the same community, then each of you can either ask someone from your own community or approach a respected third party group whom you both trust and know will give wise counsel.

If the one who refuses to listen does not want to invite anyone else into the situation, then reassure the person that the one or

---

1   Adams, *Handbook of Church Discipline*, p. 58.

two others who are being invited in will first, listen to both sides as neutral parties; second, help both of you to see the situation in light of the gospel; and third, handle the situation in the most redemptive way possible. By explaining the redemptive perspective and process, by God's grace, the person being confronted will not be as defensive and will see the meeting as a way God's people can work together for peace and unity instead of feeling as if he or she is on trial.

Understand the role of community.

Inviting others into the unresolved situation follows the Old Testament tradition that required a diligent inquiry and the evidence of two to three witnesses of a crime before conviction.[2] Therefore, when you get others involved, do so with an inquisitive and protective spirit and not with a "mob mentality." You should explain to each of those who are being invited in about their redemptive role by sharing some of the following guidelines:

1. Help discern the issues through objective listening and clarifying questions to understand root causes.[3]

2. Show the importance of pursuing peace and unity, as well as showing the severity of the situation through their presence.

3. Ensure the confrontation reflects the gospel.

4. Serve as mediators as needed.

5. Provide a safe and controlled environment should the confrontation get out of hand.

6. Encourage and challenge those involved with the gospel as appropriate so that both parties see their need for Christ and turn back to Him.

7. Serve as witnesses only if those involved refuse to submit to Christ and His Word and the matter needs to be addressed by church leaders.

---

2 Deut. 17:2-7; 19:15; Num. 35:30; 2 Cor. 13:1

3 See Appendix 7.1 for general guidelines for listening and asking questions for better understanding one another.

If a meeting does take place, then you as one of the two invited into this process can follow these general guidelines:[4]

1. *Set a time limit.* An hour and a half to two hours is a good time-frame for this first meeting. Even if a full resolution is not achieved during this time, you can make good headway into understanding the issues and the hearts of those involved as well as establishing a time and an agenda for the follow-up meeting.

2. *Lead.* One of you should serve as a leader who will guide both parties through the discussion.

3. *Listen.* You should listen to both sides, making sure you understand the context and additional background information that may highlight a bigger picture for this particular conflict.

4. *Review.* You should get a clear understanding of any and all previous attempts between both parties to resolve the issue.

5. *Assess.* Determine if there were any Scriptural violations involved. Identify any sinful attitudes and behaviors on either side.

6. *Address.* Once you understand the essence of the spiritual and practical issues involved, offer your perspective on the matter in light of the gospel.

7. *Persuade.* Help persuade the person(s) of any wrong committed. Such persuasion might be received better when it comes from those who have a good relationship with either or both parties.

8. *Pursue Peace.* Follow the guidelines from Chapter 6 to fight for, forgive and reconcile with one another.

9. *Schedule.* Setup another meeting if (1) time is needed for more personal and prayerful reflection, (2) if everyone recognizes that there is more to cover, or (3) one of the parties doesn't agree with the terms necessary for reconciliation.

---

4   Adapted from Adams, pp. 62-64.

10. *Inform church leadership.* If after several attempts a resolution is not achieved, then let both parties know that a church leader will be brought in to help fight for reconciliation.

Know that redemption is messy.

Working out issues in community challenges and grows everyone involved as much as the one who refuses to listen. The process of redemption can no longer be just a concept but must be lived out by all involved.

If you merely point the finger at the one struggling, then God will reveal your self-righteousness. If you merely get frustrated and give up, then God will reveal your ignorance of His long-suffering and mercy towards you. If you want no part in helping the one struggling because you have been personally offended, then God will reveal your self-centeredness since you see the offense as just about you. God can also reveal your dependence on your fleshly thoughts and feelings as you can be driven more by fear than by faith. God is revealing everyone's sins and causing everyone to repent and to live by faith.

Keep repentance the goal.

Remember that God has called you into gospel mission that involves ongoing faith and repentance in your life with Christ as a means of gospel change.

Rejoice with repentance. If God grants repentance, rejoice. Repentance is a work of God's grace. Too often repentance is viewed in a negative light and you can use a person's repentance as an occasion for saying "I told you so" rather than as a time to celebrate God's mercy and grace.

Keep pursuing if no initial repentance. If the person refuses to repent even after your first attempt, don't give up and immediately push for what some would call "formal church discipline." Remember that God is using all of the redemptive and intentional efforts in gospel community to discipline His people so don't consider your efforts as "informal." However, you have the freedom to inform a church leader at any point for guidance and perspective.

Remember the offended spouse and family (as applicable).

Be sure to care for and coordinate with the spouse in any situation that impacts their marriage in a direct way.

Care for all. Sin impacts everyone in its wake. So don't forget that it is just as important to pursue and shepherd the affected spouse and their one-flesh relationship, as it is to pursue and shepherd the offender.

Do what is right. Christ personally and deeply understands the searing pain associated with sin more than anyone else. Yet in His extreme suffering, He did not sin. You can easily give in to the demands of the offended spouse or allow the hurting spouse to say and do anything she wants towards her husband who hurt her deeply. God commands, "be angry and do not sin ... trust in the Lord, and do good" (Eph. 4:26; Ps. 37:3a). You need to remind yourself and others that God is and will always be central, not the one who is suffering. Also remember that God, who did not even spare His own Son, uses suffering to redeem His bride and bring glory to Himself.

Know when to inform the rest of the community.

If you are the one who has been personally offended you will need to decide when you need to let others know in your small group, or in the immediate and relevant circle of relationships, beyond the one or two others who have already been involved. Per Matthew 18:15-17, you do want to keep the circle of care as small as necessary, but when someone in the group repeatedly refuses the love of Christ and his community, then you should inform others for prayer and pursuit.

The big picture. Know that it is always good for your group to be informed at some point so that God might be glorified for His faithfulness and others can see how the gospel is played out in real life.

What to share. As a general rule if you are the one who has been sinned against, you can share the Scriptural violation(s) involved in the struggle, offer insights into your heart struggles of unbelief and lies, as well as ways in which God has demonstrated His love, mercy and grace. You should share primarily about yourself and not about others who might be involved since this can easily lead to slander and gossip. Be discerning about the details you share so that you keep from glorifying yourself as a victim.

When to share. The timing of your sharing correlates to your specific needs and also will inform what you might share.

Specific Needs	When do you Share? With Whom?	What Do You Share?
Prayer Support	As soon as possible. With all in your group.	General prayer needs: i.e. "Please pray for John and me as we are struggling in our marriage."
Practical Support	As soon as necessary. With all in your group.	Practical details: "We need help with the kids after school, grass mowing and other household repairs during this time."
Relational Support	As soon as necessary. With those you trust and can journey with you.	Any appropriate details so that others can minister the gospel in specific and detailed ways: "I am struggling with despair. I need your love and support."

Note: These quoted examples are ways Kathy could share with her small group during her marital struggles with John.

Keep confidential. If you have the privilege of hearing about the struggles and the redemption of others, you do not have the freedom to share with people outside the group unless those who share give you permission.

LEADERSHIP POINTS—LEADING IN GOSPEL COMMUNITY

1. Keep watch over yourself.

Sin is not a respecter of persons. Satan wants to take everyone down. That is why Paul wrote, *"Brothers, if anyone is caught in any transgression, you who are spiritual should restore him in a spirit of gentleness. Keep watch on yourself, lest you too be tempted." (Gal. 6:1)* Just as sin blinds and deceives those struggling with sin, you too can be blinded and deceived by sin in your attempt to help. Here are two main ways you can be tempted:

a. *Spirit-less ministry (cf. Gal. 5:25-26).* When we minister in the flesh and don't rely on God, we are more apt to miss the leading of the Spirit in the moment or miss evidences of God's grace in and through the past and present situation. As a result, we can make wrong assumptions and assertions. We can view the situation more from our own agenda (i.e., proving who is right, righting a wrong, or returning evil for evil) as opposed to God's redemptive agenda.

b. *Self-righteousness (cf. the anti-thesis of Gal. 5:22-23).* As a result of not walking in the Spirit we will produce the fruits of the flesh. You can be tempted to think that the person owes you for your sacrifice (lack of love), you can get angry (lack of joy and peace), you may want to give up (lack of patience), you can react with harshness (lack of kindness and gentleness), and give them a piece of your mind (lack of self-control and faithfulness). A warning sign for when you may be walking more in the flesh than in the Spirit is when you see the person you seek to restore as needing more help and as being more sinful than you.

2. *Don't be simplistic in dealing with sin.*

If gospel mission were as easy as saying, "stop it" (the sin, the unbelief, the doubts, etc.) and "start doing it" (righteousness, belief, etc.) then ministry and life would be a walk in the park. Even though the Scriptures teach the "put off/put on" principle (Eph. 4:17-22; Col. 3:1-17), you need to explore and address the deeper heart issues underneath the sin that compel them to cling to things other than Christ Himself. In this process you will discover what they actually believe and do not believe about God, along with the lies they may believe instead.

3. *Don't counsel from your experience.*

Those struggling with sin need to hear the hope and the power of their living Redeemer more than your personal opinion and experience. However, it is helpful for you to share how the gospel exposes and brings relief for your sinfulness and that they are not alone in their struggle. You should remind them that you need one another because you are all prone to wander and turn your back on the living God.

4.   Include community.
If those who are struggling are willing to sit down and talk through the issues with someone, then make sure you invite others into the care process so that they can learn more of the details of the struggle and they can better understand how to minister the gospel to others. Those invited into the redemptive process, who can be referred to as "sojourners," "burden bearers," or "advocates," should be available, teachable and faithful to the gospel mission. These selected individuals or couples are just as important as the primary ministry leader in carrying out God's redemptive work in this given situation.

5.   Maintain a redemptive vision.
Because redemption is messy, it is easy to get lost or lose focus on the overall goal of gospel mission when the shrapnel of sin is flying everywhere and the enemy seems to be advancing in the heart of those struggling with sin. You need to fight to remember that God is using you and others to see with His eyes and fight for His mission in the mess of life. If you lose redemptive vision you will personally hinder God's work even though He will bring good out of your sin as well.

6.   Equip the church.
See Appendix 8.1 to help evaluate your current approach to equipping the saints for the work of the ministry. You will also find some helpful guidelines for equipping the church.

A GROANING BUT GROWING COMMUNITY
Once Pastor Greg got involved, John quickly moved out of Tom and Sharon's house because he didn't want to be pressured and prodded by any of them. The less they knew—his whereabouts and his situation with Meredith—the better. John also stopped taking Tom's phone calls. How dare they get into his business! John had

a growing sense of peace as he withdrew, but little did he know this sense of calm was a false peace that fit perfectly with his fantasy life with Meredith.

On the other hand, Kathy was opening herself up more and more to those around her. She felt comfortable sitting and chatting with Sharon since she was more experienced and shared openly about her own struggles in life with Christ. She never felt judged or "preached at" even though Sharon would speak gospel truths in a bold yet loving way to help her to see when she was not trusting in God and not believing in His promises. If this wasn't enough of a blessing, Sharon did the unexpected. She told Kathy that she wanted Kathy to speak into her life as well because she knew she had blind spots and that she needed other people to help her to see and grow in Christ. Imagine, Sharon asking her to do such a thing, knowing how messed up she is with her own life and marriage. Kathy was beginning for the first time to understand the beauty of the gospel and the function of the church.

One day over coffee, Kathy shared the names of two other women in their small group who she prayerfully considered asking to join her during this time in her life. Sharon was excited to hear Kathy's step of faith, knowing that just a few months ago, Kathy barely opened up to her. Sharon was impressed with Kathy's reasons for choosing these women: (1) they didn't have perfect marriages but they expressed the incredible ways in which God had grown them by His grace, (2) they had a firm grasp of what it means to be women of God and their calling as wives, and (3) they didn't hesitate to point her back to Christ each and every time she began to lose hope or start to disrespect John. Sharon saw how God enabled Kathy to think biblically and redemptively in her selection process. At that moment Sharon and Kathy looked at each other without saying a word and smiled, for they both knew that God was at work.

REFLECT AND RESPOND:

1. Have you experienced the gospel community that is described in this chapter?

    a. As a church leader, what things do you need to continue to do or start doing so that your small groups or adult classes can grow in being a community where the gospel is lived out in the realities of life?

b. As a small group leader, what concrete steps do you need to take to develop and strengthen this vision and practice of gospel mission among those you shepherd?

c. As a church member, how can you take your existing relationships and grow deeper in the gospel with one another?

2. Take a moment to prayerfully ask the Lord to search your heart. How do you view others who are struggling with sin? Do you tend to rejoice or focus on the sin when a spouse, child or friend confesses and repents? What other truths or concepts challenged you in this chapter?

9

Redemptive Efforts
by the Church

For I solemnly warned your fathers when I brought them up out of the land of Egypt, warning them persistently, even to this day, saying, Obey my voice. Yet they did not obey or incline their ear, but everyone walked in the stubbornness of his evil heart. Therefore I brought upon them all the words of this covenant, which I commanded them to do, but they did not. (Jer. 11:7-8)

If he refuses to listen to them, tell it to the church. (Matt. 18:17a)

Let us hold fast the confession of our hope without wavering, for He who promised is faithful; and let us consider how to stimulate one another to love and good deeds, not forsaking our own assembling together, as is the habit of some, but encouraging *one another*; and all the more as you see the day drawing near. (Heb. 10:23-25, NASB)

DECEIVED AND WEARY

It had been weeks since anyone heard from John after he moved his belongings out of Tom and Sharon's house. John ran into an old high school friend who rented him a basement apartment for next to nothing. He didn't mind his sparse living arrangements since this new place allowed him to continue his relationship with Meredith without any interference.

Meredith told her husband that she wanted a divorce after seeing John's commitment to her since their chance with Tom at the restaurant. She admitted to her husband that they had become like roommates, doing their own thing, and that over time, she realized she was never really happy with him or their marriage.

John was having the time of his life. He and Meredith took advantage of every opportunity to live out their "new life" as both of them were convinced of their future together. Whenever possible, they would take road trips to different destinations where they could enjoy themselves without fear of being seen by any of their friends.

Back at home, Kathy was closer to God than ever before but she was experiencing the most difficult and painful time in her life. It was hard to explain. She could be crying uncontrollably one moment while obsessing over her life and marriage and then, in the midst of the sobs, she would experience God's grace and peace in an unexplainable way. But the separation had taken a toll on Kathy. She was weary and worn out. Even though her community was wonderful in caring for her and the kids' physical needs while providing unbelievable relational support, Kathy still felt the consequences of John's adultery and abandonment.

Morning was the start of her daily marathon, when she had to wake up at 6:00am to prepare lunches for the kids and clean up the mess in the kitchen and around the house that she didn't have the energy or time to get to the day before. Then came the battle of getting the kids up, dressed, fed and out of the house to catch the bus to school. As soon as the kids were off, she rushed to her cashier job at the grocery store that kept her on her feet for the next six hours. At the end of her shift she darted back home before the kids got off the bus. Then came the afternoon and evening stretch when she had to help the kids with homework, scramble to throw together a meal from what she could find in the refrigerator, then get the kids cleaned up and in bed. But sleep was still out of reach. Once the kids were sleeping, she would do a load of laundry while she did homework for her teaching degree. Kathy had enrolled in school two nights a week so that she could finish the education that she put on hold once they began having children. She always wanted to be a teacher and she knew regardless of what happened between her and John, she had to do this for herself and her family. By the end of the night, she had to convince herself to shower before she fell into bed out of sheer exhaustion. As her head hit the pillow, she would recite and pray through Psalm 23, which became her personal psalm that would help her to cling to Jesus, her Shepherd King.

THE SEESAW OF SPIRITUAL BATTLES

Every situation will not be as clear-cut as John's unrepentant adultery and complete abandonment of his family, along with his blatant refusal to talk with those who pursued him for his good. However, in situations with such defined actions, you have no choice but to escalate the efforts to pursue those who have completely rejected Christ.

Living in the Gray Realities of Life

More often, people will teeter back and forth between repentance and resistance, faith and fear, submission and rebellion. Some will actually ask for help. Others will follow the guidance of ministry leaders out of a desire for change or out of a sense of obligation to submit to a church leader. But more times than not such struggles go unnoticed. There may be little to no obvious changes in their outward lives as days turn to weeks, weeks turn to months. This ongoing spiritual battle shows itself in many different ways: a man who withdraws and isolates himself from community as he struggles with despair; a woman who moves from one relationship to the next as she battles with loneliness and a longing to be married; a husband and wife who have become like roommates, living disconnected lives as they wait for the right time to go their separate ways; a divorced man who is trying to figure out who he is by pursuing adventure in any shape or form; an elderly woman who is plagued by suicidal thoughts because life has not turned out as she had dreamed; a middle-age man who still flees to drugs and alcohol as he lives with regret and shame over his efforts as a husband and father; a woman who offends those around her with her sarcasm and bitterness as she lives in a constant state of fear and anxiety. Those who are barely hanging on through these gray seasons of life need patient and persistent love from those who can point them back to the Redeemer rather than aggressive, black and white "church discipline."

Creating a Redemptive Plan

In situations where chronic struggles persist in spite of the efforts of the gospel community (e.g., escalating marital strife or apathy, enduring sexual sin struggles with pornography or sex outside of marriage, cyclic struggles with substance abuse) an elder or ministry leader should come alongside and oversee the continuing care of the person or couple. In most cases when dealing with such ongoing struggles, there is no need to think or say "church discipline" but to present your efforts in a way that best expresses your love and care for them during their time of need.

In such cases it may be helpful to create a redemptive plan to provide structure, clarity and accountability. You can either propose a plan that can be modified with their help or you can develop the plan after discussing with them what you think is needed in order to bring about redemption in their situation. See Appendix 9.1 for an example redemptive plan for a married couple who has lost hope in their marriage and in each other. If you are asking, "Wait, is this part of informal or formal discipline?" you are still thinking too rigidly. What you should be thinking is, "How can I best shepherd them so that they will see and experience the love of Christ?" Don't mistake the written documentation for formal discipline, but look at the paperwork as a means of clearly communicating important gospel truths and presenting tangible pathways for redemption. Whether you decide to write out the redemptive plan or not, you need to help them to envision the power and the beauty of the gospel so that they might find hope and experience change through Jesus, their Redeemer.

The Trajectory of Turning Away

Whether one is struggling openly within gospel community or battling in isolation without others aware of the chaos, the heart can harden incrementally over time as a result of depending on oneself more than on Christ while submitting to sinful desires. Just like heart disease, which in many cases displays few or no symptoms as it develops gradually over time until a heart attack strikes, such escalating waywardness from Christ might be exposed when some illegal or immoral act is discovered: e.g., tax evasion; stealing; sexual abuse; adultery; incessant lying; enslavement to drugs, alcohol or pornography. This chronic heart condition will take one of three broad trajectories when it is exposed: (1) godly sorrow leading to repentance,[1] (2) worldly sorrow leading to despair, and (3) little to no sorrow leading to all out rebellion. Many times in dealing with

---

1   Godly and worldly sorrow is detailed in 2 Cor. 7:9-10.

worldly sorrow, God will transform the grief, first associated with getting caught and suffering the consequences of sin, into brokenness and remorse over the weight and the wickedness of their sins along with the pain they caused others. In this chapter, we will deal with those situations in which the worldly sorrow and the outright rebellion leads to a complete turning away from the living God evidenced by outward actions and expressed desires.

Pursuing Those Who Refuse to Listen

Despite rejecting the repeated pleas of family and friends to come back to Christ, those who are undeterred in their waywardness should still be pursued. If there is one thing that is clear through His story of redemption, God never gives up on His own rebellious people and He calls His church to follow His lead.[2] Therefore, God gives us a road map for such situations through the passages typically associated with church discipline.[3] These passages extend and broaden the "one another" passages so that we would know how to shepherd through the complexities and complications of sin.

At this point in the journey with those dominated by unbelief and rebellion, it is important to keep in mind three broad guidelines as we escalate and expand the redemptive efforts of the church through issuing warnings, withholding communion and telling the corporate gathering of believers:

1. *Fight for Straying Souls.* God has invited us to join our Redeemer in His radical mission of redemption through which everyone involved is changed by the gospel. When we fight for straying souls, we not only join Christ in His work but we also reflect Christ in His pursuit.

2. *Escalate Redemptive Efforts.* As those struggling become increasingly resolute in turning their backs on God, the church needs

---

2   We should be reminded that there are some who attend church, even some who are members, who are not part of God's redeemed family (cf. Matt. 25:31-46). Only God knows the hearts of people. If those within the church who have not been redeemed by the blood of Christ never repent and seek Jesus for salvation, God will "give up on them" by turning them over to their sinfulness and eternal punishment.

3   To review these passages, see Chapter 5, "*Looking at the Church Discipline Passages.*"

to gather together to fight with increasing intensity for their souls. It is important to fight not only for those who are straying but also to protect the rest of the flock from any harm. [See Appendix 9.2]

3. *Follow the Spirit.* It is important to emphasize once again that God's redemptive efforts should not be reduced to pre-determined, sequential and time-driven tasks or events. As with any gospel ministry, your redemptive efforts should follow the leading of the Spirit of Christ through His living Word and people, with patience and gentleness.[4]

WARNING AND WAITING

As we have seen already in our understanding of everyday gospel mission in community, God's people are regularly called upon to warn those caught in the downward spiral of sin. As a wayward sheep's rebellion escalates, these warnings will naturally become more frequent, and those doing the warning may hesitate to continue. But such proactive effort reflects our God who mercifully warns those who have turned their backs on Him.

God Warns Us

Throughout God's redemptive story He sends out warning after warning to generation after generation through His prophets and His living Word. Through His warnings He calls His rebellious and wayward people back to His perfect love to do His perfect will. Warnings throughout the Scriptures are solemn since God's holy judgment is real; they are serious because refusal to listen is costly; and they are specific since their focus is on redemption. God declares warnings to bring about redemption in both those who need to turn back to Him out of their rebellion (Jer. 11:6-8; 42:18-20) and those who witness the power and judgment of God's discipline (Ezek. 5:14-16).

---

4   Pastor Andy Farmer, of Covenant Fellowship Church in Glen Mills, PA, reflected on this very point, "As we reviewed our mistakes in the past we tended to place an over-emphasis on leadership and created fixed processes that reflected that tendency. We've learned that shepherding people and the church through church discipline requires a leadership that is sensitive to the real issues involved in each situation, and sensitive to how the Holy Spirit is working in the process as well."

Yet the LORD warned Israel and Judah by every prophet and every
seer, saying, "Turn from your evil ways and keep my commandments
and my statutes, in accordance with all the Law that I commanded
your fathers, and that I sent to you by my servants the prophets."
(2 Kings 17:13)

God warns us primarily to remind us that He is the only one we
need to fear, especially during times in which we live fearlessly in
our own eyes and foolishly in His (Luke 12:4-5).

God Calls Us to Warn One Another

In the same way God warned the people of Israel through His prophets, He calls us to warn one another so that we might live life under
His care and in His ways. The warnings we give to others need to
be solidly based in Scripture, and not on what we might perceive as
a "word from the Lord." Our warnings should not mislead and harm
others in any way by speaking lies or by calling others to obey unbiblical demands. Instead, warnings should be a means of guiding, correcting, and causing us to grow in the grace of Christ for our good and
for His glory. We must remember that God has called His bride to
live out this radical mission of redemption where He uses His people
in all aspects of His transforming work, including His discipline.

> Him we proclaim, warning everyone and teaching everyone with all
> wisdom, that we may present everyone mature in Christ. (Col. 1:28)

> As for a person who stirs up division, after warning him once and
> then twice, have nothing more to do with him, knowing that such
> a person is warped and sinful; he is self-condemned. (Titus 3:10-11)

We are called to warn and encourage one another as necessary in our
relationships within our homes, friendships, community and church
(Heb. 3:12-13) [See Appendix 9.3]. As we warn others, we need to follow God's lead in presenting gospel truths to them in a solemn manner that communicates His purpose, concerns and desires.

Elder Warnings

Despite the fact that people in gospel community may have already
warned those rebelling against God, there comes a time, in cases of
persistent waywardness, when elders will begin issuing a series of
warnings as the overseers of the church [See Appendix 9.4].

If the elders have not been informed before now, those in the gospel community who have been involved in the redemptive pursuit need to tell the elders the details of the given situation since they have the responsibility to oversee the redemptive discipline process.[5]

It is a sobering reality when one or more elders solemnly issue a strong admonishment and statement of intent to those who continue to resist and reject their Redeemer. We pray that by God's grace, those receiving the warning will comprehend the seriousness and insanity of their sinful attitudes and actions and turn back to Christ. Appendix 9.5 highlights some key elements of a warning, and Appendix 9.6 offers an example of an initial warning letter.

Waiting After an Elder Warning

The warning should include a period for waiting and praying for the unrepentant person to respond to the elders. There are no formulas or guidelines for how long the elders should wait. In surveying churches across the country, the average waiting period associated with the elder's warning letter ranged from two to four weeks [See Appendix 9.7]. Keep in mind that there may have been almost two to six months of pursuing, warning and waiting prior to issuing the first full elder warning.

It is crucial that we keep in mind that the waiting period that follows a warning is not the calm before the storm or a delay in dropping the hammer on those who have turned their back on the living God. Rather, we must see this time of waiting as an opportunity for the Spirit of God to work in the hearts of all involved, as a time for the church to pursue and pray for those who have been warned in intentional ways. In order to determine the next steps after issuing a warning, we need to wait and see how the Spirit is leading, which includes seeing how those who have been warned respond to the redemptive pleadings of the church leaders.

WITHHOLDING COMMUNION

In addition to warning those who have rejected Christ through their rebellion, the elders will need to face the dilemma of whether

---

5   Once informed, the elders will need to make sure all of the details have been reported, verified, and assessed so that they can best understand every aspect of the situation.

to withhold communion. Such a decision to withhold communion should not be taken lightly or overlooked. Since this act of worship has great significance this decision should be taken with much seriousness.

The Significance of Communion

Communion, or the Lord's Supper, is one of God's enduring ordinances, along with baptism, that He commands the church to carry out. Jesus described communion's rich symbolism, its purpose and its duration as He prepared His disciples for His departure before His crucifixion:

> ... the Lord Jesus on the night when he was betrayed took bread, and when he had given thanks, he broke it, and said, "This is my body which is for you. Do this in remembrance of me." In the same way also he took the cup, after supper, saying, "This cup is the new covenant in my blood. Do this, as often as you drink it, in remembrance of me." For as often as you eat this bread and drink the cup, you proclaim the Lord's death until he comes. (1 Cor. 11:23-26)

Communion reminds us that Jesus declared and demonstrated His redeeming love through His death on the cross while we were helpless, sinful and His enemies. The bread symbolizes the body of Jesus broken by God's righteous wrath that we deserved because of our rebellion against Him. The cup symbolizes the new covenant established by the blood of Jesus that was shed to cover our sins so that God's justice would be satisfied and we would be reconciled with Him. Because of Christ's finished work on the cross, we can enjoy our new life and relationship with Him and experience unceasing transformation by His grace.

Whenever we take the bread and the cup, we are reminded of our continual need for Jesus Christ as we battle with remaining sin. We are commanded through this meal to remember and proclaim the life, death and resurrection of Christ as the church in the world until He returns. What a beautiful picture of the grace of the gospel for those who have been saved by the Redeemer. What an amazing privilege to be reminded regularly as the bride of Christ that we have been bought with the blood of Christ and that nothing can ever separate us from His love. But this reminder of the gospel does not serve merely as a "memorial" of the cross;[6] it is meant to serve as the compelling reason to no longer live for ourselves[7] but to imitate Christ in obedience to the Father and join Him in His mission of redemption as we live out the gospel.

The Seriousness of Communion

Because communion is a portrait of the suffering and sacrifice associated with our new life in Christ, God warns us not to take the meal in an unworthy manner. He calls us to practice this ordinance with all seriousness, discernment and self-examination as expressed by the Apostle Paul:

> Whoever, therefore, eats the bread or drinks the cup of the Lord in an unworthy manner will be guilty concerning the body and blood of the Lord. Let a person examine himself, then, and so eat of the bread and drink of the cup. For anyone who eats and drinks without discerning the body eats and drinks judgment on himself. That is why many of you are weak and ill, and some have died. But if we judged ourselves truly, we would not be judged. But when we are judged by the Lord, we are disciplined so that we may not be condemned along with the world. (1 Cor. 11:27-32)

The church at Corinth was abusing the Lord's Supper. They were treating it like any other meal and were taking part in communion even though they were showing an overall lack of love for one another evidenced by divisions, factions, greed, and drunkenness. Therefore Paul could not commend their practice of communion and warned them that they would "eat and drink judgment" on themselves as they ate the bread and drank the cup since their lives did not reflect the very gospel depicted by the sacred meal.

Paul's warning in this passage applies to us today. Paul is not saying that we should abstain from the bread and cup if we are aware of our unworthiness before the Lord or when we are struggling to believe aspects of the gospel. These are some of the very reasons why the Lord commands us to take part in this sacred meal. He knows that we can be encouraged and strengthened in our faith as we are reminded of His redeeming death.

---

6 Gordon Fee. (1987). *The First Epistle to the Corinthians. The New International Commentary on the New Testament*, p. 558.

7 cf. Gal. 2:20; 2 Cor. 5:14-15.

What Paul is saying is that if we take communion in a flippant manner, either without honest self-examination or while willfully rebelling against God, we should expect to be disciplined by Him. God will cause us, as His people, to suffer and experience godly sorrow as He leads us to repentance so that we might submit to Christ once again and not be condemned like the world, like those who do not know Christ.

Communion is a beautiful picture of the members of the body of Christ celebrating and affirming the fact that they have been ransomed by His blood, united with Him as one, and placed under submission to Him as Lord. Even though they once professed faith in Christ and expressed a desire to be a part of His body, those who refuse to submit to Christ are not proclaiming the goodness of the gospel in their rebellion. Their hardened and unrepentant hearts shout out that they do not care that Christ shed His blood for their redemption, they do not want to be united with their Redeemer and they are no longer willing to submit to Him and His ways. Therefore, if they took part in the sacred meal, they would be doing so in a hypocritical way that would invite God's judgment upon them.

When to Withhold Communion

When discussing with pastors the issue of withholding communion, there seem to be two broad categories of thought: (1) withholding communion is linked with removal from membership and (2) withholding communion can be done independent of removal from membership. Regarding the first category, communion is a distinct privilege associated with being a part of the body of Christ since the meal is for every member of the body. Therefore, it makes sense to link withholding communion with the decision to remove someone from the church's covenant community. However, based on the 1 Corinthians 11:27-32 passage, the case can be made that withholding communion does not have to be linked directly to removing one from fellowship.

There may be times in which the elders may decide to withhold communion from those who stubbornly refuse to submit to Christ, when repeated attempts to persuade them to repent have not born fruit. The elders can make this decision any time prior to final removal or it may coincide with their removal from the church. Though Paul's exhortation is directed towards individuals within the church, the elders should exercise their pastoral oversight in this way when those who are wayward make a mockery of Christ's symbolic meal. Regardless of when the elders decide to withhold communion, such a decision should be seen as an act of mercy since it keeps those who are unrepentant from eating and drinking judgment upon themselves.[8]

Now that we have worked through the redemptive efforts of warning and withholding communion, we need to examine the command found in Matthew 18:17 regarding "telling the church."

Delivering the Final Warning

If ongoing efforts to pursue and pray for those who have turned their backs on God do not result in repentance, the elders need to send a final warning letter [See Appendix 9.9]. The final warning differs from the previous warnings in that it provides a warning of telling the church, along with the action steps that will be taken should the person refuses to repent—removal from the care and community of the church, along with being turned over to Satan. The letter also outlines the restoration process that follows Spirit-led repentance.[9]

Gathering and Telling the Church

When those who are rebelling against God choose to reject Christ in spite of the repeated attempts by family, friends and church leaders to encourage, challenge and warn them, Jesus directs that the church be informed (cf. Matt. 18:17a). What does it mean to tell the church? Why do you need to tell the church? When do you tell? What do you tell the church? We must seek the Lord's wisdom for the answers to each of these questions since we want to be found faithful in obeying God's will, carrying out His discipline in a way that brings glory to Him.

What Does It Mean to Tell the Church?

Even though Jesus' command to "tell the church" is clear, the pastoral practices are varied based on different interpretations of

---

8   See Appendix 9.8 to consider withholding communion in light of open communion.

9   Each of these action steps is described in Chapters 10 and 11.

this imperative as well as some of the realities of the contemporary church. The pastoral application of this command, "tell the church," is practiced in at least three different ways: (1) "tell the church" means tell the elders since they are God's appointed leaders of the church who plead with the people on behalf of God and plead to God on behalf of the people, (2) "tell the church" means tell the most relevant group of people who know those being disciplined rather than the entire church since those who don't know either won't care or won't take part in the redemptive efforts, and (3) "tell the church" means to tell the entire church gathering since the local church is the entire assembly of believers who have covenanted together as a community. So how should we understand the command, "tell the church"?

As we look at the context of Matthew 18, Jesus is preparing His disciples for His departure by teaching them how they are to live with one another as a community in light of His death and resurrection. Knowing that those in this community would struggle with sin, Jesus gave His disciples instructions on how to deal with one another in an escalating and expansive manner for the sake of redeeming those who are straying.

In this particular passage Jesus does not explicitly mention or address church leaders; therefore, we cannot automatically interpret His command, "tell the church," as "tell the elders."[10] However, the elders are God's appointed shepherds to care for and lead the flock and should be the ones who oversee the process of telling the church. Some church leaders who inform only the immediate community of those in rebellion use the argument that the early followers of Christ gathered in homes, where they fellowshipped and worshipped together.[11] Despite the fact that believers were gathering in homes, most commentators interpret the plain reading of the passage as a command to tell the entire gathering of believers, the corporate body of believers, not just those associated with a given

---

10   Despite the fact that commentators agree that God has given the "keys of the kingdom" to church leaders based on Matt. 16:19, many scholars point out that God addresses the entire church in the Matt. 18 passage.

11   Acts 2:42-47; 5:42; Rom. 16:5; 1 Cor. 16:19; Col. 4:15; cf. Acts 8:3; 20:20.

home.[12] Moreover, in light of the fuller action taken by the church to not associate with those who refuse to submit to Christ and His people, it would not make sense for only a small group to be informed.[13] Jesus knew that because there would be some who would reject all redemptive efforts, the entire community would need to be gathered, informed and mobilized to pray for and pursue those who are wayward. Therefore, we can understand the command, "tell the church" as informing the larger corporate gathering who have covenanted together so that they can live out the redemptive mission of God.[14] What a beautiful picture of the body of Christ responding in an ever-increasing way to serious soul needs where the stakes are enormous and the consequences are eternal.

Because of the different ways this particular passage has been interpreted and applied, there are some church leaders who choose not to tell the entire church for one reason or another. See Appendix 9.10 for some biblical reasons why the entire church should be told.

It is also crucial that we fully understand the basis for and implications of informing the corporate gathering when redemptive actions need to be escalated by the church. There are a number of factors that we need to think through to prepare for telling the church, including the actual content and manner in which the church is to be informed See Appendix 9.11 for further discussion on "How Do You Tell the Church" and Appendix 9.12 for an "Example Manuscript for Telling the Church."

Communicate and Coordinate Before Telling the Church

Communication is essential in every relationship, especially when the welfare of God's people is at stake. Every step of shepherding

---

12   Blomberg, Boice, Bruner, Calvin, France, Green, Hauerwas, Legg, MacArthur, Morris, Mounce, Ryle, and Spurgeon all interpret Jesus' command to "tell the church" as meaning tell the entire gathered community. Moreover, when you look at other passages associated with church discipline, the "assembly" or "majority" is referenced either explicitly or implicitly given the context of the passages (e.g. 1 Cor. 5:4; 2 Cor. 2:5-8).

13   "The discipline of 'shunning' a fellow Christian would not be effective unless all the other members agreed to implement the decision" (Davies and Allison, *The Gospel According to Matthew*, 785).

14   For most churches, all who are members of a given local church represent this larger covenant community.

requires intentional coordination with everyone who is directly involved, from those receiving and offering care, to the church leaders who are giving oversight. If everyone is not on the same page then it becomes far too easy to misstep as you try to care for one another in community. Everyone who is bearing burdens needs to know what is going on, how the gospel speaks to the specific issues being addressed, and how to respond with loving truth to one another amidst the suffering and sin. They also need to know how to respond scripturally if those who are wayward refuse to listen even to the church. Such communication is crucial because the enemy wants to distract and divide the bride of Christ at every turn [See Appendix 9.13].

Before the elders inform the church, they need to ensure that they have coordinated closely with the unrepentant person's family, respective gospel community, and with one another as leaders. The elders should make sure that before they tell the church they have sought to understand and evaluate every relevant detail of the sin struggles and redemptive efforts in light of the gospel. Much harm can result if the elders and the gospel community fail to reflect Christ in their understanding of sinful actions and in their shepherding of the unrepentant ones and their families. If there is a mishandling of any aspect of God's discipline then the elders run the risk of abusing their God-given authority, confusing the church about church discipline, and shaming those whose names were brought before the church prematurely or for unbiblical reasons.[15]

LEADERSHIP POINTS—BEING ALERT AS YOU ESCALATE REDEMPTIVE EFFORTS

There is much to consider as we look to escalate the redemptive efforts towards those who have refused to listen to everyone in the church despite numerous pleas and warnings. If we add such demanding disciplinary efforts to an already heavy ministry load, along with the struggles associated with our own sinful hearts, we

---

15 The elders can exercise discernment in whether or not to share specific names based on the following factors: (1) the public nature of the offense, (2) the informal or formal influence of the person within the church and community, and (3) the potential danger for church members not to know the identity of the offender.

as church leaders can fail in our shepherding responsibilities [See Appendix 9.14]. One safeguard against this possibility is to gather with fellow elders within the church to co-labor with one another so that together, we can shepherd and lead God's bride with faithfulness and integrity [See Appendix 9.15]. But here are some additional points that will help us to guard our hearts in the midst of demanding ministry so that we can "be on the alert, stand firm in the faith, act like men, be strong" and lead with love (1 Cor. 16:13-14).

1. *Believing the gospel.*
   You will spend much time reflecting on the realities of the gospel message and mission as you face both hardened and broken hearts. When you have poured out your heart and soul into those who have turned their back on God and they still refuse to listen and submit to Christ, you can find yourself wondering why the gospel is not penetrating their hearts. When you sit with those who have been sinned against in horrific ways and they cry out in their pain, shame, and hopelessness, you can wonder about God's love and why He allows such suffering and sin. When you begin to doubt the presence and power of God, you will find yourself pulling back from speaking boldly about His promises, you will hesitate to offer those you are helping a vision of God's redemptive work that can come about through His grace, and you will fear your shepherding encounters because you have not seen God's transforming power make a difference in the lives of others. This is when you need to be still and believe that God is your Creator and Redeemer.[16] This is when you need to believe that the Spirit of the living God is powerfully present in each of His people and in His world where He is making all things new.[17] This is when you need to believe that Christ's work on the cross is finished and that He has conquered sin and death.[18]

   Another significant aspect of believing the gospel is trusting that God's commands are good for your soul and that you actually reflect Christ when you obey God's will by faith. For

---

16   Ps. 46:10; Ps. 27:14; Exod. 14:14

17   1 Pet. 1:2; John 14:16-26; Rom. 8; Phil. 2:13

18   Rom. 8; 1 Cor. 15; 2 Cor. 2:14; 4:7-18; Eph. 2:1-10; Col. 2:6-15; Rev. 21-22

instance, when faced with the decision to inform the church about a given person who has rejected God, you can hesitate, knowing that such action not only flies in the face of the culture but also seems unnecessary to some in the church. But you must trust that our all-wise and sovereign God knows what He is talking about and that such action is best for His bride. This is where the rubber meets the road. God calls you to live by faith in every aspect of individual and communal living and to believe that His will and ways are the best pathways to experience and grow in His love.

2. *Knowing the dynamics of sin.*
    You will also spend much time reflecting on the dynamics and the pervasiveness of sin as you continually encounter and engage sin while seeing and experiencing its devastating effects. As you come to learn the various dynamics of sin you can more easily explore root issues that may be hindering redemption (e.g., shame can keep one from confessing sin and believing in God's grace), you can keep from being personally offended when others sin against you, and you can anticipate the possible responses of those who are suffering and those who are blinded by sin so that you can better shepherd them. God calls you to be wise as serpents and innocent as doves (Matt. 10:16); therefore you must know the schemes of the enemy so that you can be better equipped to engage in the spiritual battle.

PERSUADED AND CURLED UP

Pastor Greg informed Kathy, along with Tom and Sharon, about the elders' decision to send John a final warning letter. After constructing the rough draft and reviewing it with his fellow elders, Pastor Greg met with the three of them to see if they had any questions and if they recommended any edits. As they met, Kathy felt a lump in her throat and a hole in her stomach. She couldn't believe this was happening. Everything seemed surreal. How could John do something like this to her and the kids? By God's grace, she was able to express her jumbled thoughts and feelings to everyone during the meeting. She cried as Tom closed their time with prayer. Pastor Greg told Kathy that he and his wife were praying for them.

He also shared that if John didn't respond to the letter after two weeks, then the elders would inform the church at their next members' meeting at the end of the month.

John was enraged when he received the letter from Pastor Greg and the elders of his church. He nearly burned the letter in disgust, anticipating pure judgment and condemnation. But after a couple of days with the letter sitting unopened on the kitchen counter, John's curiosity got the best of him and he decided to read the letter. His eyes kept bouncing over sentences, skipping from paragraph to paragraph as he anxiously tried to grasp the gist of the content while trying to avoid eye contact with any accusations. At first glance the letter made no sense at all. His eyes quickly started back at the top of the page, and he tried to compose himself by taking slow deep breaths. Just as he began to focus on what the letter had to say, Meredith walked in and asked what he was reading, thinking it was a letter from Kathy. John mumbled an answer so Meredith asked again with suspicious anger. John looked up, frustrated at the interruption and told her it was a letter from the church. Without saying a word, Meredith snatched the letter from John's hands, tore it up and threw it in the trash. She knelt down to where John was sitting, took his hands and looked him squarely in his eyes and assured him that they were going to have the perfect life together. Meredith met every one of John's objections with a counter argument until she convinced him that he needed to forget the church and focus on them as a couple.

Kathy curled up on the bedroom floor as she cried herself to sleep. She had nothing left and her world was completely shattered. She kept screaming over and over again in the silence of her mind, "I can't take it anymore! When will this misery end?" When the early morning rays roused her from her restless sleep, her entire body ached. She sank deeper into despair as she played out the routine of another day but she knew she needed to get the kids to school and herself to work. She kept wondering how her husband of twelve years would respond to the elders' warning letter. She prayed for John and their family as she forced herself off the floor.

REFLECT AND RESPOND:

1. Do you know of anyone who turned his or her back on God and was disciplined by the church? Have you ever fought for

the soul of a straying brother or sister in Christ? How so? Do you see that you are capable of totally rejecting your Redeemer apart from His grace? How do you think you would respond in your rebellion if those in the church pursued you with the love and truth of Christ?

2. How has God warned you through His Word, His people, and through the circumstances of life? Do you see such warnings as an act of love?

3. How do you honestly examine yourself before God so that you can take communion without bringing judgment upon yourself? Describe a time in which you took the necessary steps of repentance to make things right before God and others before celebrating the sacred meal.

4. What are some questions, reflections and even some uneasiness that may have emerged as you read through the section about telling the church? What points did you find the most challenging and what points were most helpful in helping you think through this issue?

10

Redemptive Shame and Suffering

And if he refuses to listen even to the church, let him be to you as a Gentile and a tax collector. (Matt. 18:17b)

When you are assembled in the name of the Lord Jesus and my spirit is present, with the power of our Lord Jesus, you are to deliver this man to Satan for the destruction of the flesh, so that his spirit may be saved in the day of the Lord. (1 Cor. 5:4-5)

If anyone does not obey what we say in this letter, take note of that person, and have nothing to do with him, that he may be ashamed. Do not regard him as an enemy, but warn him as a brother. (2 Thess. 3:14-15)

EYES WIDE OPEN AND BLIND

Ever since their meeting with Pastor Greg to discuss the warning letter, both Tom and Sharon had been restless, spending most of their waking hours talking about John and Kathy's situation. They had never been involved with another couple to this degree and this experience had deeply shaken them. Never before had they seen the effects of sin so up close and personal, along with sin's agonizing after-effects. Never before had they poured out their hearts like this, only to experience such rejection and a sense of helplessness.

Tom and Sharon were also finding it difficult to keep their community group from spending inordinate amounts of time talking with Kathy about the situation during their weekly meeting since they knew others in the group were dealing with issues that also needed to be addressed. Since they began their journey with Kathy, Tom and Sharon seemed to look at life and relationships with different eyes. They were beginning to see and hear the suffering and sins of those in their group with more clarity and with a greater sense of responsibility to care for one another.

Since it had been almost two weeks since the elders sent the initial warning letter to John, Pastor Greg offered to attend Tom and Sharon's next community group meeting to offer an overview of Kathy's situation from the elders' perspective, to explain the biblical basis and the redemptive purposes of church discipline, and to answer any questions they might have about the upcoming members' meeting when the elders would inform the church about John's rebellion against God. Pastor Greg made it a point to meet with Kathy, Tom and Sharon before the group meeting so that he could best prepare Kathy for what would be a difficult meeting for everyone, especially her. Not only would the entire community group hear more details about her situation but she also knew that the church was getting ready to take definitive action towards her husband if he chose not to respond to the elders' warning letter.

John and Meredith were off on one of their weekend adventures but he just couldn't relax. Before Meredith snatched the warning letter from him, John saw the deadline that was stated in bold print towards the bottom of the letter. He knew that he had one more day before the church would do what they warned they would do if he didn't respond. In the days after receiving the letter, John had experienced a tug of war in his heart. One moment he felt deep remorse because he knew he had crossed the line and he was convinced that God and Kathy could never forgive him. The next moment, he didn't care about his old life but was convinced that God wanted him to be happy with Meredith since she made him feel like a man in ways Kathy never did. Ironically, on the day of the deadline, he felt incredible peace. He knew in his heart he was doing the right thing.

But when he thought about the church, John felt anger toward those who tried to contact him via email and phone messages. In his mind he accused them of being unloving and unmerciful hypocrites who were just as messed up as he was but didn't know it. He couldn't believe they were still trying to control his life and were now threatening to kick him out of the church.

RESPONSE AFTER INFORMING THE CHURCH

Despite the church gathering and mobilizing for prayer and pursuit, those who are straying from Christ may not respond with contrition and repentance. The church needs to keep in mind that our hope does not rest on whether or not those who are wayward will repent, but on the sovereign and faithful Redeemer who has made all things possible through His finished work on the cross. The gospel is still powerful and effective even if the rebellious ones do not repent. Jesus is still ruling victoriously even if there is no response. The church is still commanded to carry out the will of God by faith even if it seems unlikely that such actions will make any difference.

We need to be discerning when interpreting the various responses from those who have been warned [See Appendix 10.1]. Again, we must remember that gospel mission is rarely black and white. We need to rely upon the wisdom of God's Spirit and Word to navigate the difficult terrain of discipline. But in cases where warnings do not yield repentance, God calls the church to yet another redemptive measure.

TREAT AS A GENTILE AND A TAX-COLLECTOR

Jesus, knowing the hardness of the human heart, offers one last command in the Matthew 18 passage when dealing with those who refuse to listen to God and His people as they live in gospel community. Jesus clearly states that if the wayward ones refuse to listen even to the church, they should be treated as a "Gentile and a tax-collector," meaning, as those who do not know the Son of God and who are not children of the kingdom of heaven.[1]

What does it look like for the church to treat someone as "a Gentile and a tax-collector"? Most commentators and theologians throughout church history describe the implications of Jesus' command by using words like excommunication, expulsion, exclusion, dis-fellowship and removal from the church. But what is actually involved when a church removes someone from the covenant community established by the blood of Christ?[2]

---

1   Matt. 7:21-23; 18:3-4; 25:41-46; 1 John 3:4-10; 1 John 5:18-19

2   The covenant community rooted in Christ is the new covenant established by His blood, making His people members of His body.

GOD'S COMMUNITY AND CARE

Before we answer this question, we must rightly understand God's communion and care for us as His sheep. We must also understand how our ongoing rebellion impacts our relationship with God.

Sheep and Goats

When God makes His people a new creation in Christ, He establishes an unbreakable covenant with them that will last for eternity. By God's grace, nothing can separate His children from His love once He brings them into His fold.[3] Therefore, if those who refuse to listen even to the church are truly His children, their rebellious and hardened hearts cannot remove or break God's intimate union with them that He established through the blood of Christ. In other words, nothing can ever snatch His sheep from the hands of the Father and the Redeemer, not even the perverse and pervasive sinfulness of the sheep (John 10:27-29).

However, within any church, there are some people who profess faith in Christ and participate in the life of His church but who are not truly part of His kingdom. Jesus taught that everyone who calls Him Lord is not necessarily part of the kingdom He ushered into the world (Matt. 7:15ff; 25:31-46). The church cannot know definitively who is a sheep and who is a goat (unbeliever). However, God clearly states that those who know and abide in Christ not only hear but act upon the Word of God, keeping His commandments and practicing righteousness.[4] When people refuse to listen to Christ and act upon His Word by faith, they essentially deny Christ as Lord and Savior. As a result, the church can no longer affirm the faith of these individuals and must treat them as ones who are not part of the covenant community of Christ.

Only God knows those who are His true sheep and those who are not but church leaders are called to make provisional judgments. At the end of time everyone will stand before Christ, who will judge everyone righteously and separate the goats from the sheep.[5]

---

3 Paul proclaims this gospel truth, "Who shall separate us from the love of Christ? Shall tribulation, or distress, or persecution, or famine, or nakedness, or danger, or sword? ... For I am sure that neither death nor life, nor angels nor rulers, nor things present nor things to come, nor powers, nor height nor depth, nor anything else in all creation, will be able to separate us from the love of God in Christ Jesus our Lord. (Rom. 8:35, 38-39)

4 James 1:22-25; 1 John 2:3-11; 28-29; 1 John 3:24; 1 John 4:13-21; 2 John 9

5 John 10:14-18; Matt. 12:35-37; 25:31-46; John 5:22, 25-29; Rom. 2:1-16

Rebellion's Impact on God's Community and Care

Throughout God's story of redemption we see the cycle of the people's rebellion, God's discipline, the people's cry for mercy, and God's deliverance. We also see in God's story that He doesn't remove His care from us when He disciplines us; rather He shows His care for us through His discipline. Even though our sinfulness will never sever God's eternal covenant with us or stop His care for us, our ongoing rebellion against God does impact our communion and care with Him in at least two ways—God's favor and our prayers.

God's face and favor. Though God will never ultimately remove His wayward ones from His flock, He will remove His favor from them for a season as He turns His face from or against them. The Scriptures make an undeniable connection between God's face turned against His people and His judgment towards them.[6]

> Then my anger will be kindled against them in that day, and I will forsake them and hide my face from them, and they will be devoured. And many evils and troubles will come upon them, so that they will say in that day, "Have not these evils come upon us because our God is not among us?" And I will surely hide my face in that day because of all the evil that they have done, because they have turned to other gods. (Deut. 31:17-18)

Aaron's blessing is a familiar passage that illustrates the connection between God's favor and His face turned towards His people:

> The LORD bless you and keep you; the LORD make his face to shine upon you and be gracious to you; the LORD lift up his countenance upon you and give you peace. (Num. 6:24-26)

When you contrast this passage to its antithesis, you see that when God's face is not favorably turned towards His people, His blessings, protection, grace and peace cannot be presumed. God takes a loving disciplinary posture towards His rebellious people so that they would experience the brokenness and the affliction associated with their unrelenting sinfulness. But God doesn't want us to see only our sin. He also wants us to see the merciful power and loving provision of the cross as we come back to Him.

---

6   Gen. 33:10; Lev. 20:1-5; Pss. 27:9; 132:10; Ezek. 7:21-22

God and our prayers. When God turns His face away from His people and removes His favor, He also refuses to hear their sinful and self-centered prayers.[7] Why would God listen to and answer prayers offered from those who have turned their backs on Him and refuse to listen and submit to Him, especially when the intent of such prayers is to advance their own individual kingdoms and not His kingdom? It is important to remember that God turns His face away, removes His favor and refuses to listen to godless prayers in His loving discipline in order to humble arrogant hearts and turn them back to Himself so that they might receive His abundant compassion and forgiveness.

Now that we better understand God's community and care, let's take a look at what is actually involved when a church removes someone from the covenant community established by the blood of Christ.

Removal From Covenant Community

In order to have a right understanding of what it means to remove someone from the church, we need to look at two inter-related aspects of relationship with Christ and His people:

Covenant Community of Christ = Being in Community and Experiencing Care

These two aspects of community and care are inter-related because one implies the other. In other words, being in community with Christ and His people includes care from Christ and His people. And care from Christ and His people flows from communing with Christ and His people. Such intimate covenant community, established through the cross of Christ and sustained through the Spirit of Christ, is a picture of the church enjoying and benefiting from her relationship with her Redeemer.

Therefore, to remove someone from the covenant community known as the church, you remove them from the community of God's people and from the mutual care experienced in community:

---

7   The connection between God's face and prayer is seen in Ps. 102:1; Dan. 9:17; 1 Pet.3:7, 12.

Removal from Covenant Community = Removing Community and Care

BINDING AND LOOSING

Some people may ask, "What right does the church have to remove anyone?" To answer that question, we must come back to a primary identity of the church. By God's design and calling, the church serves as an ambassador of Christ who represents the Savior King in this world. Knowing His ambassador has no actual power Jesus stands behind and supports the church as she steps out to fulfill her role:

> Truly, I say to you, whatever you bind on earth shall be bound in heaven, and whatever you loose on earth shall be loosed in heaven. Again I say to you, if two of you agree on earth about anything they ask, it will be done for them by my Father in heaven. (Matt. 18:18-19)

We as the church do not determine what is to be bound or loosed, prohibited or allowed, but instead, we carry out what God prohibits and allows as He has made it known through His Holy Scriptures. As ambassadors of Christ we declare His message and carry out His mission in the same way Jesus declared His Father's message and accomplished His Father's mission. As ambassadors we have no authority and agenda other than God's authority and agenda found in His Word. Therefore, we need to understand if God commands the church to remove those who are rebelling against Him, and if so, how this is consistent with the gospel.

A Response to Adultery

In order to understand God's will regarding removing rebellious sheep from the fold, let's take a look at this question from the perspective of Jesus and His bride, the church. In God's story of redemption, Jesus, our Redeemer, claimed us as His blood-bought bride, brought us into intimate union with Himself and promised we would spend eternity dwelling in His perfect love and glory. Given this divine analogy of marriage, when a bride refuses to follow and submit to the leadership of her husband, dishonors and disrespects him, develops affections for another man and then gives herself to her adulterous lover in an intimate way, the covenant relationship is compromised and the intimate union has been defiled. What is a husband to do in this situation?

Until His bride recognizes her sins, ends her adulterous relationship, and returns to her husband with a broken and repentant heart, the marriage cannot continue as if nothing is wrong. The husband needs to deal with his wife in ways that he knows will not only honor the marriage but will also help his bride to see the seriousness of her sin and to realize that her true love and life is with her husband. Perhaps she will come to her senses as she finds herself removed from her house, cut off from the provision and protection of her husband, separated from his fellowship and love, and left to fend for herself in an evil and wicked world. Moreover, her husband's consistent and tender promise of abundant compassion and forgiveness upon her return eventually prompts her to come back, trusting that she will experience mercy and not condemnation.

When we remember that every member of the body of Christ is also a part of the bride of Christ, we can see why God demands action be taken against those guilty of such rebellion and spiritual adultery. Therefore, given the significance of Jesus' command to treat as a "Gentile and a tax-collector," what does it mean for the church to remove communion and care from those who refuse to submit to God and His people?

THE CHURCH REMOVING COMMUNITY AND CARE

By removing those who are rebelling against God from covenant community, the church is acknowledging and trusting in God's sovereign will to accomplish His redemptive purposes: in restoring a wayward sheep, saving a lost sheep, or removing a goat that is not part of the flock. We have already seen that there is nothing that can ultimately separate God's rebellious people from His communion and care, but He does use decisive and purposeful actions to deal with their waywardness and to bring about His divine desires. God commands the church to take two inter-related redemptive action steps against those who have turned against Him: (1) remove community and care and (2) turn them over to Satan.

Remove Community and Care[8]

God gives clear direction to His church that they are not to associate with those who profess to follow Christ but refuse to trust and obey Him. The language is absolute and directive:

---

8   See Appendix 10.2 for an overview of the importance of church membership.

- "Let him ... be removed from among you ... [c]leanse out the old leaven ... do not associate ... purge the evil person from among you" (1 Cor. 5:2, 7, 11-13).

- "Avoid such people" (2 Tim. 3:5; Rom. 16:17).

- "Have nothing to do with them" (2 Thess. 3:14; Titus 3:10).

- "Do not receive him into your house or give him any greeting" (2 John 10).

Community cannot be removed without also removing the care that comes with close, intimate relationships. You cannot separate the one from the other. However, we must keep in mind that the actual loss of care that results from being removed from gospel community reflects God actually caring for His people through His redemptive discipline. There are several aspects of community and care that are impacted when fellowship is broken. Those removed from covenant community will no longer enjoy:

- The relational support and accountability of friends from within the church.

- The mutual benefit of serving others in the church.

- The sense of community and identity associated with a group united in membership and purpose.

- The mutually beneficial interactions in various contexts such as neighborhood functions, sporting events, workplace, and social gatherings.

- The business arrangements that emerge from within the church circles. Members of the body of Christ will need to address such business-related agreements on a case-by-case basis and evaluate them using their Spirit-led consciences as a guide.[9]

The church must remember that such separation and withdrawal from those removed from the church is actually an acknowledgment first to God that His ways are best even when they don't make sense to us and seem foolish to the world. Next, such action declares to those removed that everything is not right between them

---

9   Acts 24:16; Gal. 5:1-26; Heb. 13:18

and God and with His people. Lastly, such action acknowledges to one another that the bride of Christ is more important than any one member, but that together as a community, the church needs to fight for the souls of one another.

Turn Over to Satan

The most shocking and symbolic act against those who have turned their backs on God is to "turn them over to Satan."[10] When you first hear this phrase you can't help but take a deep breath, knowing this is a serious command. Such a command can provoke a twisted view of God, making Him appear detached and judgmental, ruling with an iron fist and getting rid of anyone who doesn't obey Him. Nothing could be further from the truth.

Yes, God does demand that the church deal deliberately with those who persistently rebel against Him by withholding communion, removing community and care, and turning them over to Satan. God's steadfast love and faithfulness compels his certain discipline. God knows that the spiritual battle is real and fierce. Souls are at stake. His glory is on the line.

Therefore drastic action needs to be taken. Especially in moments like this, God calls His people to trust and obey His thoughts and ways over their own inclinations. We have already seen that the wisdom and power of God shine forth in the midst of the foolishness and weakness of men and women. Listen to Paul convey God's counter-intuitive command to the church at Corinth:

> When you are assembled in the name of the Lord Jesus and my spirit is present, with the power of our Lord Jesus, you are to deliver this man to Satan for the destruction of the flesh, so that his spirit may be saved in the day of the Lord. (1 Cor. 5:4-5)

Radical actions are required for radical redemption. God is fully aware that His people are prone to get entangled by remaining sin, and the flesh-driven soul needs to be broken and humbled. God stops at nothing to bring His people back into His loving arms, even if it takes delivering them to Satan for a season of suffering.

What does it mean to turn someone over to Satan? How does the church obey this command? Simply put, the very actions of treating someone like a Gentile and tax-collector—removing Him

---

10   1 Cor. 5:1-5; 1 Tim. 1:18-20; cf. Job 33:29-30.

from the community and care of the church—serves as a declaration that God and His people have turned the wayward person over to the desires and devices of their sinful flesh, the world and Satan. The overarching goal of such action is redemption, specifically the destruction of a rebellious and deceived heart so that He "may come to [his] senses and escape from the snare of the devil, after being captured by him to do his will" (2 Tim. 2:26).

Removal Reflects the Rebellion

As we reflect on the steps associated with removal from the church, it is important to see the two-fold declaration involved. First, those who have turned their backs on God have declared three broad desires through their own words and actions:

a. They desire a life without God by refusing to submit to His will.

b. They desire a life without the community and care of God's people by refusing to listen even to the church.

c. They desire a life that reflects the will and ways of Satan.

In other words, their rebellion reflects a "self-imposed exile."[11]

Second, as the church leaders inform the church about the extreme waywardness of those who once professed faith in Christ, the church is simply acknowledging these three realities already declared by those in rebellion. By the time God's discipline reaches this point, those who are wayward have repeatedly refused to listen to their Redeemer and others who love them. They have also turned their backs on God and His people who have pursued them. In essence, when the church removes those who refuse to listen to and submit to God and His people, the removal reflects what those who are in rebellion have already made known to Christ and His body.[12]

You still may find it hard to believe that someone you know could ever submit themselves to the wiles of Satan. Paul warns us of this very real possibility by reminding us how we once were captured and compelled by evil.[13] But somehow, even after we have

---

11   Davies and Allison, p. 804.

12   Mounce, *New International Biblical Commentary: Matthew*, p. 129.

13   Rom. 6:17; Eph. 2:1-3; Col. 1:21; Titus 3:3.

confessed Christ, Satan can lure us in to do his will (2 Tim. 2:26). Hearts once submissive to Christ can be hardened. Affections that were once satisfied in Christ can become insatiable and will stop at nothing to get what is desired. Relationships once cherished can now be detested and seen as unloving and judgmental. Christ, once professed as Savior and prized as the source of hope and joy, now seems irrelevant. When such disorientation seems like the way, the truth and life, we are now ensnared by Satan.

Is Removal Too Harsh?

Some of you may still think that removing those who oppose God and His ways and turning them over to Satan is too harsh. We must remember that such "harshness" has holiness in view. God's discipline flows from His love so that we, as His people, may share in His holiness, enjoy His goodness and exalt Him as our God. Ultimate "harshness" is seen in the cross.

God's wrath was carried out against His own Son, but not for the Son's sake. Rather, it was for our sake. In the heights of His love, the Father sent Jesus to bear our real shame as He bore our real sins. In the depths of His love the Father caused Jesus to suffer the judgment and wrath that we deserved and He died our death so that we might live a new life as a redeemed and righteous people in Christ.

So we must understand that God demonstrates His redeeming love when He allows us to endure the pain of discipline in the present so that we might reflect our righteous God, worship Him with our whole lives and be saved at the day of judgment. God's discipline can only be understood through the lens of the gospel and within the context of His grand story of redemption. Otherwise, God's discipline serves no purpose and might be understood as detached, unloving and harsh.

The unfathomable mercy of God's discipline is that He stops at nothing to redeem His people. The unsearchable wisdom of God's discipline is that He accomplishes His will in ways the world denounces as foolish. The unparalleled love of God's discipline is that He never gives up on His adulterous bride. The inexplicable grace of God's discipline is that He calls us to participate with Him in His glorious work of redemption.

We must trust that God always enables our obedience as we step out by faith. This is the incomparable and radical life and mission of the church. Ultimately, through what we commonly refer to as church discipline, God calls His church to do what reflects the gospel message and what accomplishes His gospel mission. Nothing more. Nothing less.

REDEMPTIVE SHAME AND SUFFERING

As we come to the point of removing those who relentlessly rebel against God, you might struggle with what seems to be unnecessary exposure and shame. In order for us not to lose perspective, we must focus primarily on the gospel of our suffering Savior who was put to shame for our redemption. As we keep the gospel message and mission central in our focus, God's glory will always take precedent over the shame and suffering imposed on His wayward people as the church carries out God's discipline by faith.

As harsh as it may seem, when the church removes those who have turned their backs on God, the people of God are participating in the kind of judgment that is intended to bring biblical shame upon the unrepentant person (2 Thess. 3:14; Eph. 5:11-14). Our holy Creator will not be mocked by the sin-hardened rebellion of His creation. Throughout Scripture, we see that biblical sin results in biblical shame before a holy and sinless God (Jer. 17:13; Ezra 9:6; Dan. 9:8). But in keeping with the gospel, this intentional shame is redemptive and merciful since such shame results in godly sorrow, which in turn, points us back to Christ, who bore our shame and guilt and set us free from the wages of sin.

SIN DYNAMICS ASSOCIATED WITH REBELLION

Church leaders and members need to be aware of two common sin dynamics that show up regularly when shepherding those who refuse to listen and submit to Christ and His people:

1. *Diving Deeper Into Sin.* It is not uncommon for those who are disciplined by the church to sink deeper into sin either before or after being removed. Looking from the perspective of human nature, such escalating behavior might be explained by a defeated or defiant mindset. For example, "I might as well go the rest of the way since I already messed everything up!" Or, "To hell with God and the church, I'll show them I can do anything I want." But looking from the

perspective of the spiritual battle, such degradation might be the manifestation of rejecting God and being handed over to Satan for the destruction of the flesh. Ultimately, God uses the actions and attitudes meant for evil to break and humble the rebellious hearts of his own.

2. *Doubting or Denying the Faith.* By the time those who are wayward receive a final warning or are removed by the church, they will express clear doubt or denial of their faith in Christ. This progression makes sense on several levels. First, from the viewpoint of spiritual warfare, the unrepentant person is senseless and doing the will of the enemy (cf. 2 Tim. 2:25-26). He has been deceived through the lingering and cancerous lies that now seem like truth and the truths he used to believe now seem like lies. Second, from the viewpoint of sin dynamics, how else can one justify their continuing actions that reflect a complete rejection of God other than to question their beliefs? To believe the gospel truths at this point would undermine their entire justification for their sinful lifestyle and reveal not only their foolishness but also their fantasies. Third, from a relational viewpoint, they may be so ashamed and full of guilt that no other explanation seems to make sense. They may think that God will never forgive them so they, in turn, give up on God. It is ironic that they denounce the only one who can rescue them from their dilemma.

THE AFTERMATH OF REMOVAL

After the church has removed those who refuse to heed the warnings of the covenant community, there can be a variety of responses. For the church leaders, this can be a time to take a deep breath to rest and reflect on all that has taken place. The lessons learned in every shepherding situation should help the leaders identify what issues need to be addressed through teaching and training, in addition to ways God might be adjusting the church's vision and purpose. Another reality is that church leaders may be worn out because they might be dealing with one or more discipline situations simultaneously while carrying out other important responsibilities associated with the overall life of the church.

Unfortunately, in many cases, it only takes a few days for the "buzz" associated with the removal to wear off and for people to go back to their own lives and routines. However, those who have been directly involved with the affected family members will still feel a certain weight as they offer continuing care. They too are weary and can be overcome by the chronic suffering and the consequences of sin piled on top of the demands of their own lives.

Therefore, the church should not take a "hands off" approach after the removal. Church leaders should be aware that there is a ripple effect across the entire church after removing those who refuse to listen and repent [See Appendix 10.3].

If the church goes back to "business as normal," then the church leaders can be accused of caring only about flexing their "pastoral authority," especially if they appear to be more concerned about disciplining wayward individuals than about the individuals themselves and if they forget about shepherding those who have to deal with the wake of suffering and sin. These accusations may be totally unfounded, but given the overwhelming demands of ministry, one can easily see how such perceptions can arise. Therefore, church leaders need to offer strategic instruction to God's people so that the church can participate in and experience God's redemptive work.

Instructing the Church

Church leaders and members alike tend to struggle with the practical implications of removing those who are unrepentant from the covenant community of the church. However, it is crucial for church leaders to provide guidance to the church so that everyone will understand their responsibilities in the months and years to come. As in all things, we must keep God's story of redemption as our paradigm so that, when faced with situations not clearly addressed in the Scriptures, we can respond in ways that reflect the gospel message and accomplish His mission [See Appendix 10.4].

LEADERSHIP POINTS—BEING WISE BEFORE, DURING AND AFTER REMOVAL

God calls His shepherds to lead His people in ways that reflect God's redemptive ways. As with anything in life, when we minister in the flesh apart from the Spirit's leadership, we can fall into the trap of removing people for the wrong reasons, and we will miss learning valuable lessons.

Don't Remove for the Wrong Reasons

The church needs to know that removing someone from the covenant community of the church is a significant action and should not be abused. A person may be threatened or actually be removed for all the wrong reasons:

1. Church leaders may want to flaunt or abuse their authority. By doing so they fail to recognize that the only authority they have is what has been entrusted to them through the Word of God. Leaders should move towards removal only when it is clear that those who refuse to repent are rebelling against God as understood from His Word, not when they want to get rid of some difficult people.

2. Church leaders may threaten removal as a form of manipulation to prompt the person to repent or change before even trying to understand and deal with the associated heart struggles. In other words, the threat of removal might reflect laziness and coercion on the part of the leaders.

3. Church leaders can prematurely remove someone because of a legalistic and systematic approach to church discipline. For example, the leaders may think a person needs to be removed because of an instance of adultery since a Christian man would "never do such a thing."

4. Church leaders can prematurely remove someone because they want to set an example for the rest of the church.

5. Church members may threaten such action as a form of manipulation or as a means to hurt someone who wronged them.

If there is any evidence of God's grace working in the lives of those who are rebelling, then hold off on the removal. Look for any signs of repentance and fruit of the spirit and don't automatically doubt or disregard such evidence out of your suspicion or your pre-determined judgment. Remember that God calls us to keep fanning the flames of His Spirit in one another since our hearts are deceitfully wicked and we are prone to turn our backs on the living God.[14]

Learn Valuable Lessons

It is always beneficial to debrief and reflect on any major pastoral situation, especially after removing someone from the covenant community. During the debrief, review the following aspects of the shepherding process:

1. *Lessons learned from the family.* Was there consistent and appropriate care offered to the family of those removed throughout the time leading up to the removal? Who walked alongside the spouse and can they continue in their ministry roles? Who have been journeying alongside the children? What practical needs were covered and not covered (for example, cutting the lawn, car repairs, meals, etc.)? Who will be the main ministry leader overseeing the family's ongoing care? What are the family's current needs, and possible future needs, given the removal of their family member?

2. *Lessons learned from community.* Is there anything that should be included in the next small group training based on the lessons learned from this particular situation? Did the community seem to understand their God-given responsibility outlined by the "one another" commands? Did the small group leaders contact their ministry leader in a timely manner? Was an elder informed in a timely and appropriate manner? How effective was the community in caring for those involved? Did the community persevere or burn out? What changes need to be made in the shepherding plan?

3. *Lessons learned as leaders.* Did we respond with the appropriate sense of urgency in a timely manner? How was the follow-up and communication with everyone involved through the entire process? When did we lead well and when did we fail to lead—with the family members and community group, with the various attempts to call the person back to Christ, with the

---

14 Heb. 3:12-13; cf. Richard Sibbes, "It should encourage us to duty that Christ will not quench the smoking flax, but blow on it till it flames" (*The Bruised Reed*, p. 50).

process and procedures of membership meeting, with identifying and addressing issues that emerged after the public removal of the unrepentant person? How did God grow us through this pastoral situation? What are we learning about shepherding the flock? Has this situation exposed any areas of weakness in our preaching, teaching and equipping ministries?

EXPOSED, ENRAGED AND ESCAPE

To his surprise, John slept soundly throughout the night despite his refusal to respond to the elders at his church. John smiled as he got out of bed the next morning, more refreshed than ever compared to all of the mornings during the previous months. He could not understand why the burden of his new life seemed like it had been lifted but he gladly reveled in this new feeling as he looked forward to his new life free from the past and free from the hounding of the church. Finally!

In the days that followed, he heard about the upcoming church members' meeting where they were going to tell the members how he abandoned his wife and children for another woman. John was filled with rage as he thought about the church defaming his name and causing his family to suffer public shame. That night, he couldn't sleep as he tossed in his bed, obsessing about the nerve and stupidity of the church. He pulled himself out of bed when his alarm went off, then stumbled into the shower to try to wake himself up. As he stood underneath the steady stream of flowing hot water, John rehearsed what he would say to Pastor Greg when he called to give him a piece of his mind. After showering and getting dressed, John called the church office and asked to speak to Pastor Greg. When the secretary said that the pastor was unable to come to phone, John delivered his venomous message to the secretary. He threatened that if they brought up his name before the church and publicly humiliated his family, he would sue the church for everything it had. Without giving the secretary a chance to respond, he slammed the phone on the hook.

John could not stop thinking about the church's hypocritical and judgmental actions. A few days later, John ran into two men from church at the local hardware store. He complained to them for almost twenty minutes, telling them his side of the story, explaining how his wife "drove him into the arms of another woman," how Tom and Sharon had the nerve to tell him what to do and how Pastor

Greg never once took the time to understand his struggles and help him work through the mess. The men walked away confused by John's explanation and they began to question Pastor Greg as well as Tom and Sharon and their community group.

John's inner storm continued. The only way he felt calm was when he was with Meredith. After a while, however, even she didn't provide enough relief for him. John tried to combat his fading pleasure by making their frequent weekend get-a-ways more exotic and decadent. But it didn't take long before he maxed out three credit cards and fell two months behind in his rent and utilities. When Meredith realized that John's money had run out, she decided that their fling was over. She mumbled underneath her breath as she walked out, "I thought you were different than my ex-husband. You are a loser just like him."

John couldn't believe his life. Not only did he wreck his family life, but now he was in financial ruin. He was over ten thousand dollars in debt, delinquent in all of his bills and being hounded by credit collectors. Even worse, his boss fired him for poor performance and for exceeding his allowable sick and vacation days due to his long weekend jaunts.

REFLECT AND RESPOND:

1. Reflect on how removal reflects the rebellion of those who are wayward. How is removal a redemptive action of the church?

2. Reflect on the redemptive shame and suffering associated with removing those who relentlessly rebel against God. Share how you might be struggling with what seems to be unnecessary exposure and shame.

11

The Battle for Repentance and Restoration

For when I kept silent, my bones wasted away through my groaning all day long. For day and night your hand was heavy upon me; my strength was dried up as by the heat of summer. *Selah*. I acknowledged my sin to you, and I did not cover my iniquity; I said, "I will confess my transgressions to the LORD," and you forgave the iniquity of my sin. *Selah* (Ps. 32:3-5)

For such a one, this punishment by the majority is enough, so you should rather turn to forgive and comfort him, or he may be overwhelmed by excessive sorrow. So I beg you to reaffirm your love for him. (2 Cor. 2:6-8)

Put on then, as God's chosen ones, holy and beloved, compassionate hearts, kindness, humility, meekness, and patience, bearing with one another and, if one has a complaint against another, forgiving each other; as the Lord has forgiven you, so you also must forgive. (Col. 3:12-13)

Broken, Busted and Bottomed Out

Pastor Greg gathered the elders together to pray through and discuss John's phone threat, which had greatly unnerved Shirley, the church secretary. They reviewed the church by-laws and covenant to make sure these documents contained a description of the church discipline process, to include informing the church of those who refused to repent and submit to Christ. After meeting for over two hours with an extended time of prayer, each of the elders agreed that they needed to step out by faith to follow the Lord's command found in Matthew 18:17 by informing the church about John's way-wardness and encouraging them to pray for and pursue John, as well as to support and care for Kathy and the kids.

During a regularly scheduled members' meeting on Wednesday night, the elders first presented the proposed budget for the upcoming year. Immediately following, a team who just came back from a mission trip to Serbia shared their experiences of God's redemptive work through the prayerful and persistent labors of a missionary family sent from their church. Afterwards, Pastor Greg announced all of the new members who joined the church since the last quarterly meeting, then gave an overview of how church discipline flows from God's story of redemption. Pastor Greg knew that most of his people did not have much experience with this aspect of church life so he wanted to lay some groundwork before sharing the relevant facts about John and Kathy's situation.

As he moved into the portion about John's rebellion, stillness came over the people as they sat at the edge of their seats taking in every word that was shared. Pastor Greg welled up with tears as he looked at the section where Tom and Sharon huddled around Kathy, together with their community group. Kathy let out a loud sob as Pastor Greg described John's rebellion and his scriptural violations, along with an abbreviated chronology of the church's redemptive efforts to call John back to Christ. After encouraging the church to pray for and pursue both John and Kathy, Greg explained that if John didn't respond with a desire to repent within the next two weeks, then he would be removed from the church. Pastor Greg warned the people against any gossip or slander, explaining that all that they heard was a family matter and that they should not share anything with anyone outside the church. Pastor Greg closed the meeting with a time of prayer as he encouraged everyone to gather in groups of three to four to pray for John, Kathy and their children. He also encouraged the church to pray for one another and their own hearts, reminding them that everyone is prone to wander.

With nothing left in his wallet or bank account, John decided to move to Chicago where his younger brother, Mark, agreed to take him in after hearing his brother's desperate plea for help. John knew there was nothing left for him in his hometown and his home church. He needed a clean break. Mark's apartment was sparse, typical of a single man who spent nearly all of his time at work, but it served as a refuge where John could get away from those to whom he owed money and from those who knew about his situation. For the first time in a while, John was able to be still. He could feel his chest rise and fall with every breath as he began to re-play the tape of his life, particularly of the past eight months.

God's Ongoing Discipline

God does not sit in heaven anxiously wondering if His chosen ones will finish the journey of faith. God's story of redemption written for each of His children is already complete, from birth to rebirth, from death to life everlasting (cf. Ps. 139:16). God's sovereignty doesn't allow anyone to snatch His children from His hands nor separate them from His love, even when the culprits are members of His rebellious and adulterous body. But only God knows His sovereign will. Only God knows those who are His sheep and those who will never enjoy His everlasting love and glory.

But how can the removal of unbelievers be redemptive discipline? When the church removes those who never repent and submit to Christ for salvation, God does His redemptive work in the church by removing "the leaven" (cf. 1 Cor. 5:6-8; cf. Gal. 5:9), thus exalting Christ by protecting His bride's purity as well as deterring sin within the body of Christ. The sober reality is that removal is not redemptive for those who never experience the sweetness of saving grace through repentance and faith in Jesus Christ. Even though God uses the removal of unbelievers to bring about redemptive change in His church as a whole, those who never repent will experience the wrath of God's judgment. Ultimately God's purposes and plans are accomplished as His people trust and obey His commandments as they carry out His discipline.

As we allow these gospel truths to serve as our immovable foundation for understanding God's discipline, we can be confident that God will bring His people back to Himself through repentance and faith in His way and in His timing. But none of us know the details of God's wondrous and mysterious drama of redemption. He calls us to wait with patience, to pray without ceasing and to give thanks always. One thing we can know for sure—when we wait, pray and give thanks to God, we will experience His deep transforming work in our own lives as we are sustained and shaped by His faithful and all-satisfying love. But if we try to deal with the pain and disappointment of life with mere emotional responses, obsessing and scheming of ways to make our lives work apart from His wisdom, and allowing discontentment and despair to drive our disposition, we will miss the redemption that comes through trusting and obeying Christ. We may also miss experiencing His love in deeper and more personal ways. Such redemptive realities apply to all of God's people, including both the offender and the offended. These realities remind us that the Lord is continually redeeming each of us for His glory. But how does God deal with those removed from the church?

God Gives Us Over to Ourselves

God knows the wickedness and the stubbornness of the human heart. He is neither intimidated nor ignorant of how to deal with those He created in His own image. Nor is He stumped by the schemes of the enemy. We must recognize that when God commands the church to release His own who are wayward into the hands of the world and Satan, He is neither done with His work nor confused about what to do. Every measure of God's discipline is designed for redemption. Listen to what God does when we refuse to listen to Him and fail to heed His warnings:

> But my people did not listen to my voice; Israel would not submit to me. So I gave them over to their stubborn hearts, to follow their own counsels. (Ps. 81:11-12)

> For although they knew God, they did not honor him as God or give thanks to him, but they became futile in their thinking, and their foolish hearts were darkened. Claiming to be wise, they became fools and exchanged the glory of the immortal God for images resembling mortal man and birds and animals and creeping things. Therefore God gave them up in the lusts of their hearts to impurity, to the dishonoring of their bodies among themselves, because they exchanged the truth about God for a lie and worshiped and served the creature rather than the Creator, who is blessed forever! Amen. (Rom. 1:21-25)

When we fail to listen and submit to God, He does what is necessary to break our stubborn and hardened hearts—he gives us over to our own sinful desires and lifestyle. Is this to say that God gives in to sin? Of course not! God uses what is meant for evil for His redemptive purposes. God allows the decisions and consequences of our sinful lives to reveal a spectrum of realities: the wickedness in our hearts, the vanity of the world, His holiness and beauty, our desperate need for Him and the incomparable grace of the cross. Does this mean that God releases us from His grasp? Never! Nothing can ever remove us from His hands or separate us from His love.[1]

God's Affliction and Conviction

When those removed from the church are turned over to the world and Satan, God knows they will experience intense affliction not only as a consequence of their own sin but also as a consequence of His discipline. In other words, the destructiveness of sin and the righteousness of God work together to accomplish the Lord's re-demptive work. How else will those who have turned their backs on God desire His true light unless they are overcome by darkness and deceit? How else will they yearn for the goodness of the Lord unless they have tasted the wretchedness of evil? How else will they cry out to the Lord in desperation unless they weep in utter misery and hopelessness?

In Psalm 38 King David offers a timeless anatomy of the human soul that is afflicted by the living God in response to deep and abid-ing sin. Let's take an up close and personal look at how God afflicts those whom He loves so that they come to their senses and return to Christ.

The psalmist, in response to God's unrelenting conviction, opens with a plea for the LORD not to rebuke him in anger or to discipline him in His wrath as he lays wounded by the arrows of God's Spirit and pressed down by God's tender but firm hands that will never let him go (vv. 1-2). The psalmist then describes his restless body and soul that have become odorous and infected because of his foolish sins and by the righteous anger of God (vv. 3-5). Broken, humbled and emptied by suffering, the psalmist is awakened afresh to his sinfulness, knowing there is nothing good that dwells within him, and he cries out from the chaos of his heart (vv. 6-8). He knows that every inch of his body and every ounce of his spirit are laid bare before the penetrating and searching eyes of his sovereign God, yet he still cries out to Him in hope that his LORD will hear, draw near

---

1   See Chapter 10, "God's Communion and Care."

and save him out of His intervening mercy (vv. 9, 15, 21-22). Charles Spurgeon describes God's affliction and conviction with vivid imagery:

> God's law applied by the Spirit to the conviction of the soul of sin, wounds deeply and rankles long; it is an arrow not lightly to be brushed out by careless mirthfulness, or to be extracted by the flattering hand of self-righteousness. The Lord knows how to shoot so that his bolts not only strike, but stick. He can make convictions sink into the innermost spirit like arrows driven in up to the head ... he shoots at their sins rather than them, and those who feel his sin-killing shafts in this life, shall not be slain with his hot thunderbolts in the next world... One drop of divine anger sets the whole of our blood boiling with misery... Deeper still the malady penetrates, ill the bones, the more solid parts of the system, are affected. No soundness and no rest are two sad deficiencies; yet these are both consciously gone from every awakened conscience until Jesus gives relief.[2]

Only Jesus can provide deep, cleansing and renewing relief from divine affliction and conviction. God's discipline is unceasing and always drives us back into the arms of Christ where we find infinite compassion and pardon. But God works mightily not only through His Spirit but also through His people.

Participating in God's Continuing Discipline

The church plays a vital role in the lives of those removed from the church in the weeks, months and years that follow. As God relentlessly presses down and pursues the rebellious ones and God's people continue to pray, there will be times in which the wayward ones will emerge out of the suffocating darkness to seek relief. The people of God need to be ready for any and every opportunity that may arise.

A husband who abandoned his wife and children approaches you to find out how his family is doing, to talk about his struggles and to ask you about the chance of making things right despite the overwhelming mess. A wife who refused to listen to the church when she married an unbelieving man calls you to see if she can talk about a few things that have been on her mind. When you head to the

---

2   Spurgeon, *The Treasury of David*, Vol. 1, pp. 198-199.

coffee shop one afternoon, you run into a former deacon who was removed for stirring up dissension and disunity within the church over a financial issue, and he opens up about his loneliness. Don't shy away from such opportunities out of fear or apathy. Don't refuse such opportunities out of a legalistic mindset [See Appendix 11.1]. God opens the doors of wayward hearts in subtle and various ways.

THE BATTLE FOR REPENTANCE

God afflicts and convicts His wayward children so that they might experience the wickedness and weightiness of their rebellion against Him and turn back to experience His love and forgiveness. But the enemy tries to harden and blind the hearts of God's people so that they will remain disoriented in their sin and remain confused and distant in their relationship with their Redeemer. Satan knows that:

> Excusing sin, and heading for and extenuating it, and striving against the Spirit and conscience, and wrangling against ministers and godly friends, and hating reproof, are not the means to be cured and sanctified.[3]

The enemy does all he can to distort our view of God and defile our relationship with Him. In fact, our sinful flesh, the world, and Satan constantly set off roadside bombs that throw out shrapnel of unbelief as the triad of evil tries to prevent the very thing that will enable a deeper, more intimate and personal relationship with our Savior King: turning to God in repentance and faith in our Lord Jesus (cf. Acts 20:21):

> ... observe that Satan, in hiding the love of God from you, and tempting you under the pretense of humility to deny his greatest, special mercy, seeks to destroy your repentance and humiliation, also, by hiding the greatest aggravation of your sin.[4]

In our unbelief we will not repent if we fail to see and experience both our deep sinfulness and God's radical love. Not until we are aghast by the vileness of our hearts will we run desperately towards our Redeemer for refuge. Not until we are overwhelmed by the love

---

3   Baxter, *Directions for Hating Sin.*
4   ibid.

and mercy of God will we submit in humility before our Savior for rest. This two-fold realization of our sinfulness and God's love is intertwined, enabled by faith, and leads to repentance (cf. Rom. 2:4).

THE PATH OF REPENTANCE

By God's grace, there will be times when those removed from the church come back and express their desire to make things right with God and His church. Such a move requires a step of faith as they are aware of the heartache associated with their sinful choices. They have also wrestled with the shame of their godless living and the fear associated with the uncertain but necessary steps of reconciliation. In many situations those who return to the church may not exhibit clear and definitive repentance, but instead their repentance may have a mixture of sin and remnants of blindness given the nature, duration and intensity of their waywardness. As the psalmist described himself while in the depths of his rebellion, "I was senseless and ignorant; I was a brute beast before you" (Ps. 73:22).

In some situations, God can bring about immediate clarity and wisdom but in most cases those who turn back to Christ after a period of running from God will still be partially blinded by the disorienting haze of sin. Even though, by the grace of God, they see their overriding need for their Redeemer, they will need time to journey with brothers and sisters in Christ as God untwists their perverted thinking, sheds light on their wickedness and rekindles their affections for Christ. This journey may take weeks or months, but is all part of the path of repentance.

This notion of ongoing and increasing repentance does not apply only to those removed from the church but to each one of us. Let's see if you can relate to the follow dynamic. As God brings more and more clarity and conviction of your sinfulness, you are able to confess more fully. As you develop a growing understanding of your sinfulness, you will become more desperate for Christ and His finished and gracious work on the cross. As you grow in your personal understanding of the cross of Christ, you will experience and be compelled more and more by His love. As you grow in believing God's love for you, you will turn to Him more fully and more frequently in the midst of your ongoing struggles and temptations. With each cycle, your repentance grows deeper, more frequent, and with greater fervor.

Our ongoing growth in repentance flows from our growing understanding of God's mercy. Believing more and more that God laid every bit of our wickedness onto His Son who nailed it to the cross and covered it with His blood makes the reality of turning back to Christ in repentance more and more attractive. Even more, although God knows the depths of our sin, He does not reveal the full weight and wickedness of our sins all at once, for if He did, we would be utterly destroyed. God reveals our sinfulness incrementally, showing us more of our wickedness while showing us more of His love. This increasing exposure of our sin and His love leads to increasing repentance. It seems most merciful that our Redeemer will not reveal the fullness of our sins until He reveals the fullness of His glory. Full exposure of our sin and God's glory will not come until we are finally immersed and secured in His glorious grace as we dwell together for all eternity as His consummated bride.

GOSPEL RESTORATION

Throughout the Scriptures, God brings His wayward people back to Himself and His people so that He might restore their relationship with Him. Everything about the gospel life is supernatural and is enabled by the Spirit of God—from our awareness, confession, and repentance of sin to our forgiveness and reconciliation with God. Such gospel practices require faith and result in redemptive change for all involved. But how should the church respond to someone's repentance, especially after a long period of waywardness? What does restoration look like? What steps should be taken?

God's Cycle of Restoration

Before we begin to answer these and other questions, it is important for us to look again at God's story of redemption so that we can more fully understand restoration from His perspective. Throughout the Old Testament we see God's restorative love over and over as He deals with the people of Israel: they rebel against Him in their wickedness, God disciplines them in His righteousness, the people cry out for mercy and God delivers them and restores His relationship with them out of His mercy.[5] Psalm 85 and other passages capture

---

5   Passages like Ps. 106; 1 Sam. 12:8-13 and Jer. 50:4-20 offer snapshots of this
     cycle of the people's rebellion and God's restoration.

the beauty of God's restoring grace as He withdraws His wrath and turns from His righteous anger so that His people can once again enjoy His salvation (cf. Ps. 85:1-5).

But God's restoration is more than a judicial transaction. In His redemptive story, God primarily pursues and restores His wayward people so that He might restore His relationship with them. In other words, restoration is all about relationship. Not just a relationship in concept but a relationship where His love and faithfulness meet our sinfulness, and where His righteousness and peace kiss and overwhelm our rebellious hearts (cf. Ps. 85:10-11).

Not only does God restore His relationship with us but He also showers us with His blessings. Because of His steadfast love and mercy (Ps. 51:1) God restores us so that we might rejoice in Him (Ps. 85:6), dwell with Him in His glory (Ps. 85:9), be immersed in ultimate peace found only in Him (Isa. 57:19), and be captivated by the joy that comes with His salvation (Ps. 51:12). He also restores us so that our hearts and souls will love and obey Him (Deut. 30:1-6). In other words, God restores us primarily for His glory, but also for our good so we might experience every blessing associated with our supernatural life with the one true living God.

God's restorative mercy is clear throughout the Old Testament. But God's story under the old covenant serves as a signpost to a more complete restoration that unfolds in the New Testament. God's restorative relationship towards His rebellious people is most powerfully revealed through the life, death and resurrection of His son, Jesus Christ.

God's Powerful and Pursuing Mercy

After sharing the parables of the lost sheep and lost coin (Luke 15:1-10), Jesus tells a story about a prodigal son who is restored through the radical love of a father (vv. 11-32). Through these parables, Jesus reveals God's merciful love as He seeks after those who are lost and wayward and meets them with open arms when they return to Him. As a result, those in the heavens and earth celebrate God's powerful and redemptive work in the hearts and souls of His rebellious people.

As we look at the parable of the prodigal son, we can make the mistake of focusing mainly on the prodigal's foolishness and eventual change of heart. But we must recognize that the Heavenly

Father is the one who pursued and drew this wayward son back by His powerful mercy and love, which in turn, led to the son's repentance and faith. Spurgeon highlights this very point, "The eyes of mercy are quicker than the eyes of repentance. Even the eye of our faith is dim compared with the eye of God's love. He sees a sinner long before a sinner sees him."[6] God never gives up on His people and will always restore those who are truly His sheep and He will complete His redemptive work in them (cf. Phil. 1:6).

The second half of the parable of the prodigal son (vv. 25-32) is equally as instructive in how we should respond to those who turn their backs on God but who later return, repent and seek restoration. We as the church can respond just like the "older brother" by focusing more on the sinfulness of prodigals than on the mercy and love of our Redeemer. When we fail to focus on God's merciful work, we can be filled with skepticism, cynicism and even resentment as we dwell on their previous wrongdoings, lies and manipulation, which in turn keep us from celebrating God's powerful grace that brings His wayward people to repentance. Such sin-centered and human-centered perspectives expose our own wickedness, which is no different than that of the prodigal's. Such perspectives also expose our self-righteousness, which arrogantly questions God's righteousness and wrongly believes that our own righteousness is based on the law rather than on faith in our perfect Redeemer (cf. Rom. 10:1-13).

Knowing how important it is for us to completely understand restoration, Jesus lived out the truths revealed in His parables. Jesus offered an undeniable picture of gospel restoration through two significant events at the end of His ministry on earth: Peter's denial after Jesus' arrest and Peter's restoration after Jesus' resurrection.

God's Affirming and Forgiving Love
Before His arrest, Jesus shared with Peter that Satan would sift Him like wheat and that Peter would deny knowing Him (Luke 22:31-34). It didn't take long before Jesus' prediction came true, despite Peter's self-confident proclamation that he would never do such a thing. At the very moment Peter denied knowing Jesus for the third time, "the Lord turned and looked at Peter. And Peter remembered what Jesus

---

6   Spurgeon, "Prodigal Love for a Prodigal Son," p. 158.

said to him, 'Before the rooster crows today, you will deny me three times.' And he went out and wept bitterly" (Luke 22:61-62).

We might imagine that when Jesus looked at Peter, Jesus' love and compassion overwhelmed Peter's shame and guilt, in a way similar to when the father fixed his gaze on his prodigal son (Luke 15:20). In that split-second encounter Peter remembered Jesus' prophetic words, fell under godly sorrow and turned back to Christ in repentance. In the midst of his remorse, Peter was able to experience Jesus' forgiving love through the brief but penetrating glance from his Lord.

But Peter's full and explicit restoration came after Jesus' death on the cross. In one of His first appearances after His resurrection Jesus appeared to His disciples and ate breakfast with them on the beach (John 21:15-19). It was then that Jesus asked Peter, "Do you love me?" Peter confessed, "Yes Lord; you know that I love you." Jesus then commanded, "Feed my lambs." This question, confession and command occurred three times between Jesus and Peter, perhaps corresponding to the three times Peter denied knowing Jesus. Full restoration soon became evident as Peter repeatedly confessed his love for the Lord and as Jesus repeatedly commanded Peter to care for His people, along with a final command to follow Him in suffering and death for the glory of God. Jesus knew that Peter needed to love Him more than any other so that he would give his life for the sake of the gospel. Jesus showed that restoration required a renewed declaration of love and involved a renewed call to service.

God's Intimate and Interceding Oneness

We must believe that what was true for the people of Israel and for Peter is true for us today as God declares, "All day long I have held out my hands to a disobedient and contrary people" (Rom. 10:21). But now under the new covenant established by the blood of Christ, God's personal and intimate restoration is more fully revealed and experienced through the ongoing ministry of Jesus, our High Priest. God rescued His people once and for all through the personal sacrifice of His Son Jesus Christ, who bore the wickedness of our sins and absorbed the wrath of God so that we would be restored to a right relationship with God. God not only restored our relationship with Him, but He did so in the most intimate way—God placed His Spirit within us, the people of God, in ways promised in the Old Testament.[7]

Does this mean that we will never stray from God since we are eternally restored through Jesus Christ? Of course not! But we must see the beautiful and patient mercy of Christ who holds out His hands to us in spite of our continual rebellion against Him, just as God did for the Israelites. Christ offers an infinite supply of redeeming grace to us as His chosen ones not because of anything we have done or will ever do, but because of what He has done and will continue to do as our High Priest who intercedes for us (cf. Rom. 11:5-6; 8:26, 34). Jesus also continually calls us to come to Him and approach His throne of grace with confidence in our time of need (cf. Matt. 11:28-30; Heb. 4:14-16). Remarkably, by God's grace, our ongoing rebellion against Him can never sabotage our personal and intimate restoration in Christ. Therefore, whenever we, as God's people, stray from Him, regardless of the severity of our sinfulness or duration of our waywardness, God will restore us since nothing can separate us from His love because of our undeniable and unbreakable oneness with our Redeemer.

Despite the clear picture of restoration that God has woven into His story of redemption, He also provides specific and concrete instructions in the letters given to the New Testament churches. God makes sure that we connect the dots between His eternal realities of redemption and the temporal realities of suffering and sin within the church so that we can serve as ministers of reconciliation.

God's Mission of Restoration for the Church

Before Paul instructed the Corinthians on how they should restore a man they disciplined, he referenced the difficult interactions he

---

7   Grudem, in reference to John 14:17 and 7:39, explains that even though the Holy Spirit worked within people in the Old Testament, "the more powerful, fuller work of the Holy Spirit that is characteristic of life after Pentecost had not yet begun in the lives of the disciples. The Holy Spirit had not yet come within them in the way in which God had promised to put the Holy Spirit within His people when the new covenant would come (see Ezek. 36:26, 27; 37:14), nor had the Holy Spirit been poured out in great abundance and fullness that would characterize the new covenant age (Joel 2:28-29). In this powerful new covenant sense, the Holy Spirit was not yet at work within the disciples" (Grudem, Wayne. *Systematic Theology: An Introduction to Biblical Doctrine.* Grand Rapids, MI: Zondervan Publishing House, 1994, p. 637).

personally had with them as a church. But in spite of the pain, he reaffirmed His abundant love for them (cf. 2 Cor. 2:1-4). Then in a parallel manner, Paul addressed the pain that the man they had disciplined had caused the church (v. 5) and encouraged them to reaffirm their love for Him, "turn to forgive and comfort him, or he may be overwhelmed by excessive sorrow. So I beg you to reaffirm your love for him" (v. 6-8).

Paul appealed to the church, "by example rather than by command,"[8] to forgive and love the man whom they disciplined while "in the presence of Christ" (v. 10). Paul wanted his affectionate and redemptive approach taken with them to serve as an example of how they should deal with the man who caused them many tears and much pain through his grievous sin. Moreover, just as Paul did not want to overextend his apostolic authority by demanding the church's repentance in how they sinned against him (cf. 2 Cor. 1:23-24; 13:9-10), Paul did not want the church to overextend their discipline of this man so as to cause him excessive sorrow and to give Satan a foothold within the church based on a spirit of unforgiveness and harshness (2 Cor. 5:11). Paul's exhortation for the Corinthians to forgive the man they disciplined seems to coincide with Jesus' teaching about forgiveness that follows the passage associated with church discipline (Matt. 18:15-20), where Peter asks about forgiving those who sin repeatedly along with Jesus' parable of the unforgiving servant (Matt. 18:21-35).

But Paul's example points to an even greater example of tenderness in the face of heartache and sin—how Christ forgives, comforts, reaffirms His love and restores us to a right relationship with Himself despite the way we continually reject Him out of our self-centered and wicked unbelief (cf. 1 John 1:9). However, Christ does not merely want us to be recipients of His relentless kindness, mercy, love and reconciliation. God calls us to forgive, love and reconcile with others by the power and grace of His Spirit, just as He does with us, so that we might reflect Him and His gospel message, and as a result, bring glory to Him.

Paul's appeal for the Corinthians to restore the repentant man also reflects the gospel mission to which we, as the church, have been called as a result of being made new creations in Christ (cf. 2 Cor. 5:17). God

---

8   Hughes, *The Second Epistles to the Corinthians*, p. 71.

calls us to be ministers of reconciliation, ambassadors, not only to proclaim the message of God restoring His people to Himself through Jesus Christ (vv. 18-20), but also to live out this reconciling message both with those in the church and in the world.

Given our brief survey of how God restores His wayward people throughout His story of redemption, we now have a better understanding how we, as the church, should respond to those who are seeking restoration. But practically, what does this look like? What steps should the church take in restoring a prodigal brother or sister? Let's now take a look at some practical issues involved with restoration.

LEADERSHIP POINTS—LEADING THROUGH REPENTANCE AND RESTORATION

There are few situations in pastoral ministry that require more intentional shepherding and wisdom than restoring a wayward brother or sister who has been removed from the church. Church leaders play a critical role in setting the vision, establishing the course and navigating the difficult waters in this redemptive journey. But by His grace, God provides His story of redemption to serve as a consistent and substantial framework to guide us through the complexities of restoration.

Church leaders have to be careful not to create a double standard for those who are being restored, since they can be overly swayed by the flagrant rebellion of the offender, the painful suffering of the one(s) offended, along with the suspicious reaction of those in the community. Pastor Marlin Jeschke addresses this key issue in restoration:

> The perennial temptation of the church is to demand more for restoration higher than for baptism, to make the conditions for restoration higher than for the original incorporation into the body of Christ.... But it is inconsistent with forgiveness to hold restored members in a state of perennial disgrace, or to make them "pay" with continued humiliation, or to put them on any other probation than that under which all believers always live.... there is not one kind of forgiveness sought by admonition and another by the more drastic means of excommunication and restoration. There is only one gospel, and only one kind of spiritual life it offers.[9]

---

9   Marlin, *Discipling the Brother*, pp. 138-39.

Some may argue that you do have to be more careful in assessing one's repentance in the case of church discipline versus that of a new convert, since the one who was removed once professed faith in Christ. Needless to say, the consequences of offering a false assurance of salvation are equal, if not greater, than prematurely restoring someone who was removed from the church. In either case, God's wisdom is needed and the gospel needs to be applied consistently.

As you provide pastoral leadership during the redemptive efforts it is important for you to remember that the church plays a key role in God's restorative work. Even though God is the one who convicts, enables faith and repentance, and ultimately restores, He calls us to attend to the real and necessary details of restoration. Whether it is the deceitfulness of the enemy, the busyness of ministry or the apathy of the flesh, you may struggle to give the necessary time or energy to shepherd all of those involved in a way that reflects the faithfulness of God. The following broad guidelines will help you to be more faithful in serving those God has entrusted to your care.

1. Develop a Restoration Plan.

You may hesitate to create a restoration plan out of laziness ("I don't have time or it will take too much work"), pride ("I will remember all that needs to be done") or fear ("This might appear too formal and it may scare off those involved"). Here is the bottom-line: if you fail to develop a plan, more than likely you will not address the necessary details associated with the restoration and the person being restored will not have a clear understanding of what is expected. Moreover, the person being restored may not be held accountable for the essential elements of the restoration since the family and community will not know the scope and details of the restorative efforts. In other words, if you do not develop a restoration plan, you risk confusing everyone and being negligent in your shepherding responsibilities.

You can see the basic components and customized sections in a sample restoration plan found in Appendix 11.2. You will see that the restoration plan is both broad and specific. The plan should focus on relationships with God and others. Additionally, the plan should also provide some specific action steps but not serve merely as a checklist. It should also be flexible so that it can be updated and adjusted as needed.

2. Develop a Shepherding Plan for the Family.

You should develop an intentional and parallel plan to shepherd, and even protect as necessary, the offended family member(s). It is all too easy to focus primarily on the one being restored rather than giving the family member(s) the care they may need during this period of restoration.

3. Seek Outside Counsel.

You may need to seek help from individuals or agencies outside of the church if there are situational details that require additional pastoral experience, specialized knowledge (for example, such as drug and alcohol detoxification and treatment, or psychiatric issues) or legal expertise (like child protective services, emergency protective orders, family court issues, or criminal activity). Be sure to protect the confidentiality of those involved when seeking counsel. Also be aware of and obey mandatory reporting laws based on state regulations.

4. Create a Redemptive Community.

Church leaders will need to decide whether those being restored should be placed back into a regular small group or if they should be immersed in a select redemptive community. In general, if the one being restored exhibits a level of spiritual and/or mental instability that might confuse, divide or pose a risk to others, then it may be wise to place the person in an intentional redemptive community rather than a regular small group. See Appendix 11.3 for guidelines for establishing a select redemptive community during a restoration process.

5. Seek Reconciliation Privately Before Publicly.

Church leaders should shepherd those being restored through a process of confessing their sins, asking for forgiveness and seeking reconciliation first with those in their own family, then working outward to those within their small group, neighbors and co-workers as needed. Once those being restored attempt to reconcile their private relationships by God's grace, then church leaders can decide when to bring them before the large church gathering to reconcile with the church as a whole and to celebrate God's merciful restoration. It is important to see that reconciling relevant relationships before being fully restored to the church is an essential outworking of repentance rather than proving one's repentance. Such intentional redemptive work reflects trusting and obeying Christ by faith and in humility, something God calls all of His people to do as a reflection of the gospel.

6. Shepherd the Church Community.

Wise pastoral leadership is needed to address a variety of reactions from church members regarding those being restored. There might be some in the church who don't approve of the restoration, those who are confused by the redemptive approach, and those who might demand a quicker process. Remember that many in the church may not fully understand God's overarching story of redemption, let alone His discipline or ongoing work of restoration. Don't let sin and Satan divide those involved. Fight for unity. Forsake disunity. The enemy does not want the church to see and experience the beauty and grace of God's redemptive work through repentance and reconciliation.

7. Coordinate with Another Local Church.

There may be times in which those who were removed from the church decide to attend another church. When the Lord brings them to repentance and they seek to be restored to God, then the leaders at the current church should contact and coordinate with leaders at the church who removed them. Church leaders should use this situation to help those being restored to see and experience the beautiful reality of God's universal church along with the power of His grace, forgiveness and love. If excessive shame is the primary reason for not wanting to return to the previous church, they can be encouraged to believe that there is no condemnation in Christ and that the church welcomes them back with open arms and with joy. If the nature of their offense makes it difficult or impossible to stay in the previous church (for example, child abuse or extreme abuse towards a spouse still a member of the church), even though there maybe total forgiveness and genuine encouragement to stay, church leaders may agree that it may be wise for them to be members of another community within the realm of gospel freedom. In such cases, leaders from the different churches should work together to continue God's redemptive work but also make sure those at the new church take the necessary precautions. Moreover, church leaders need to guard against undermining the leadership of another church in situations where there is overlap in family, friends and/or circumstances.

8. *Consider Communion*

In most situations restoring the privilege of communion corresponds to fully restoring the repentant one back into the covenant fellowship of the church. But there are situations when those being restored require extended time journeying on the path of repentance. They may need extended time to gain clarity about their sinfulness and certainty in the gospel as they emerge from a prolonged period of rejecting God and His truths while believing the lies of the enemy. Extended time may be needed to seek forgiveness and reconciliation with those they hurt deeply, to complete a recovery program that might serve as an indicator of the genuineness of their repentance or to address other areas for repentance in the wake of their destructive rebellion.

In these and other instances, those desiring restoration may cry out to believe as they struggle to live one day at a time by faith while battling an overwhelming sense of guilt and shame from their rebellion, along with being tossed by relentless waves of unbelief. If this wasn't hard enough, their daily struggle to exist may be complicated by the lingering after-affects of drugs or alcohol on their mental clarity. Their ability to participate in communion prior to being restored fully may be a needed tangible expression of grace, helping them to experience the gospel that was once intimate, but now seems so distant. Church leaders may decide in such complex situations that it might be helpful, and not contradictory, to reinstate communion before full restoration.

9. *Celebrate the Restoration.*

As Jesus instructed through His parables, there should be great rejoicing and celebration by all when those who once turned their backs on the living God repent and come back to their Redeemer. The church should express the same degree of joy and thanksgiving to a person being restored as a person being baptized, given that the same grace and work of the Spirit are required in both cases. The church should freely forgive, comfort and love those God has restored.

Those being restored should not be anxious or shameful about coming before the church, knowing that Christ absorbed every ounce of shame associated with their deep sinfulness. Nor should they be fearful of judgment since there is no condemnation or fear in the presence of perfect love—Christ Himself. Instead, those being restored can stand before their church family with tears of gratitude for being rescued from the realm of darkness and brought back into the realm of light, freed from the snare of the enemy and back to the bosom of the Redeemer, and re-oriented from foolish and selfish living to humble and sacrificial service to the King.

What are some elements that should be included in a gathering where you will announce and celebrate the restoration of those whom God has disciplined and brought back to Himself? First, whenever the elders bring any discipline issue before the church, whether they are informing the church about a wayward member who refuses to return and submit to Christ or announcing the restoration of a brother or sister, they should offer a short teaching on God's redemptive discipline. In the case of restoration, the elders can provide an overview of when and why the person being restored was removed from the covenant community of the church, then share when and how the person approached the elders to be restored to God and the church. The elders should then highlight the restoration process, explain the implications of the restoration as it relates to the person's family and the church and invite those who were part of the redemptive community to join their brother or sister in front of the church. The person being restored can be given an opportunity to address the church family in a pre-determined manner followed by the elders announcing the restoration. The gathering can crescendo with a celebration of the Lord's Supper, with the elders first serving the one being restored along with those in the redemptive community, and then they can serve the rest of the body. The time of celebration can end with corporate singing and prayer. See Appendix 11.4 for an example of a restoration manuscript.

How can the church develop a vision and culture of joyous repentance and restoration? Here are a few ways that the church can grow in celebrating God's mercy and love:

a.   Remind one another that God knows the depths of our sins from birth to death, yet He still chose to save us, claim us as

His people and restore us over and over again despite our ongoing rebellion against Him.

b. Celebrate God's mercy in repentance any time and every time.

c. Help one another to see and express evidences of God's grace in and through the details and routine of life.

d. Remind one another of God's ongoing work of redemption and how He is changing all of His children through the gospel.

Stirred to Repent and Seek Restoration

After a week of sleepless nights and hours of reflecting on his life without the distraction of anyone or anything, John began to remember the God of his salvation. Flooded with shame and guilt, John sobbed like a baby as he cried out to Jesus for mercy. His mind was overwhelmed with doubts and fears as he began to see how he had destroyed his life with Kathy and his children. Thoughts and questions blared like an endless pre-recorded message, "I can never go back now." "How can I ever begin to make things right?" "Can Kathy and the kids ever forgive me ... will they ever take me back?" "How can I ever show my face around the people at church and work?" "Turing back will be too hard ... I should just try to start over again."

But by the grace of God, one verse kept ringing in his heart and mind, "being confident of this, that he who began a good work in you will carry it on to completion until the day of Christ Jesus" (Phil. 1:6, NIV). John wondered what this passage really meant. Was this a promise from God? If so, did this promise apply to him? His friend Tom kept coming to mind as well. Should he dare call him? What would he say to Tom? How would Tom respond? Even though there were disagreements, Tom always seemed to be there for him and he definitely proved that he cared through his constant pursuit.

After drinking four cups of coffee, John took a deep breath, picked up his cell phone and called Tom. After three rings, John almost hung up as he second-guessed calling but a moment later he heard Tom's voice.

Seeing John's name in his caller ID, Tom panicked as his mind raced in countless directions. But he said a quick prayer and answered the call. There was silence. Tom asked, "John, is this you?" More silence. Tom asked again with more anxiety and nervousness, "John, are you there? Talk to me!" Finally after what seemed to be a very long thirty seconds, John whispered, "Tom, can you help me?" Tom immediately replied, "John, so good to hear your voice. I am so glad you called. I have been worried sick over you. Of course I will help you! I will do everything I can to help you, my friend."

John was taken back that Tom didn't hesitate in his answer despite their last few encounters. Tom asked, "John, where are you?" John said, "I am in Chicago. I have been at my brother's apartment for the last week. I finally stopped long enough for everything to catch up and sink in." After expressing gratitude that John was okay, Tom asked, "John, what kind of help do you want?" John hesitated. Finally he started crying, as he answered, "Tom, I have no idea if it is possible but I want to be get things right with God, with Kathy and the kids, with you and Sharon and everybody else at the church. I am so sorry for all the things I have done ... can you help me?"

Tom couldn't believe what he was hearing, but it was exactly what he, Sharon and their community group had been praying for since all of this began. Tom responded, "Absolutely. I will not only help but I will walk with you every step of the way if you want. You know someone needs to call Pastor Greg. Do you want to call him or do you want me to?" John said, "I know that I eventually need to talk with him but would you mind calling him right now? I have nothing left in me." Tom said, "Sure thing, John. You know you have a place to stay when you come back." John breathed a sigh of relief, "Whew ... I was hoping you would let me stay with you ... I don't want to be alone anymore."

Tom expressed how excited he was about his repentance and desire to be restored to God and His people. Tom couldn't hold back the tears as he prayed for John before they got off the phone.

REFLECT AND RESPOND:

1. Reflect on the Lord's ongoing discipline of someone removed from the covenant community of the church. How can God's affliction of an unrepentant person be seen as loving?

2. How is your understanding and approach to repentance more legalistic than gospel-centered?

3. How does seeing God's restoration throughout His story of redemption give you a better understanding on how to restore those who have been removed from the church?

4. What aspects of the restoration process do you find most challenging as you consider the culture and context of your own church?

12

The Cost of Gospel Mission

Remember these things, O Jacob, and Israel, for you are my servant;
I formed you; you are my servant; O Israel, you will not be forgotten
by me. I have blotted out your transgressions like a cloud and your
sins like mist; return to me, for I have redeemed you. (Isa. 44:21-22)

Or do you not know that the unrighteous will not inherit the kingdom of God? Do not be deceived: neither the sexually immoral,
nor idolaters, nor adulterers, nor men who practice homosexual-
ity, nor thieves, nor the greedy, nor drunkards, nor revilers, nor
swindlers will inherit the kingdom of God. And such were some of
you. But you were washed, you were sanctified, you were justified
in the name of the Lord Jesus Christ and by the Spirit of our God.
(1 Cor. 6:9-11)

Unsure But Willing

John sat anxiously in Pastor Greg's office, wondering if he made
a mistake calling Tom and coming to see the pastor. He felt like he
was sitting on death row waiting to be judged and executed. John
knew that his future was filled with uncertainties regarding his life
with Kathy and their children. How could they ever forgive him?
How could Kathy trust him ever again? Did they have a chance at
reconciling as husband and wife?

John's obsession-induced daze was dispersed when Pastor Greg
startled him as he walked in with a warm greeting. John instinctu-
ally stood up, and Greg expressed his gratitude for John's return as

they embraced warmly. Greg then took a step back, and while holding onto John's shoulders and with tears in his eyes, shared how it broke his heart to remove John from the church but that he had prayed that God would never stop pursuing him with His redemptive love.

They sat together for almost two hours as John unpacked the details of his adultery and the struggles in his heart, often breaking down in tears as he heard himself describe the realities of his own sinfulness. Greg patiently and passionately countered every doubt and unbelief declared by John as he wrestled to understand how God could ever forgive him and why life was still worth living. John stated in no uncertain terms that he would do everything he needed to do to show his love for Kathy and his children and to be reconciled with them.

Greg gave John an overview of some general "next steps" for John to begin the process of restoration. As John sat and listened, he felt a struggle rising up in him. Part of him wanted to dive head first with no reservations, but another part of him wanted to push back and run. There were no guarantees and so many unanswered questions.

Greg noticed John's internal struggle. He challenged John by saying that working through the reconciliation process would be one of the hardest things he had ever done, but God would grow him as a man as he would learn to follow Christ by faith. Greg also encouraged John by telling him that Christ had already paid the price for his adultery and, despite knowing all of John's sins past, present and future, Christ still chose to save him by His grace. John sat stunned and broken by the beauty and power of the gospel.

John shared that he waited to call Kathy until after this meeting. He wanted to make sure he didn't do anything to compromise his chances of reconciling with his family. Greg told John that he and others within the church would journey with him and Kathy for however long it would take. Greg asked John to let him know when he had his initial conversation with Kathy so that he could talk with her to see how she was doing and to share with her a gospel perspective on the situation.

John left encouraged but tentative. He knew that he couldn't do this in his own strength and that God would have to work powerfully for Kathy to forgive him and reconcile their marriage. Only time would tell.

Where Do We Go From Here?

Whether you made it through to this point of the book or you skipped the previous chapters by starting with the last, you still need to ask yourself, "Where do I go from here?" Let's take a moment to consider where you might be regarding God's discipline and His church.

Response #1—"I still don't see the need ..."

If you still do not see the need or the urgency to join God in redeeming His people through discipline, then you may need to think more about His mission, the nature of His church and the overarching purpose for all we do. God's mission in His story of redemption is to make Himself known, to spread His glory (cf. Isa. 6:3; Ps. 72:19; Hab. 2:14). One of God's primary means for spreading His glory is through His church.

Specifically, God brings glory to Himself through His relationship with His people (Matt. 22:37-38) and through His people reflecting Him in their relationship with one another in the world (Matt. 22:39-40). But because we still battle with indwelling sin, we need to love and fight for one another so that we mature in Christ and do everything for the glory of God (Col. 1:28-29; 1 Cor. 10:31). God spreads His glory by displaying His love through His redeeming discipline.

Response #2—"I see the need. But give me a list of sins or a step-by-step guide to deal with 'those' people who need to be disciplined."

If you are still looking for a formulaic approach to church discipline and a list of sins to serve as a guide, then you may need to think more about how God patiently and graciously deals with you in your ongoing battle with sin. He uses the everyday issues of life to help you grow in your understanding of your sinfulness, His goodness and His pervasive and powerful love through the cross of Christ. You may also need to be reminded that life and relationships cannot be reduced to a list of do's and don'ts, given that we live by God's grace.

If you struggle with questioning how those who need to be disciplined by the church can even be Christians, then you need to spend more time searching for the unbelief and lies that drive your thoughts, affections, desires and actions. You also need to assess whether you put more weight on your performance as a Christian or in Christ's performance—his sinless life and atoning death. You need to see yourself as no different than those who have turned their backs on the living God. No one is beyond the deceptive and destructive ways of Satan.

Response #3—"I see the need but lack the time, energy and confidence."

If you understand God's calling for His church but are hesitant to carry out His discipline, then you may need to think more about your identity in Christ, as ministers of reconciliation and His appointed shepherds for His flock. If you are not serving and leading out of your God-given identity, then you may want to consider whose agenda and mission you are striving to fulfill and whose glory are you protecting.

If you are struggling with the fears of the flesh, then be reminded of God's call to live by faith, which includes shepherding and leading by faith. You should also be reminded that God does not leave the church to her own devices to carry out His commands. Christ is with us always, intercedes for us and leads us victoriously (Rom. 8:34; 2 Cor. 2:14). We need to deny ourselves, take up the cross and follow Him by faith, knowing that He will accomplish His mission and He makes His power known in our weakness (Matt. 16:24; 2 Cor. 12:9).

Response #4—"I see the need, but how do I get from where we are as a church to where we need to be?"

If you see the need to step into God's mission but are unsure how you might proceed, then prayerfully reflect on your Redeeming God and His bride (Part 1), on understanding the fullness of God's discipline through His church (Part 2) and on how the church is called to engage in everyday gospel mission through community (Part 3). It is important that you believe and embrace God's radical life and mission for yourself so that you can help your church envision their calling, equip them with the basic knowledge and skills needed for ministry, then encourage them to engage in everyday gospel mission.

Be patient and prayerful as you teach, lead by example and shepherd your church through the struggles of suffering and sin as a gospel community. You can proceed with confidence knowing that Christ will enable the steps you take to follow His commands and trusting that He will redeem everyone in the process. By His grace, God will develop a culture of community and care within your church where every person will grow in understanding and connecting gospel truths to their lives and help one another to do the same. As a result, the church will grow in their love for Jesus as they experience His love in personal and tangible ways and witness His redemptive power to change lives.

THE COST OF MISSION

Regardless of where you and your church are, everyone must accept the fact that gospel mission is serious work that involves suffering, requires faith and aims to redeem those involved. Mission also recognizes legal liabilities and deals head on with the complexities of life. Consistent with Paul's instruction to Timothy, we must prepare, practice, persist, and progress as we labor in the gospel. Why? As Paul writes, "in doing so, you will save yourself and your hearers" (1 Tim. 4:15-16).

Mission Involves Suffering

Fighting for the cause of Christ is not only serious, but involves suffering: dealing with ongoing sin, chaotic situations, inconvenient hours, overwhelming details, timely follow-up, time-consuming coordination, relentless spiritual warfare, false accusations, and never-ending expectations, all with little relief. When we minister in the flesh apart from the power and perspective of the gospel, we will eventually shrink back and fall away from such suffering. If we give up the fight and give in to the temptation to overlook the difficult pastoral situations and fail to follow through with various aspects of church discipline, we will not do our part to build up the body in love and advance the kingdom of God. In other words, we will not carry out the gospel mission entrusted to us.

Not only must we stay in the fight, but also we must fight with wisdom and in the power of the Spirit. We will burn out if we merely fight fiercely against evil. Instead we need to learn how to endure patiently with it.[1] We must remember that such long-suffering is the way of the cross and reflects our Christ.

---

1   Calvin. *1 & 2 Timothy & Titus*, p. 131.

We are called to share in the sufferings of Christ for the redemption of others and for ourselves. Such sacrifice is costly but results in an eternal reward. "Beyond war is victory, beyond athletic effort a prize, beyond agricultural labor a harvest and beyond suffering is glory."[2] God's call to step in and stay in gospel mission is clear, but it requires prayerful and steadfast faith in our Victor, Jesus Christ (cf. 1 Cor. 15:57; 1 John 5:4).

Mission Requires Faith

It is impossible to please God without faith (Heb. 11:6). Therefore, every aspect of gospel mission has to flow from believing and trusting in our Redeemer rather than other people, our circumstances and ourselves. Gospel mission requires faith because we must believe that Christ and His living Word are our only means to understand our world and ourselves and the only means to bring order out of disorder. Next, as we minister to others in the midst of suffering and sin we must believe that the same gospel we trust can change those God entrusts to our care. Too often we do not see the gospel that saves us as the same gospel that brings about radical transformation in hardened and rebellious hearts. Third, we must also believe that God is accomplishing His work through us as Christ is redeeming His bride through discipline. We have to discern and follow the Spirit's leading as we step out by faith to pursue and fight for others during their time of need. God invites us into His redemptive work that He will complete at the day of Christ. Lastly, gospel mission requires faith because we must believe that our ministry to others reflects God as He ministers His Word *to us* and *through us* to others.

Mission Mutually Redeems

God intends gospel mission to be mutually redemptive, to be a two-way learning and growing process, never one-way. With all of life, God always ministers to us as we minister to others. We miss out on this transformational opportunity when we arrogantly and self-righteously think we have it all together and that we have already learned all that we need to know. Solomon writes about the

---

2   Barrett , *The Pastoral Epistles*. p. 102, cited in Gordon Fee, *1 and 2 Timothy, Titus*, p. 243.

mutuality of ministry and Charles Spurgeon describes this biblical dynamic:

> Whoever brings blessing will be enriched, and one who waters will himself be watered (Prov. 11:25)

> We are here taught the great lesson, that to get, we must give; that to accumulate, we must scatter; that to make ourselves happy, we must make others happy; and that in order to become spiritually vigorous, we must seek the spiritual good of others. In watering others, we are ourselves watered. How? Our efforts to be useful, bring out our powers for usefulness. We have latent talents and dormant faculties, which are brought to light by exercise. Our strength for labour is hidden even from ourselves, until we venture forth to fight the Lord's battles, or to climb the mountains of difficulty. We do not know what tender sympathies we possess until we try to dry the widow's tears, and soothe the orphan's grief. We often find in attempting to teach others, that we gain instruction for ourselves. Oh, what gracious lessons some of us have learned at sick beds! We went to teach the Scriptures, we came away blushing that we knew so little of them. In our converse with poor saints, we are taught the way of God more perfectly for ourselves and get a deeper insight into divine truth. So that watering others makes us humble. We discover how much grace there is where we had not looked for it; and how much the poor saint may outstrip us in knowledge. Our own comfort is also increased by our working for others. We endeavour to cheer them, and the consolation gladdens our own heart.
>
> Spurgeon, *Morning and Evening, August 21.*

If we avoid engaging in the very thing through which God designed to grow us, we will remain immature and we will not experience the power and depth of His love. Consequently, His church will not be built up in love and reflect His glorious grace on this side of heaven.

Mission Recognizes Liability

God calls us to be wise as serpents and innocent as doves (Matt. 10:16). This biblical principle applies especially to church discipline. Church leaders and members can say and do things out of ignorance or sinfulness that might increase legal liability. Despite the fact that the church functions in a litigious culture, we must not waiver in embracing and engaging in gospel mission, knowing that God has called us to join Him as He redeems His bride and advances

His kingdom in this world. Leaders need to minister within state regulations and federal law while not being bound by fear of accusations and lawsuits.

1. Churches have great latitude in the discipline of their members as long they carry out such discipline in a manner reflective of God's Word and His redemptive work. But increased legal liability typically emerges out of some common missteps within churches: Failing to be consistent in following written guidelines. For example, touting a highly developed training program for ministry leaders but allowing those who have not been trained under this program to oversee the care and discipline in a given situation.

2. Failing to act with the same urgency required by law. If the church delays for days or weeks in reporting suspected child abuse, then they can be accused of mishandling the situation and be responsible for inflicting more harm.

3. Failing to keep necessary notes and records. Regarding notes, if a church leader fails to take notes on major actions and comments made by those who later accuse the church of spiritual abuse and defamation, the church would not have notes that might prove otherwise. Regarding records, the church may require new members to sign a membership agreement form on which they acknowledge reading and submitting to the church by-laws and covenant. If the church fails to keep track of such documents, the church would not be able to show evidence of signature of those who are disciplined and claim they never agreed to such practices.

4. Failing to be loving and redemptive in church discipline. If church leaders and members deal with those rebelling against God with condemning judgment, shameful treatment and derogatory remarks, they will not only fail to reflect their Redeemer but will actually hinder the gospel mission, as well as open themselves up for legal action.

Appendix 12.1 offers some general guidelines for minimizing your legal liability as you carry out God's discipline through His church.

Mission Deals with Complex Issues

We do not get to pick and choose whom God places in our path or the set of issues that drive their struggles. Additionally, life is not black and white. We all encounter situations in ministry that are complex and demand continual prayer, patience and persistence. As we journey with one another over time, we will have to deal with complicated and difficult situations that may not be explicitly addressed by Scripture.

At what point do you discipline someone struggling with an addiction? What if someone who is rebelling against God has been diagnosed with a physiologically-driven disorder like Bi-Polar or Schizophrenia? Because we want to provide each person with the best possible care, there are times we will need to consult and work with professionals in the community so that those we are shepherding will benefit from needed expertise, and receive needed services. But we must not slip into the mode where we merely pass off those who seem too difficult or require outside help.

In every situation, regardless of the particular issues of the body and soul, we must remember that God created each person in His own image. He is sovereign over everything in His world and calls everyone to live according to His ways. To live any other way results in certain disorder. However, we need to constantly ask for wisdom to know when those who are struggling with psychiatric disorders, in particular, can be held accountable for their actions. In such cases the focus shouldn't be solely on the sinful behavior but on the repentance and faith that follows any such actions. Despite any prevailing weakness we face, the Spirit of God can still convict us concerning sin and righteousness and judgment (John 16:8).

As the church we are called to employ the seemingly "limited" means of church discipline in dealing with God's wayward people. Such an approach seems foolish to the world but has unlimited power to change hearts through the power of the gospel. Government leaders, on the other hand, employ the seemingly "unlimited" resources of the police, the court and prison systems, social agencies and even the military to control a person, though with absolutely no power to change hearts. Let us step out in faith as we serve our Savior King and shepherd His people, all for the glory of God.

RECONCILED AND RESTORED

Kathy was shocked when she received a call from John after he met with Pastor Greg. She had a hard time processing all she was hearing as she sat listening to her husband's tender yet tentative voice. She was so quiet that after John shared what he initially planned to say, he asked if she was still on the line. Kathy didn't know whether to cry for joy or sadness as waves of thoughts and emotions overwhelmed her. She affirmed that she was listening but asked if she could call him back after she had a chance to process everything.

In the days that followed, Kathy met with Pastor Greg, along with Tom and Sharon, and honestly shared her ambivalence towards John. How could she ever trust him again? Where would they start to address all of the mess that John had created and put their family through? Was John truly remorseful and repentant or was he coming back only because he had nothing left? Pastor Greg acknowledged Kathy's questions and concerns. He realized that Kathy was also on a redemptive journey, like John, that neither would have chosen for themselves. But given the realities of their suffering and sin, God was calling them to trust in Christ alone for their separate journeys, believing that He can and will take what was meant for evil and bring about redemption. By God's grace, their separate paths would become one intertwined journey, but only God knew when and how.

The next four months were tumultuous as Pastor Greg met regularly with John and Tom to work through John's questions, fears, and doubts as he grew in his understanding of his sinfulness, not only against Kathy, but primarily against his Redeemer. The grace of Jesus was becoming more tangible to him with each passing day. Kathy met regularly with Sharon and another woman from their small group as they read and reflected on how suffering strips away the peripheral distractions and by God's grace, compels us to approach the throne of grace in our time of need. Many of the passages she had read before were now coming alive to her in ways she never understood before.

A few weeks after John's return, he and Kathy started meeting weekly with Pastor Greg so they could process all that had happened together as a couple. It wasn't until two months into the restoration process that Kathy grew in confidence that she and John had a chance as husband and wife. She knew that she was not able to forgive and reconcile with John in her own strength. It would take the grace and power of Christ for her to even consider such steps. She was also growing in her understanding of her sinfulness and how much she had been forgiven in Christ.

It was when John and Kathy were out on their "first date" together, laughing and crying as they sat at their favorite coffee shop after dinner, when Kathy stopped, looked John straight into his eyes, and told him that she forgave him and wanted to fight for their marriage. They fell into each other's arms as they wept for joy for all God was doing in their lives. The next day they called Tom and Sharon and shared the incredible news of their reconciliation.

Pastor Greg was deeply encouraged by God's redemptive work, not only with John and Kathy, but also with each person in their small group, including himself. He and the other elders knew that God was gracious in allowing them as a church to experience His compassion and forgiveness. They excitedly planned a gathering for the members so that they could restore John to membership and celebrate God's merciful work.

The word had spread of the Smith's reconciliation and the auditorium was overflowing for this special members' meeting. There was not a dry eye while Pastor Greg highlighted the painful yet redemptive journey for both John and Kathy. Everyone watched and listened in amazement, as John and Kathy stood arm-in-arm, surrounded by Tom and Sharon and their small group, giving a brief testimony about God's powerful and redeeming love. Pastor Greg spoke on behalf of the elders and affirmed God's work in John's life and announced his restoration to the church family. The members responded with joy as they stood, clapped and shouted praises to God for His amazing grace. Communion followed with the elders serving John and Kathy, along with their small group, who then served the rest of the body. The night ended with everyone singing, "In Christ Alone."

> In Christ alone my hope is found,
> He is my light, my strength, my song;
> this Cornerstone, this solid Ground,
> firm through the fiercest drought and storm.
> What heights of love, what depths of peace,
> when fears are stilled, when strivings cease!
> My Comforter, my All in All,
> here in the love of Christ I stand.[3]

---

3   First stanza of Stuart Townend, Keith Getty's "In Christ Alone"

REFLECT AND RESPOND:

1. What questions do you still have about God's discipline through His church?

2. Which concerns you most when you consider the sections related to the "cost of mission"?

3. What necessary steps do you need to take to minimize your legal liabilities?

4. How is your Redeemer stirring your heart as you consider the extraordinary power and beauty of God and His loving discipline?

Appendices

Appendix 6

Understanding and Applying the "One Another" Commands[1]

God provides clear instruction for how we are to live together as the body of Christ through His one another commands. Since these passages may be so familiar, it is important to prayerfully and intentionally work through this appendix so that you can better understand how these commands guide you in everyday gospel mission.

Take a moment to think about a particular situation that God has placed before you so that you can think through your particular situation in more concrete terms as you read through the four broad categories of one another commands: (1) Loving God and One Another, (2) Engaging One Another with the Gospel, (3) Fighting for One Another in Suffering and Sin, and (4) Forgiving and Reconciling with One Another.

Reflect on the "whys" and the "hows" of each of the sections and then take time to honestly assess yourself by working through the evaluation questions. Be encouraged if you see that God has given you the grace to reflect Him through your life with others. Be prayerful as God reveals ways you may be falling short of loving those around you. Confess your sinfulness and turn back to your Redeemer for compassion and forgiveness.

Share with your spouse, family and community what the Lord is teaching you through better understanding these one another commands. As you embrace the vision of this radical life with Jesus, you will be more effective in helping others to understand and engage in God's radical mission of redemption.

Loving God and One Another

God is clear in His Word that He is God and we are not. He also summarizes all of the law, prophets and writings by His double love command. Therefore, everyday gospel mission can only be accomplished by ...

---

1   This appendix does not cover all of the one another commands.

> 1. Loving God first and foremost
>
> 2. Loving God by loving others

1. *Loving God first and foremost.*

   a. **Why?** Because He first loved us as our Creator and Redeemer and He poured out His love in our hearts through His Spirit.[2]

      i. God demands all of our affections because He is the only one worthy of worship.

      ii. Our vertical relationship with God determines and drives our horizontal relationships with others. We are compelled to love others primarily because of God's love working in us and secondarily because of our love for Him.

   b. **How?** By making it our ambition to please God by not living for ourselves, but for Christ in all areas of life. We also love God by loving others in general and by loving our enemies in particular.[3]

   c. **Evaluate.** How do you fail to love God personally—through your thoughts, affections, desires, and actions—and relationally—through your love for others?

2. *Loving God by loving others*

   a. **Why?** Because loving others reflects our love for God and reflects the love of God. Such gospel-driven love fulfills the royal law, or the law of Christ, while binding everything together in perfect harmony. God grows us primarily when we love one another in a way that reflects the gospel. If we fail to love one another, we will "bite and devour one another."[4]

   b. **How?** By loving others the same way Christ loves us—in a sacrificial, self-denying, submissive, servant-like and redemptive manner so that everyone involved would experience the love of God in a deeper, more experiential and transforming way. The primary

---

2   Deut. 6:4-5; Gen. 1-2; Exod. 20:2-4; Rom. 5:5

3   2 Cor. 5:9; Heb. 11:6; Gal. 2:20; Rom. 12:1; Matt. 22:39-40

4   1 John 4:18-21; 1 Thess. 3:12-13; James 2:8; Gal. 5:14; cf. Matt. 22:37-40; Gal. 6:1-2; Col. 3:14; 1 John 4:12; Gal. 5:13-14

way we love others is through comforting and challenging one an-other with the gospel so that we all grow in our love for God and others.[5]

c. **Evaluate.** In what ways is your love for others conditional or partial? Does your love for others reflect your agenda where you either love to receive or you love because you have received? In other words, is your love for others more about your own glory and pleasure or about God's glory and pleasure? What is the purpose of your love for your friends, spouse, and children—how does your love for others point them to Christ?

ENGAGING ONE ANOTHER WITH THE GOSPEL

We all struggle with relationships. Whether it's because of time con-straints, differences of opinions, clashing personalities, fear of being known by others, apathy in caring about others, or a lack of experience in sharing lives in a transparent and in-depth way, we have to fight to develop lasting and meaningful relationships that help us to grow in the grace of Christ. God calls us to engage one another with the gospel by ...

1. Building one another up in the gospel
2. Speaking the truth in love
3. Stirring one another up to love and good words
4. Staying away from gossip, slander or complaining about others

1. *Building up one another in the gospel.*

a. **Why?** Because God calls us to build up the entire body of Christ in love. Also because the days are evil and our hearts can become unbelieving and hardened, and turn away from God.[6]

b. **How?** By helping one another live out the gospel through every day interactions:

i. Connecting everyday conversations with the gospel. Be in-tentional in looking for ways the gospel offers perspective and informs the issues at hand.

ii. Encouraging and challenging one another to live by faith in Jesus in concrete ways.

---

5   John 13:34; 15:12; Eph. 5:1-2

6   Rom. 14:19; 15:2; Eph. 4:15-16, 29; 1 Thess. 5:11; Rom. 14:19; Eph. 5:15; Heb. 3:12-15

iii. Encouraging and challenging one another to live a life of repentance where we grow in seeing, confessing, and repenting of our sins while turning back to Jesus and trusting in His finished work on the cross.

c. **Evaluate.** Do you tend to build yourself up by subtly tearing others down through sarcasm, cynicism, and failing to encourage and affirm them? How easy is it for you to receive a compliment? To offer a compliment? How often do you get into gospel conversations when you hang out with one another? What do you tend to talk about, perhaps your favorite sitcoms or movies, the sport of choice, work or the latest fashion or sales event? How do you need to step out of your comfort zone so that you might be able to talk about what really matters in life and what will yield eternal fruit?

2. *Speaking the truth in love.*

a. **Why?** Because the ministry of the Word always instructs and corrects, encourages and challenges, comforts and confronts so that we all grow up in every way in Christ. Also because God confronted the wickedness of our sins by declaring His love for us on the cross.[7]

b. **How?** By sharing gospel truths that offer the needed grace for the moment. Speaking the grace of the gospel is accomplished by addressing three main areas:

i. Sharing how you see evidence of God's grace in each other's lives and situation.

ii. Confronting each other's sinfulness with gentleness, humility, kindness, meekness and patience, knowing we have the same struggles and realizing that if left unchecked, the person will more than likely become more deceived and hardened and eventually turn away from God.[8]

iii. Helping each other to see how God is using things meant for evil for His ongoing work of redemption in and through their everyday lives and in the lives of others.

c. **Evaluate.** How do you look for evidence of God's grace in another person's life? Which end of the spectrum do you tend to lean— speaking more truth without love or more love without truth?

---

7   Eph. 4:15; 1 Thess. 5:14; Col. 3:16; 1 John 4:9-10
8   Gal. 6:1-2; Col. 3:12-14; Heb. 3:12-15

Reflect on and explain your tendencies in this area. What keeps you from sharing truth with love—apathy, fear of man, anger? How do you need to grow in being able to see how God can redeem a sinful situation for His glory?

3. *Stirring up one another to love and good works.*

a. **Why?** Because God calls us to love others through our concern and care for one another. Self-love results in selfishness and self-centeredness and destroys community. Moreover, God calls us to not only be hearers of the Word but also doers of the Word. Also as we stir up one another in this way God grows us in the gospel.[9]

b. **How?** By considering others more important than ourselves and by looking at life through the lens of the gospel, we will identify and step into opportunities that not only allow us to express loving concern but also demonstrate loving care. Our faithful and loving deeds will spur others on to do the same. Here are some fool-proof ways to stir up love and good works:[10]

    i.   Serve one another.

    ii. Outdo one another in showing honor.

    iii. Contribute to the needs of one another.

    iv. Show hospitality and welcome one another.

    v. Help one another see how God can do His redeeming work in the midst of their suffering and sin.[11]

c. **Evaluate.** When was the last time you were able to stir up another person to love and good works? How do you need to grow in serving others and being more hospitable? How do you need to grow in helping others catch a redemptive vision of a given situation?

4. *Staying away from gossip, slander or complaining about others.*[12]

a. **Why?** Because we love others by talking with them rather than talking about them. We also run the risk of being a source of strife

---

9   Heb. 10:24-25

10 Phil. 2:3-4; John 13:14; 1 Cor. 9:19; Gal. 5:13; Rom. 12:10b, 13; Rom. 15:7; 1 Pet. 4:9

11 Even though this point is not an explicit one another command, such effort is an essential aspect of the ministry of the Word (cf. Gen. 50:20; Phil. 1:6)

12 Eph. 4:9, 31; James 4:11; 5:9; Prov. 11:13

and division within the body of Christ when we speak evil of others.

b. **How?** By loving one other in spite of differences in personalities and preferences. By dealing directly with the person who sinned against us or with the one who is struggling with unbelief in the midst of suffering.

    i. When you are working through a conflict with a spouse or with someone else, be sure to talk only about yourself to others and to talk about how God is using the difficult situation to expose your own sinfulness. If you start talking about the sin of the other person, then what seems to be innocent and helpful "venting" is really sinful slander.

    ii. Don't mask your gossip through "sharing a prayer request" or through "seeking godly counsel."

    iii. Seek counsel from one who has biblical wisdom if you are unsure how to handle a situation, but do so with care and confidentiality. Do not share the name of the person(s) involved and do not share details that will reveal the identity of the offender.

    iv. If someone comes to you and asks for counsel about a situation in which he is directly involved, encourage him to deal with the offender in private so that he will not become guilty of gossip or slander. If someone comes to you and asks for counsel about a situation in which he is not directly involved, try to discern if he is drifting into gossiping, slandering, or complaining. If he is, warn him about it. If he has Biblical concern about the situation, ask him to encourage those directly involved to engage with each other.

c. **Evaluate.** Do you justify talking about others rather than talking with them? What keeps you from engaging them with the gospel—being apathetic towards them or about your relationship with them; desiring the guilty pleasures associated with slander and gossip more than their redemption by the grace of God; struggling with your own issues and time demands; fearing the other person's reaction?

FIGHTING FOR ONE ANOTHER IN SUFFERING AND SIN

As the body of Christ, we are in a relentless spiritual battle, both individually and collectively, because of our own indwelling sin, the world, and

Satan. God grows and matures us in the gospel as we enter the fray with our brothers and sisters in Christ, as well as when we allow others to enter into our lives with the gospel. We fight for one another in our suffering and sin by ...

1. Bearing one another's burdens
2. Praying for one another
3. Pursuing for the sake of redemption
4. Approaching one another privately and personally first
5. Confessing sin to one another

1. *Bearing one another's burdens.*

a. **Why?** Because Christ bore our burdens on the cross out of His love for us; therefore, by bearing one another's burdens we fulfill the law of Christ. On one hand, we are not designed to bear the weight and penalty of our own sin, but on the other hand, God designed us to bear the burdens of others in both suffering and sin, so that collectively, we build up the body of Christ in love.[13]

b. **How?** By understanding the particular struggles of one another and ministering Christ and His gospel truths during times of suffering and sin so that we might grow in faith, hope and love in Christ. We should also speak in ways that offer grace for the need of the moment.[14]

    i.   Strengthening the weak—God calls us to hold onto, cling to, put our arms around those struggling with self-control and who are weak spiritually.

    ii. Rebuking the rebellious and idle—God calls us to rebuke and admonish those who profess to know God but are actively rebelling against Him. We are also called to rebuke the idle—those who are lazy and don't live responsibly.

    iii. Encouraging the timid—God calls us to encourage those who are anxious and worried, who lack courage, who are discouraged and have become despondent.

    iv. Being patient with all—God calls us to be patient (long-suffering) with everyone, since God is infinitely patient with us. By God's grace, patience is a fruit of His Spirit (cf. Gal. 5:22-23).

---

13 1 Cor. 12:26-27; 13:7; Gal. 6:1-2; Rom. 12:12, 15; 15:1-3; Eph. 4:2; Col. 3:16
14 Eph. 4:29; 1 Thess. 5:14; Rom. 15:1-3; 2 Cor. 12; Rom. 12:9; Heb. 4:14-16; 10:19-23

c. **Evaluate.** Do you tend to take a "one size fits all" approach when dealing with others? What do you struggle with the most in your own heart when you are bearing the burdens of others?

2. Praying for one another.

a. **Why?** Because such an act of faith and dependency reminds us that God is the one in control. Praying for others also reflects God since Christ and His Spirit are continually interceding for us with groanings too deep for words according to the will of the Father. God delights in hearing our prayers and "the prayer of a righteous person is powerful and effective."[15]

b. **How?** By drawing near to the throne of grace on behalf of others. By praying that God will complete the work that He began in them. By asking God for mercy and grace that He would take what was meant for evil and work all things together for good to those who love Him and are called according to His purpose.[16]

c. **Evaluate.** What rhythms or practices do you have in place to pray for others? When you pray for others in their presence, how would they describe your prayers: consistent with Scripture, with personal conviction as if you believe what you are praying, with hope grounded in the gospel? What is it like when you minister to others in the flesh, reflected by your prayerlessness or praying only when you don't know what to do?

3. Pursuing for the sake of redemption.

a. **Why?** Christ pursued us when He rescued us from darkness and death and He still pursues us all the days of our lives.[17] Phrases found in the "one another" passages like, "if he listens to you, you have won your brother over," "restore in gentleness," "so that none of you may be hardened by the deceitfulness of sin ... and fall away from the living God," "save his soul from death," and "snatching them out of the fire" all point to the over-arching purpose of God's pursuit and discipline: redemption.[18]

b. **How?** By calling one another back to Christ while hating what is evil and clinging to Christ. As in the parables of the lost sheep, lost coin, and lost son, the church should pursue a straying member

---

15 1 Thess. 5:17; Rom. 8:26, 34; James 5:16

16 Heb 4:14-16; 10:19-23; 1 Thess. 5:17; Phil. 1:6; Gen. 50:20; Rom. 8:28

17 Ps. 23:1

18 Matt. 18:15; Gal. 6:1; Heb. 3:12-13; James 5:20; Jude 22-23

with intentionality so that by God's grace, the person repents and is restored to Christ, thus saving his soul from death.[19]

c.   **Evaluate.** What do you do when you are aware of someone strug-gling in suffering and sin? What would others share about how you pursue them with the gospel in their suffering and sin? How would they describe your approach and the type of care you offer? Would they say your approach and care reflect the power and the grace of the gospel or primarily pragmatism?

4.   *Approaching one another privately and personally first.*

a.   **Why?** Because you should first deal with those directly involved in the suffering and sin so as not to bring undue shame, risk slan-der or cause division in community. Such private and personal pursuit also reflects how God loves us.[20]

b.   **How?** By directly approaching and dealing with the person with whom there is strife or with whom there is some concern associ-ated with a given life struggle.

   i.   Assess the "next steps" based on the person's response and outcome of the initial and subsequent gospel conversations.

   ii.   Ask the person who they think should also get involved from their community to help bear burdens and to provide the best possible redemptive care.

   iii.   In the case of blatant and persistent rebellion, if the person refuses to listen to you and submit to Christ through obeying His Word after several attempts, you will need to invite oth-ers into the situation even if the person doesn't want others to know.

c.   **Evaluate.** What fears do you face when you need to confront oth-ers in their suffering and sin? When someone sins against you or when you are told someone has something against you, do you tend to talk about the person with others before you talk directly with that person? What are some of your underlying motives when you gossip or slander others? Have you ever been in a situation when everyone but you knows about the strife between you and some-one else? How does this occur?

---

19   Rom. 12:9; 1 Thess. 5:21-22; Luke 15; James 5:19-20

20   Matt. 18:15; Ps. 23:6

5. *Confessing sins to one another.*
   a. **Why?** So that we can be humbled and encouraged as we confess our desperate need for the gospel and our steadfast belief that there is now no condemnation in Christ. Confessing the sins of our hearts against God and expressing His truths frees us from the deception of sin and reminds us of the cross. We also need to confess sin to one another when there is strife and division so that we can pursue peace and unity.[21]

   b. **How?**
   Confessing your sin struggles to one another by ...
      i. Sharing God's conviction
         a. *Confess specific* **unbelief and lies**. Share ways in which you are not believing the gospel and specific lies you choose to believe, all of which fuel your struggles.

         b. *Confess your* **sin against God**. Share specific biblical commands you disobeyed, gospel truths you rejected, and how you rejected God Himself. You need to see and understand how your sin is evil in God's sight.[22]

         c. *Confess your* **failure to love**. Share ways in which you failed to love God and others because of your sins.

         d. *Confess your* **need for Christ**. By this point the specific ways you need Christ will be apparent. The more we depend on Christ for all things, the more we grow in submission and humility in every way.

      ii. Sharing God's grace
         a. *Express* **God's love**. Share ways in which God has shown His love to you by pursuing you, calling you back to Himself, redeeming your thinking, affections and ways, and giving you a bigger and deeper understanding of the cross of Christ.

         b. *Express what* **repentance** *looks like*. Repentance is not only recognizing your sin but includes returning to Christ and seeking to follow Him in faith and obedience. How does God tend to open your eyes to your sinfulness, convict you and bring you to repentance?

---

21   Rom. 12:16, 18; 14:18-19; Col. 3:14-15; Heb. 12:14-15; James 5:16

22   See Rom. 1:18-32 and 2 Sam. 12:9-10 for scriptural examples of how we reject God's laws, truths, and God Himself; Ps. 51:3-4

c. *Express what* **faith** *looks like.* What is God calling you to do even if the situation never changes? How will the details of your life look different when you walk in the Spirit rather than in the flesh?

d. *Express your* **thanks.** Give thanks and praise for God's mercy and grace for what He is doing in your life.

Confessing your sins against others by ...

i. Starting with the steps associated with confessing your sin struggles (previous section).

ii. Sharing God's conviction
   a. *Confess your* **sins against them.** Share specific ways you sinned against them. Do not add any excuses, defend yourself, or shift blame.

   b. *Confess your* **failure to love them.**
      1. Share specific ways you failed to love them. Review 1 Corinthians 13 beforehand so that you can be reminded of how God loves you. This and other passages will provide a good starting point for you to better understand and describe your sins against them in a biblical way.

      2. Share the specific ways you hurt them. Also take this time to ask them to share with you how you hurt them so you can better understand the extent and the consequences of your sins against them.

   c. *Confess your* **need for Christ.** By this point the specific ways you need Christ will be very apparent with regard to your relationship with one another.

iii. Sharing God's grace
   a. *Express* **God's love.** Share ways in which God has shown His love to you in this difficult situation, in your relationship with them, and in their gracious response or gospel-driven desires after being sinned against.

   b. *Express what* **repentance** *looks like.* What will look different in your relationship with them? How will your attitude and behavior change as a result of your repentance?

   c. *Express what* **faith** *looks like.* Share how you pray God will change you and your relationship as you live by faith—

you being less demanding and less insecure because you are now finding your identity and worth in Christ; less angry because you find contentment and satisfaction rightly in Christ and not in your relationships; more grace and humility as you recognize the gracious and humble ways Christ deals with you. Also by faith you will accept whatever consequences are associated with your offense and you will make any necessary restitution.

d. *Express your* **thanks.** Give thanks and praise for God's mercy and grace for what He is doing in their lives and in your relationship with them.

c. **Evaluate.** What ways do you struggle with judging others when they confess their sins? Do you lean more towards rejoicing or demanding more evidence of true repentance when someone confesses their sin to you? What are some of the ways in which God enables you to see your own sin? What keeps you from confessing your sins to others, not only to those you sinned against but also to others in the community? Is there anyone to whom you need to confess but have been putting it off?

FORGIVING AND RECONCILING WITH ONE ANOTHER

Gospel community is messy because of our ongoing sin against one another. Knowing this, God makes it clear that we are to forgive and reconcile with one another so that our relationships in community reflect His relationship with us. God calls us to forgive and reconcile with one another by ...

1. Putting off bitterness, anger, and vengeance
2. Pursuing peace and unity
3. Loving and forgiving as Christ loves and forgives us
4. Reconciling with one another

1. *Put off bitterness, anger, and disunity.*
   a. **Why?** Because bitterness, anger and disunity...
      i. Are contrary to the message and mission of the gospel and do not reflect our redeeming God.

    ii.   Sink deep poisonous roots in our hearts that keep us from fully loving God and others.

    iii.   Disrupt the peace and unity of the body of Christ.[23]

b. **How?** By first trusting God for the grace, desire and strength to do His will.

    i.   Realizing the immeasurable forgiveness you have in Christ—past, present, and future. No one will ever sin against you more in frequency or magnitude than the way you sin against God.

    ii.   Believing that Christ bore your guilt and shame associated with all of your sins and the sins committed against you.

    iii.   Seeing yourself and the one who sinned against you as the same—both in desperate need of Christ and His gospel work.

c. **Evaluate.** What bitterness might you be struggling with right now? If nothing comes to mind, then consider past conversations with others when they gave you some feedback regarding your anger, sarcasm, cynicism, bitterness, or vengeful spirit. Do you struggle with anger towards others when they keep you from getting what you want or when you can't control the circumstances in life? Can you think of any relationships in your life that need to be reconciled? Do you tend to shy away from addressing "broken" relationships?

2. *Pursue peace and unity.*[24]

a. **Why?** Because the health of the church, the integrity of the gospel, and the glory of Christ are at stake.

b. **How?** Intentionally moving towards one another by faith with redeeming love while remembering that forgiveness and reconciliation are the goal. Who should make the first move? You should. God gives us no choice in who goes first because He knows our worship and witness is impacted when there is strife with others:

Go if anyone has something against you ...

    i.   *So if you are offering your gift at the altar and there remember that your brother has something against you, leave your gift there before the altar and go. First be reconciled to your brother, and then come and offer your gift.* (Matt. 5:23-24)

---

23   Prov. 10:12

24   1 Pet. 3:11; Rom. 12:18; 14:17-19; Heb. 12:14-15; Eph. 4:1-6; Col. 3:12-15

Go if you have something against anyone ...

    ii.   *And whenever you stand praying, forgive, if you have anything against anyone, so that your Father also who is in heaven may forgive you your trespasses.* (Mark 11:25)

  c. **Evaluate.** What excuses do you tend to make when you fail to pursue peace and unity with a brother or sister in Christ, with a family member, or with a neighbor? How does such unrest and disunity impact your worship of God and the witness of the body of Christ?

3. *Loving and forgiving as Christ loves and forgives us.*

  a. **Why?** Because Christ calls us to deny ourselves, take up our cross and follow Him. He calls us to reflect Him in all that we do, especially in these two foundational aspects of gospel community.[25]

  b. **How?** By prayerfully trusting God and His call to love and forgive one another like Christ instead of relying on our own understanding and desires—expressed perhaps by our ambivalence or opposing thoughts and by our lack of desire to do so. When we trust God more than ourselves, we reflect our Redeemer and experience change by the gospel.[26] We love and forgive others like Christ by ...

    i.   Putting off bitterness and pursuing peace and unity.

    ii.   Loving those we might consider our enemies by being compelled more by Christ's steadfast love for us than by the hurt and desire for justice that flows from being sinned against.[27]

    iii. Entrusting those who sinned against us to Christ. If Christ is their Redeemer, then His blood covers their sins and they will receive abundant compassion and pardon as they repent. If Christ is not their Redeemer, then Christ will deal with them according to His sovereign will for them, either through merciful redemption or eternal condemnation.

    iv. Living out our identity as the bride of Christ. We have been ransomed and redeemed from the bondage of sin and have been set free to live in the grace of the gospel for the glory of our redeeming God.

  c. **Evaluate.** Think about the immoral woman who bathed Jesus with her expensive bottle of perfume in Luke 7:36-50. Explain the

---

25   Mark 8:34; Eph. 4:32-5:1-2; Col. 3:8-9, 12-15

26   Prov. 3:5-8

27   Matt. 5:43-46; Luke 6:27-36; Rom. 12:9-21

correlation between her being forgiven much and her loving much. How is your understanding of the depth of your forgiveness in Christ reflected by the way you love God and others?

4. *Reconciling with one another.*

a. **Why**? Because God has reconciled us to Himself through Christ and He has given us the ministry of reconciliation as ambassadors for Christ. We also must reconcile with one another because Christ desires His bride, and body, to be one flesh as a way of reflecting that we love Him and abide in Him.[28]

b. **How**? By forgiving and loving one another in Christ.

 i. Believing not only that we are able to live as one in Christ, but that we are one in Christ.

 ii. Knowing that reconciliation is always possible when we put our faith in Christ and not in ourselves or another person.

 iii. Note that forgiveness is distinct from reconciliation. Forgiveness enables reconciliation. But a relationship can't be reconciled if repentance is not experienced and forgiveness is not mutually offered between those involved. In circumstances involving abuse or other issues of safety, reconciliation is not advisable if further harm is possible from the perpetrator.

c. **Evaluate**. Take a moment to think of those you have forgiven because they deeply sinned against you. What evidence exists that shows that you are truly reconciled with them? What excuses and rationale do you use to keep from fully reconciling broken relationships even though you might have told yourself and others that you have forgiven them?

---

28 2 Cor. 5:16-21; Mark 11:23-24; John 14:21; 15:10

Appendix 7
Gospel Care in Redemptive Relationships

In Chapter 6, we saw the big picture of gospel care. Here you will find some additional information that will help you to better understand those who are struggling with suffering and sin so that you can proclaim the gospel in personal and specific ways.

Understanding with the Gospel

1. **Listen and explore for evidences of God's grace in the person's life.** One of the best ways of encouraging and building another up in Christ is by pointing out how you see Christ at work in the person's life. Again, this is a huge departure from our normal mode of confronting another person, where our agenda is to point out blame, express hurt, and get the person to confess and ask for forgiveness.

2. **Listen and look for evidence of unbelief and lies.** What truths about God and His gospel are not being believed? How might the fears or anger expressed reveal lies that are being believed? Realize this approach is far different than charging in with accusations, shouts of Scriptural violations and demands for repentance. You actually need to understand the person so that you can both learn and grow in the gospel.

3. **Listen to and explore the heart struggles.** Understand the person's struggles within the context of where they are in life so you know how you can offer the gospel in personal and relevant ways to specific issues. Understand the primary thoughts, emotions, actions, desires, and affections involved in the heart struggles and see how they may be consistent with or contrary to the gospel.

4. **Explore and share life struggles.**
   a. As you listen and explore the heart of the one who offended you, you might be compelled to explore more of the person's life so that you can help them to see significant influences, themes or patterns over the years that contribute to the struggle of unbelief and the lies being believed.

   b. Share how you also struggle with similar issues (if you have) and confess any sin you might have committed associated with the situation being addressed or since the incident.

5. **Note the language and details shared.** You can use their words and unpack their struggles in light of the gospel. By using the person's own words in your encouragement and correction, the person often is less defensive and can more clearly see the sin and ugliness in his or her heart.

6. **Explore gospel opportunities.** How can each of you see ways in which the gospel can impact or address the situation?

PROCLAIMING THE GOSPEL

1. **Understand the realities of spiritual blindness.** Sin confuses and distorts thinking and perspectives, compels emotions and affections, and drives desires and decisions. Remember that only God can clear the confusion and change the heart. Do not rely on excessive and harsh truth telling to bring about change. Only God's Spirit convicts.

2. **Connect to the cross.** Christ and His cross should be your constant reference.

   Remember when addressing a brother or sister in Christ:
   a. God made both of you in His image. Therefore, know that when you are living in the flesh and not in the Spirit, your souls are deceived and disordered. God has called each of you into the ministry of reconciliation where you can reflect the gospel through your love, forgiveness, and efforts to pursue peace.

   b. Christ died for you and for the one who sinned against you. Therefore, He calls you to deny yourself, take up your cross, and follow Him in all that you are and do. Both of you are deeply sinful and in desperate need for the Redeemer.

   c. How you have been sinned against does not compare in magnitude or frequency to your continual sin against God.

d. Christ died for the shame and sin involved in the strife between you and the other person.

e. Christ suffered in every way for you, enables everything He calls you to do by His Spirit, and changes you through every act of obedience by faith.

When you are addressing an unbeliever who has offended you, know that the same truths above apply but with the following nuanced differences:

a. You need to remember that since unbelievers do not know God, not only are their souls deceived and disordered but they are not able to understand the root cause of their chaos. As the believer, don't forget that when you are living in the flesh and not in the Spirit, your soul is also deceived and disordered. But because you know God, you have been called into the ministry of reconciliation. God calls you to reflect the gospel through your love, forgiveness, and efforts to pursue peace.

b. You need to remember that Christ calls you, as a believer, to deny yourself, take up your cross, and follow Him in all that you are and do so that those who do not know God will experience the gracious love of the gospel. Both you and the unbeliever are deeply sinful and in desperate need of the Redeemer.

As the one who knows Christ and who has been redeemed by His grace, you are entrusted to live out the gospel with the unbeliever who offended you. One of the beautiful things about the gospel is that the same truths apply to both believers and unbelievers but only those who know God are able to trust and obey.

3. **View the situation through gospel lenses**. How does the gospel change your perspective of the situation, of yourself, of the other person? Each of you should strive to be compelled more by the love of Christ than by your own agendas. Offer a redemptive vision for growth and change for each of you—specifically how God can redeem you both through ongoing repentance and faith, as well as through love, forgiveness and reconciliation that reflects the gospel.

4. **Share God's grace**. Convey particular ways in which you see God's grace in the situation and in the person's life. Know that God offers His grace through both gospel comfort and confrontation. We need to remember God's discipline is always evidence of His grace towards us because such discipline is used to help us grow in righteousness.

5. **Adjust your rebuke as necessary**. You may need to change your approach and words based on the person's response throughout the conversation.

    a. The person might see and confess his own sin through the power of the Holy Spirit as well as through the redemptive approach you took.

    b. The person may become defensive and deny any wrongdoing. You can minimize a defensive response by using the person's own words of admission to help you show how the situation was offensive. It may be helpful to agree to re-address the matter after a time of prayerful reflection.

    c. As the Lord gives grace, the gospel truths you offer in love will first encourage and revive the soul of the offender, and as the Spirit of God provides clarity of sin and brings conviction, the offender will realize he has been rebuked and will respond with gratitude.

6. **Speak gospel truths in love**. Address areas of unbelief and lies and show how the gospel addresses their situation.

    a. *Read a specific passage(s)*. Sometimes when the living Word is read the Holy Spirit will open up blind eyes and the Word read will carry more authority and weight than if you summarize the passage.

    b. *Share a summary of a passage*. At other times, you can take a passage and speak the truths directly to the person or situation without even opening the Bible, helping the person to connect the gospel with the particular issues needing to be addressed.

        Example: A friend may express fear of being rejected by you. After taking the time to listen and explore the fullness of her struggle you can offer the following truths from Psalm 27 wrapped in a personal and heart-felt response,

        > I am glad you shared this fear with me. I understand I let you down and I hurt you as a result. Will you forgive me? Please know that I will probably let you down again, not because I don't care about you, but because I am deeply sinful. That is why we both need Christ. He tells you to not fear, for He is your light and your salvation ... He will not abandon you but will hold you close (cf. Ps. 27:1, 10).

c. *Minister Christ and His Word in creative ways.* Use metaphors and illustrations so you can help the person to see what God might have the person to see and do in response. Here is a helpful hint in choosing metaphors to convey gospel truths: use illustrations that emerge from their concrete examples of life and struggle, or use images that come to your mind, as you listen and seek to understand what they are saying.

d. *Share honestly how God has confronted you with the same truths.* Such humility will be evident through the conviction with which you share as well as the compassion you display in your time with the person.

7. **Discuss next steps.** What next steps need to be taken in order to pursue reconciliation? What sins need to be confessed and forgiven? Explore what repentance and faith looks like.

   a. Remember that only God enables repentance (Rom. 2:4; 2 Cor. 7:9-10). What does repentance look like in this situation?

   b. Remember that only God enables faith and without it, one cannot please God (Eph. 2:8; Heb. 6:11; Rom. 8:8). What does living by faith look like in this situation?

   c. Realize that the faith that one needs to see and trust Christ for salvation is the same faith needed to see and trust Christ when battling a deceived and hardened heart.

   d. Pray for the Lord to pour out His grace upon the person.

8. **Explain the spouse's role in redemption.** If a spouse is involved and affected by the person's sin you will have to help the spouse to view the sin in light of the gospel. You will also help the spouse to focus more on Christ and His redemptive agenda than on the deep pain caused by the sin and the resultant self-protective or even vengeful posture.

Appendix 8

Equipping Gospel Community

As a church leader, one of the most time-consuming yet rewarding responsibilities we have is to equip the church for gospel ministry. As leaders we wrestle long and hard with this very issue. We struggle with *what* to train—there is so much to teach in so little time; *when* to train—there are so many competing activities with work and family schedules; *how* to train—there are a range of approaches that include lecture, dialogue, small groups, personal study, and "on-the-job" training.

But for many church leaders, we think we are equipping the flock by offering a rotating set of classes in which we lecture on a curriculum that reflects the approach of our own biblical and theological training in college or seminary: Old and New Testament, Church History, Evangelism, Missions, Spiritual Disciplines, Worship, etc. Although we come away with more knowledge and insight about God and the Bible with this type of training, we often fall short of knowing how to apply such knowledge to real life. We wrongly think that we are fulfilling Jesus' call to "make disciples" through classroom teaching, because we wrongly assume that people can readily connect the theological concepts to the concrete issues of life. But more times than not, people either don't know how to make the connection or they don't take the time to reflect and seek application. Often, we don't even make the connection for ourselves as leaders.

A Three-Pronged Approach to Equipping
One of the most helpful illustrations that shaped my approach to equipping ministry leaders and members in community is a leadership development model from J. Robert Clinton first seen in the Global Church

Advancement (GCA) Church Planting Manual.[1] You can quickly grasp the model by visualizing two parallel rails connected with cross-ties similar to a railroad track.[2]

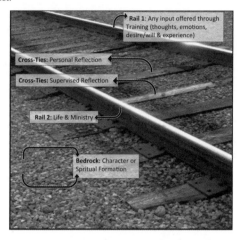

Rail 1: Any input offered through Training (thoughts, emotions, desire/will & experience)

Cross-Ties: Personal Reflection

Cross-Ties: Supervised Reflection

Rail 2: Life & Ministry

Bedrock: Character or Spiritual Formation

The first rail represents any knowledge that affects our thoughts, emotions, desire and will. The second parallel rail represents the experience found in life and ministry. The cross-ties represent ongoing reflection, both personal and supervised. And the bedrock on which the railroad track lies represents the developing character of the person that results from the equipping process.

When any of these rails or cross-ties is missing, or is not fully addressed, the equipping process will suffer. For instance, if you are equipping potential small group leaders how to lead gospel-centered small groups, you can easily spend eight hours teaching them the best content over a weekend (rail 1). But if you do not give these apprentices an opportunity to "get in the driver's seat" to actually lead a group (rail 2—ministry), then they will forget the training. Though they can apply most, if not all, of the concepts to their own relationships and family life (rail 2—life and ministry), most will not see the connection. Even if you place them immediately in a small group leadership position, they will struggle to carry out all that was taught if they do not take the time to learn from their actual experiences (cross-tie—personal reflection). Moreover, if you

---

1   *GCA Foundations for Church Planting*, (2008), Learning Module #5, p. 7; J. Robert Clinton, *Leadership Training Models: A Self-Study Manual For Evaluating And Designing Training*, 2006.

2   Image taken from: http://www.intheiropinion.com/2009/04/articles/federal-statute-other/federal-regulation-of-railroad-roadbed-design-and-construction-does-not-preempt-state-requirement-of-switchyard-walkways/

do not take the time to observe these new leaders as they actually lead a group or do not sit down with them on a regular basis to listen to their concerns, help them think through various situations and explore their hearts related to life and ministry (cross-tie—supervised reflection), they will take longer to develop as leaders and they run the risk of developing bad habits, burning out or hurting others due to not being adequately equipped and not receiving sufficient oversight.

But let's take a look at an intentional and relational approach to equipping. For example, you are in a discipleship relationship with a young man who serves as a small group leader along with his wife. He asked you to mentor him because he has watched you love and invest in not only your wife and children's lives, but in many other men who lead small groups. As you are making your way through the gospel of John, you teach (1st rail) him about Jesus' commandment to love one another just as He has loved us (cf. John 13:34). You take the time to illustrate Christ's sacrificial and self-denying love in ways that engages his heart and mind and he walks away motivated to love others.

But he has not been equipped at this point. It is not until he experiences (2nd rail) the challenges of loving his wife and co-workers, as well as the needy person in his group, will he begin to understand that Jesus' command is easier said than done. But the equipping process is still not complete.

As he sits and prayerfully reflects (cross-tie—personal reflection) on the difficulty of loving others in sacrificial and self-denying ways for the purpose of redemption, he begins to see his deep sinfulness and insecurities. God wants him to see his sinfulness but He doesn't want him to stop at his sin. God also wants him to see his present need for Christ. But his shame and guilt keep him from rounding the corner to the cross.

When he comes to you, you notice he is down on himself and is focused on his failures. As you listen and explore his heart with various questions, he begins to reflect more deeply (cross-tie—supervised reflection) so that he sees not only his need for the gospel but he also sees in a more personal way the depth and beauty of the cross. He realizes that God is loving him when his sinfulness is revealed through his struggle to love others and He calls him back to Christ where he can find mercy and forgiveness. But God is also pouring out His grace upon him because he is beginning to see that God loves him more deeply through the cross of Christ than he ever imagined. After a tearful and enlightening time with you, he walks out with more confidence in Christ and more gratitude for his Redeemer (bedrock of character).

As you address similar gospel dynamics in the following months, you see that this young man is able to more readily see his sin and his Christ in the midst of everyday life and that God is producing spiritual fruit in him. It is at this point that the first phase of equipping has taken place. The next phase is when you encourage and challenge him as he now walks alongside other men in a similar fashion. He will be equipped even more as he now teaches others and helps them to more deeply reflect on how the gospel connects with the details and difficulties of life.

EQUIPPING THE CHURCH

Why is equipping so important for gospel community? In order to be faithful to God's mission of redemption, which involves His continual discipline through His living Word (the Bible) and church (his people), you, along with your ministry leaders and members, need to know how the gospel is worked out in community. Yes, God has given us the "one another passages" so that we not only have the overarching framework for community life but we also have specific commands and principles to use when we encounter the gray areas of life associated with suffering, sin, and unbelief.

As God's entrusted shepherds, the elders need to be intimately aware of the spiritual battles that are raging in the homes and hearts of those to whom they give oversight. But they can't fight this battle alone. The church leaders need to involve others as everyone follows Christ. Remember that God is redeeming every man and woman in gospel community. This is why it is crucial for you as a leader to equip the saints for the work of ministry.

1. **Know that Redemption is Costly and Chaotic**. As a leader, you are immersed in the messiness of the church. Every week you see the direct and indirect consequences of sin in the lives of those under your care. To read about progressive gospel growth is one thing, but to see and experience such change in gospel community in the midst of suffering and sin is another story. Do you tend to view God's redemptive work as clear-cut and formulaic (a+b = c: if you do "a" and "b", you will get "c")? It only takes looking at your own life for you to realize that gospel change is slow, sometimes more "down" than "up" in movement, and at times, barely recognizable. There are times in which you might even question God and your salvation. In fact, because you are human and sinful there are times you need others to point out where God's grace is evident in your life and circumstances. Your understanding of redemption influences the way your leaders and members view redemption. Given these realities, you need to be aware of some common missteps when we forget that the process of redemption is costly and chaotic:

a. *Simplistic View.* If you see God's work of grace as "linear" or in black and white terms, your people will develop the same skewed perspective as you. More than likely, you and others will fall into a formulaic approach to life and ministry.

b. *Quick to Judge.* One of the worst mistakes you can make when dealing with others who are struggling with sin is to question their salvation as your first response. You can easily forget that we struggle with sin both outwardly and inwardly on this side of heaven. Such quickness to judge reflects more the self-righteous Pharisee who looks down at others than the humble tax collector who asks for mercy (cf. Luke 18:9-14).

c. *Impatient and Harsh.* When you fall into the trap of thinking that you can bring about change in someone through your biblical or psychological knowledge, persuasive or eloquent speech, or whatever other gift or talent you possess, you can deal impatiently with those who are struggling in their suffering and sin. Your approach and words can be harsh because you think they should "get it" or be further along in their journey.

2. **Be personally involved.** The constant demands of ministry are overwhelming. So many different people and issues pull you in a number of different directions. You can't possibly take personal lead in all of the pastoral situations in your church. Your tendency may be to delegate and distance yourself from the relentless skirmishes so that you can focus on other things. Again, this is a major reason for you to dedicate time to equipping other ministry leaders. Here are some things to keep in mind:

a. *Delegate but don't default.* You can feel good about identifying leaders to take the lead in the various pastoral issues. For a brief time, you can even brag about the number of leaders you have involved but if they have not been equipped for the task you assigned them, your delegation can fall apart, can cause more harm than good, and cause those involved to burn out sooner than expected. Proper delegation requires more supervision on the front end, but your investment of time and energy will pay off in the long run.

b. *Be available.* Your leaders will need access to you as they have questions, and you will need access to them as you give them regular oversight. An important tension you should hold is knowing if and when you should get involved. And when you do get involved, should your involvement be direct or indirect? For example, even though you have informed those involved in a pastoral situation that a certain ministry leader is taking the lead, you might still receive calls and emails from the church member in crisis. Before responding directly, you should let the ministry leader know about the calls and have him follow-up. There may be times in which you may need to meet with everyone as you step in to re-assess the situation so that you can offer additional guidance.

    c. *In the case of one refusing to listen.* Depending on the issue, you may or may not be aware of the sin struggle that has emerged from the community where a person is refusing to submit to Christ and His Word. The benefit of equipping your members and ministry leaders is they will be able to handle such shepherding issues more effectively and you will be involved less directly. However, you need to train your people so that they know that they should never hesitate to call you when either the urgency of the situation demands it or they decide they need additional guidance after prayerfully reflecting on the situation (see Table 1 and 2 in chapter 7).

3. **Involve others.** Even if you are taking the lead in a particular situation, you must get others involved so that they can help bear burdens, offer comprehensive care, and be exposed to and equipped for real gospel ministry. Again, when you involve others, you will have to take the time to offer the necessary instruction and guidance so that everyone knows his or her role. The beauty of gospel ministry is that God makes evident those who should be involved based on their desire to help, their giftedness, their availability, and love for the person(s) in need. So prayerfully ask the Lord to raise up people and constantly look to see who the Lord is raising up.

4. **Remember people are at different places on the journey.** This particular point brings us back to the fact that redemption is messy. Because God is redeeming everyone involved, not just the one struggling, you need to watch out for everyone's various perspectives and responses. Everyone is on a growth curve regarding the gospel, which includes, but is not limited to, an increasing understanding of God's glory and beauty, his or her own sinfulness, and the cross of Christ. You should anticipate that there will be some people who can step directly into difficult situations and maintain a redemptive vision while others will step into the mess and get confused, resort to legalistic thinking, or give up because bearing such burdens seems overwhelming.

APPENDIX 9.1

Example Redemptive Plan[1]
(for a married couple)

GOD'S MISSION—REDEMPTION[2]

God's mission involves redemption—redeeming us as His own people as He uses us in His redemptive work with others, both in and out of the church. Even as Christians, we struggle to live out the gospel in the midst of suffering and sin. As weary and wayward sojourners we all need help every step of the way to better understand, believe, and walk in a way pleasing to the Lord—a way that brings glory to Him by building up His body in love (Eph. 4:16) and advancing His kingdom in a dark and dying world (cf. Matt. 28:18-20). Every member of Christ's body needs one another to remember that this life is a journey towards home where we will live forever with our Redeemer. Every member of Christ's body needs one another in order to conform more and more to Christ (Heb. 3:12-13; 10:23-25), as we all are being prepared for the final and ultimate marriage to Christ, all by the grace and power of the Holy Spirit.

Such inter-dependent body life is a picture of the church living out the gospel. We reflect our redeeming God as we help one another to hold fast to Christ (1) while we struggle with unbelief in our suffering and sin and (2) while we strive to worship God with our whole lives (cf. Rom. 12:1).

---

1   This example plan should be used only as a guide as you prayerfully develop the specific plan for your church. You want to make sure the wording, tone and emphasis of your plan is consistent with your own church and specific to the details of the situation being addressed.

2   The first two pages of this plan serve as a necessary foundation for the redemptive plan. You can reduce this introductory material but consider that most people do not have this understanding of life, community and church.

Such whole-hearted living declares and demonstrates the gospel to believers and unbelievers and brings glory to God! This redemptive mission is God's purpose for our lives in Christ.

GOD'S PROCESS OF REDEMPTION

Because God knows our continual struggles, He lovingly and persistently disciplines us through His Word and people so that we will conform increasingly to Christ in our life of faith and repentance. Since God uses the church to carry out His redemptive mission, this plan should be seen as a practical way that we, as the church, can lovingly shepherd and journey with you as we all grow in the gospel.

OVERALL APPROACH

- We will come alongside you with a spirit of love and gentleness (Gal. 6:1-2), not condemning since there is no condemnation in Christ (Rom. 8:1), and hopeful since we have an unwavering hope in Christ (Rom. 5:5).

- We pray you will realize the beauty of God's love through gospel community as we explore the deep hurt and brokenness underneath each of your fears, doubts, and confusion. We assure you that you are not alone in this redemptive process—we all need the same gospel and grace.

- We will journey with you as God uses the details and difficulties of life to grow you as a man/woman of God. We pray you will find increasing faith and hope in Christ and experience His love as He accomplishes His purposes in and through your life. We are confident that Christ can bring about change in your life and marriage that will be above and beyond what you could ever ask or think (cf. Eph. 3:20).

WHY A REDEMPTIVE PLAN?

- We as elders decided the best way we can love you is to step in and establish a redemptive plan in the midst of your chaos and struggle. Because of the nature of your chronic marital struggles, your desperate cry for help and your battle with weariness, we want to support and love you in an intentional manner.

- This plan is written out so that you might understand the big picture of God's redemptive mission, the tangible "next steps" for redemption and the intentional community committed to journey with you as you all grow together.

- Some realities to be aware of ...

- You may grow bitter and resentful if you do not see this plan from God's redemptive perspective.

- You may wrongly think you are alone even though people who love you and who are sacrificing to care for you are surrounding you.

- You may wrongly see others who are trying to help you as those who are out to get you, who don't understand you, who are trying to hold you back and ruin your life and who are condemning, judging, or shaming you.

- You may be tempted to blame others for your situation and not accept your own sinfulness, and as a result, you will not experience the deep love of God through Christ.

Next Steps for Marriage and Family

- By faith and by the power of the Holy Spirit, John, you are to love and lead Kathy by faith as her husband and Kathy, you are to love and respect John as his wife.

- Work through the following gospel materials per a given schedule with others involved in this redemptive plan and those in your CG:
  - Porterbrook Character modules—*Gospel Living, Gospel Relationships and Gospel Change.*
  - *The Realities of Marriage: What Did You Expect?* by Paul Tripp
    - Attend City Church's next Redeem Marriage event.
    - At some designated point, attend and participate in weekly marriage counseling and complete assigned homework.
    - Arrange your work and home schedules to maximize time together as a couple and family. Avoid weekend trips with family and friends that will separate you as husband and wife.

Next Steps for Care and Community

- Attend weekly CG with Tom and Sharon Davis. Be intentional to share with them your deep need for Christ and gospel community and ask for prayer as each of you strive to be the man and woman God desires you to be in your marriage and family.

- Know that any relevant information discussed can be shared with those involved in the redemptive community so that we can fight against divisive talk and hidden sin.

- Attend and participate in weekly individual counseling as required and complete assigned homework.

- Receive and follow the guidance of those leading in this redemptive plan as they will address many practical aspects of living out the gospel.

- Attend weekly Sunday services and serve together as husband and wife in whatever ministry area that coincides with your desires and schedules.

- Attend the next Redemption Group.

FAILURE TO SUBMIT TO CITY CHURCH LEADERSHIP IN THIS REDEMPTIVE PROCESS

- John and Kathy, it is our prayer that God will use this redemptive plan to bring about gospel change in your life and marriage. However, if either of you choose not to submit to the various portions of this plan in any way, you will have to discuss with City Church elders at Midtown your reasons for not following this agreement.

- We recognize that sanctification is a process and only God determines the timing and the degree of gospel change, as well as the means for such change. We also know the Holy Spirit enables gospel transformation through faith and perseverance (1 Pet. 1:2-9; Gal. 5:22-23; James 1:2-4) but God calls us to live out the gospel with intentionality (Eph. 4:1; 5:1-2) "to work out your salvation with fear and trembling; for it is God who is at work in you, both to will and to work for His good pleasure" (Phil. 2:12-13).

I have read, understand, and agree to all aspects of this redemptive plan, *all by the grace of God.*

Printed Name	Signature	Date

Printed Name	Signature	Date

Elder Printed Name	Elder Signature	Date

Appendix 9.2

Elders Escalating Redemptive Efforts

The following list offers some of the major steps that can be taken by the elders to shepherd those brothers and sisters who increasingly refuse to follow Christ despite many warnings:

1. **Inform the elders.** If the elders have not been informed before now, they will need to be briefed and meet with those involved so that they can best understand the situation. The elders cannot lead in escalating redemptive efforts when they are unaware of the situation. As God's appointed leaders in the local church, God holds the elders responsible for the leading, feeding, and caring for the flock. As the Apostle Paul instructs:

   > Pay careful attention to yourselves and to all the flock, in which the Holy Spirit has made you overseers, to care for the church of God, which he obtained with his own blood. I know that after my departure fierce wolves will come in among you, not sparing the flock; and from among your own selves will arise men speaking twisted things, to draw away the disciples after them. Therefore be alert, remembering that for three years I did not cease night or day to admonish everyone with tears. (Acts. 20:28-31)

   > Obey your leaders and submit to them, for they are keeping watch over your souls, as those who will have to give an account. Let them do this with joy and not with groaning, for that would be of no advantage to you. (Heb. 13:17)

Some people may hesitate to inform the elders for fear of breaking confidentiality or being guilty of gossip. The two passages above reveal several truths that will help you see that such fears are commendable, but not applicable when it comes to caring for the bride of Christ:

a. God appoints elders as overseers to care for His blood-bought bride.

b. God commands elders to pay careful attention to not only themselves but to all the flock.

c. God knows that the enemy is relentless in his warfare against the flock and the devil seeks to draw believers away and destroy them.

d. God calls elders to be alert and to keep watch over the souls of those entrusted to their care.

e. God will hold the elders accountable for the ministry He has given them.

God calls every person of His body—members and leaders—to love one another. But because of the special calling God gives elders, He holds His appointed overseers accountable for how the body bears burdens and builds itself up in love. Therefore, the elders need to know when there is a shephearding situation that warrants them being informed.[1] The following practical considerations complement the biblical reasons why elders need to be informed:

a. Elders can offer gospel guidance to help those in community who are struggling to know what they should and should not do in response to a given situation.

b. Elders can assess and envision the situation with more gospel clarity given their experience in knowing and applying the Word of God to real life struggles.

c. Elders can shepherd those in community who are responding to a given life struggle, knowing that there can be tendencies to over-react with legalism or cheap grace, inactivity or over-activity, fear or anger, and hopelessness or false hope.

d. Elders cannot oversee situations of which they are not aware.

---

1   Review Chapter 7, Table 1 to see situations in which elders should be informed immediately.

e. Elders cannot equip the body through real ministry situations if they are not involved.

Both the biblical and practical reasons why elders are to be informed are made possible only through the grace of God and the power of His Spirit. Moreover, God's grace will guide and enable the elders so that:

a. Elders will not swoop in with a rod of discipline when informed. Instead the elders' hearts will break with compassion and display steadfast faith knowing that the gospel is powerful enough to change anyone and any situation, all for God's glory.

b. Elders will not judge those they hear about since they know that they too are sinners in need of the gospel. In fact, such knowledge will enable the elders to discern the needs of the flock that can be addressed through preaching, teaching, and more intentional shepherding efforts through both gospel gatherings on Sundays and scattered gospel communities throughout the week.

c. God redeems not only those needing help and those who are helping to bear burdens, but God also helps the elders mature as God's shepherds as they struggle, suffer and lead through the difficult pastoral situations.

Now that we have a better understanding of why elders should be informed, let's take a look at additional ways of dealing with those who are straying. These efforts should only be considered once the elders have taken the time to prayerfully assess the situation after meeting with everyone involved.

2. **Offer warnings.** If those straying refuse to listen to their gospel community, then the elders need to offer warnings so that they might realize the seriousness and weight of sin plus the beauty and weight of God's love and forgiveness found in Christ.[2]

3. **Withhold communion.** In 1 Corinthians 11:27-32 Paul warns us to not take communion lightly, especially if we have unsettled sins

---

2 Refer to Chapter 9 for a detailed discussion about offering warnings.

before God and others. When the elders offer a verbal warning, they should take the time to explain the significance of the 1 Corinthians 11 passage and tell them they should abstain from taking communion unless they return and submit to Christ.[3]

4. **Exclude from service.** Those who are blatantly rebelling against God and His church should be asked to step down from any and all places of service. If those serving in the church are not willing to serve God with a life of faith and repentance, then they are in no position to serve others since they may say or do things contrary to the gospel which, in turn, may mislead others or may cause division. Those who are unrepentant should be removed from the outset if the nature of their rebellion is serious, as determined by the church leaders.

5. **Exclude from community.** In most cases those who refuse to repent do not want to stay in gospel community since they think everyone is against them. They can also think that no one loves them because no one seems to agree with their decisions and desires. But there might be situations when those fighting with God stay in community for the wrong reasons. They may try to create division and doubt within the community and towards church leadership or try to undermine God's Word through their own reasoning and actions. In such cases, they will be told that they are no longer allowed to be a part of the church's covenant community.

6. **Exclude from church gatherings.** More times than not, when people get to this degree of hardness, they stop attending corporate worship. However, if they do remain, and through their attendance they stir up division and confusion among the people, they should be told that they cannot attend the various gatherings on the church campus.

7. **Inform the church** (cf. Matt. 18:17a). Once the elders see that those who are wayward have refused all redemptive attempts, they should agree to bring the matter before the entire church gathering so that they can be informed and mobilized to pray for and pursue those who are in bondage, doing the will of the enemy.[4]

---

3   Refer to Chapter 9 for a detailed discussion about withholding communion.

4   Refer to section, *"When will the church gather?"*

APPENDIX 9.3

The "Who" and "Where" of Warnings

It is helpful to see that warnings are part of the confronting and correcting aspect of the ministry of the Word. When we think about warnings in this way, we can see how warnings can be rightfully issued in every context of life.

1. **In Everyday Relationships.** As you experience deep and intentional one-on-one relationships with others, undoubtedly you will see sin struggles in one another. As the Lord provides opportunities and as you strive to be a faithful friend, there may be times in which you warn a friend who is involved in some self-destructive behavior, enslaved by a bitter and vengeful heart, develops an apathetic posture towards God, or expresses a longing to escape an unfulfilling marriage. Your warning serves as a flare to get their attention, to signal danger and to remind them of God's unrelenting holiness and love.

2. **In Small Groups.** Warnings can issue from a gospel community of brothers and sisters in Christ in a variety of ways. Biblical warnings can take the form of gentle reminders, intentional corrections, firm but loving rebukes, to include solemn declarations of God's wrath against wickedness and waywardness. It's helpful to remember that warnings are one of the ways you can fight for the souls of one another.

   a. *Naturally in community.* For example, week after week one of the men in the men's accountability time during your small group gathering gripes about his wife and marriage. Each time the men in the group help this one man to see not only the selfishness in his perspective and the sin in his own heart but also the gift that this man's wife is to him. You encourage and challenge one another to be men who love and sacrifice for their wives knowing that God grows you as men as you love and lead like Christ. But one week, this man breaks down and confesses that he has become emotionally connected with a woman at the office. The men speak boldly yet lovingly to him as you all warn him of what he risks losing, how he is being unfaithful to his wife as he is living out a fantasy, and how he is rebelling against God through his adulterous heart. Each of you calls him back to Christ and commits to journey with him through this dangerous season of his life.

 b. *Intentionally as a community.* There may be times when those you have warned through a series of private discussions still refuse to hear and live out the gospel. In such cases others can be invited in from your community to assess the situation, to offer clarifying and corrective perspectives and to warn as necessary.

3. **In Elder-led Situations.** Once an elder gets involved, he will take the lead in the shepherding situation. Based on the development of events and the trajectory of those who refuse to listen, the elder will issue a warning on behalf of God as one of His appointed shepherds who has the responsibility of caring for and protecting the flock. Elders will either issue the warning verbally or in written format based on the willingness of the unrepentant person to meet and the number of warnings already presented.

 a. *Verbal warnings.* If the person who is rebelling against God is willing to meet in person, the elder should do whatever it takes to make the face-to-face meeting happen. You should always try to meet in person since everyone involved will benefit from the dynamics of a give-and-take conversation along with experiencing the full array of emotions and desires expressed through the verbal and non-verbal communication.

 b. The person may be unwilling to meet with the elder in person but may be willing to talk with him on the telephone. Even though the elder will not experience the full benefit of a face-to-face encounter, he can at least have a conversation that may allow him to explore the heart, proclaim the gospel in more relevant and personal ways based on the details of the discussion and arrange a time in which they can continue the discussion.

c. *Written warning.* If the person refuses any contact, the elders may have no other choice but to send a written warning letter. The elders may decide to send the warning letter via the postal service and simultaneously through email. When sending an actual letter, you should get it certified so that you can track the receipt of the letter.

4. **Before the Church**. When the elders decide to inform the church about a given shepherding situation, they will convey the scriptural violation(s), the pertinent points of the elder warnings and the respective waiting periods so that the members will understand the essence of the rebellion and the redemptive efforts already taken by the church. God uses such public warnings to sober those who hear the warnings and to provide an example of the consequences of sin and of a failure to submit to God and His people.

Appendix 9.4

A Series of Elder Warnings

The elders can issue a number of warnings based on the situation and response of those who have been warned:

- An initial warning. An elder can issue a warning when he discerns that the hearts of those he is shepherding have become hardened by their continual refusal to listen to gospel truths—they seem to be on a trajectory of turning their back on the living God.

- Follow up warning(s). With each warning comes a waiting period to allow time for the Holy Spirit to do His sanctifying work as those who received the warning stop and reflect on all that is going on. Follow-up warnings are offered in the following circumstances:

  - *Because of the cycle of sin.* Sometimes those who are struggling will repent and submit for a season then cycle back into a pattern of rebellion. In such cases, the elders will need to warn them each and every time the cycle repeats. The elders need to decide when they need to issue a final warning in spite of the predictable repentance that seems to follow.

  - *Because of no response.* In many cases, the elders will issue another warning if those who were initially warned fail to respond. The follow up warning can either be another warning or it may be presented as a final warning before informing the church of their waywardness and refusal to submit to God and His Word.

- Final warning prior to telling the church. The elders may issue a final warning at any point after their initial warning or immediately, depending on the particulars of the rebellion and given circumstances. In most cases, the final warning is put in the form of a written document that explains the rebellious situation from God's perspective and His discipline the church is called to carry out. When people fail to respond to this final warning, it generally leads to informing the larger church gathering and, eventually, removing them from the covenant community of the church.

Appendix 9.5

What's in a Warning?

What's In A Warning?

What does it look like for church leaders to issue a warning to those who refuse to turn back and trust God? There are some essential components that you need to consider so that your warnings not only capture God's redemptive purpose but also convey His concerns and desires. Before you deliver a warning message in person or through letter, you need to consult with the other elders in your church so that together, you can talk through: (1) the biblical and theological content, (2) the tone of the message, (3) the clarity of each section, especially when summarizing the ways the person has rejected and rebelled against God, (4) the concreteness of the "next steps" associated with each option and (5) the emphasis of the gospel throughout the warning.

If the person is married, take the time to review the warning with the spouse so that the spouse can ask questions, offer feedback and also feel a part of the process. This can help the spouse feel cared for as she reads and comprehends all that is involved in the redemptive efforts. The following is a global outline for a warning. You can see two full warning examples in Appendices 9.6 and 9.9.

The following outline highlights the essential components of a warning:
1. Opening Section
   a. Express thanks for the opportunity to meet or express regret in not being able to meet face-to-face.

   b. Express your love for them and your desire to care for them as one of their pastors.

   c. Make clear God's call to repentance, which consists of returning to Him by faith and obedience, while receiving His abundant compassion and forgiveness.

2. Section highlighting the rejection of God through Scriptural violations.

3. Section highlighting the goodness and mercy of God's discipline.

4. Section highlighting the redemptive efforts and subsequent responses.

5. Section explaining the two broad biblical options
   a. Option 1—Repentance and Restoration
      i. Explain what repentance and faith looks like for this situation.

      ii. Explain what the restoration process looks like with this option.

   b. Option 2—Refusal to Repent
      i. Describe possible action steps that can be taken
         1. Withhold communion if not already done.

         2. Excluded from serving if not already done.

         3. Excluded from various forms of church gatherings—Sunday services, small group, and church-sanctioned events.

         4. Inform their community group.

         5. Inform the church.

         6. Removed from the church's covenant community.

      ii. Describe possible actions steps assigned to church members[1]
         1. For family—Maintain relationship as appropriate. Live out the gospel with the person as a means of redemption.

         2. For non-family—Do not hang out with the person in a casual setting which makes it seem that nothing is wrong.

         3. For all—Pray for and pursue the person through whatever means the Lord leads. When you do cross paths, offer the love of God and ask the person to return to Christ. Do not act as if everything is normal.

      iii. Explain what the restoration process looks like with this option.

      iv. Convey the deadline for responding to a designated elder.

6. Closing Section
   a. Express again your love for them and your desire to care for them.

   b. Make a final plea to return to Christ.

   c. Express commitment to pray for the person and their family.

---

1   Described in more detail in Chapter 10.

Appendix 9.6

Example Initial Warning Letter[1]

Date

Name
Address
City, State Zip Code

Dear John,

We greet you as fellow members of the body of Christ. As your pastors, we come to you with heavy hearts, guided by God's Word and His Spirit. We love you and desire to care for you in the midst of your confusion and rebellion. Your refusal to meet face-to-face requires us to write this letter which serves as an initial warning in the escalating church discipline process found in Matthew 18:15-17.

Our efforts to pursue you and to pray for you have one goal—for you to turn back by faith and obedience to Jesus Christ where you will find abundant mercy and forgiveness (cf. Isa. 55:6-8).

[Scriptural Violations][2]
John, we love you enough to confront you with the gospel, which you once trusted, proclaimed and lived out. Your adulterous relationship with Meredith (Exod. 20:14; Matt. 5:27-30; Heb. 13:4) and abandoning Kathy and your children (1 Tim. 5:8; Eph. 5:22ff; 6:4; Deut. 6:5-9) represent a clear rejection of God's Word and will.

[God's Discipline]
Please know that when you live contrary to God's commands, you not only blatantly sin against Him but you also experience great suffering—

---

1   This example letter should be used only as a guide as you prayerfully develop the specific letter for your church. You want to make sure the wording, tone and emphasis of your letter is consistent with your own church and specific to the details of the situation being addressed.

2   Headers serve as a guide to outline what needs to be addressed in the warning letter. They should not appear in the final document.

from your soul being disordered by sin and from God's discipline. But know that God disciplines you because He loves you (Heb. 12:6):

> It is for discipline that you have to endure. God is treating you as sons. For what son is there whom his father does not discipline? If you are left without discipline, in which all have participated, then you are illegitimate children and not sons. Besides this, we have had earthly fathers who disciplined us and we respected them. Shall we not much more be subject to the Father of spirits and live? For they disciplined us for a short time as it seemed best to them, but he disciplines us for our good, that we may share his holiness. For the moment all discipline seems painful rather than pleasant, but later it yields the peaceful fruit of righteousness to those who have been trained by it. (Heb. 12:7-11)

Please see God's goodness and mercy in this passage. God disciplines us for our good so that we may share in His holiness (v. 10).

John, we pray that you will realize that you have fallen into the trap of the enemy and you are believing his lies (cf. 2 Tim. 2:25-26). What you think is life is really death. The joy and pleasure you seek leads to eventual despair and pain (cf. Prov. 5, 7).

[Response Requested]
John, please contact Pastor Greg as soon as possible so that you both can talk face-to-face about your situation. You have not crossed "the line of no return." Forgiveness and restoration is always possible through Jesus Christ.

We assure you that if you desire forgiveness and restoration, we will journey with you every step of the way as we fight the good fight of faith together by the grace of God (cf. 1 Tim. 6:11-12).

[Next Steps If No Response]
If you do not respond to this initial warning letter within two weeks of the date above, we will continue our efforts to pursue you and pray for you. However, if after a series of ongoing attempts to call you back to Christ does not result in your repentance, we will issue a final warning letter prior to telling the entire church about your refusal to submit to Christ at a members' meeting in the near future.

[Closing]
John, please know we love you and desire for you to experience the joy of your salvation in Christ. Seek the Lord for wisdom and strength to do His will. Seek Christ, for He is calling you to come to Him in the midst of your pain, you weariness, and your confusion (cf. Matt. 11:28-30).

Grace and Peace in Christ,

The Elders of City Church

Appendix 9.7

Waiting after Warning

Here are some factors to consider as you determine the designated waiting period:

1. **Based on the severity of the offense**. If those under warning have committed a heinous crime (e.g. murder, rape, abuse of a minor, and other crimes that involve issues of physical violence) the church leaders will need much discernment in determining if the waiting period should be any different from those associated with "lesser offenses." More, not less, time may be needed in such cases, especially if law enforcement agencies are involved. The offending church member may be so distracted by the legalities and in shock by the magnitude of the situation that additional time to sort out the issues of the heart may be required. In such cases, there will be several tensions that the elders need to keep in mind:

   a. *No remorse*. If the offender shows no remorse then there may be little to no waiting period and the elders will immediately remove the person from the covenant fellowship of the church. Removal from membership is not part of the punitive process but is part of the redemptive process.[1]

   b. *Remorse*. If the offender expresses remorse, the elders will need to allow a sufficient waiting period to watch for the fruits associated with godly sorrow that leads to repentance. Church leaders should still take the proper precautions during this waiting period for the

---

1 A full discussion of removing an unrepentant person from the church's covenant community is addressed in Chapter 10.

safety of the church in spite of the offender's expressed remorse. Moreover, the elders need to prayerfully decide whether or not to remove the person from the covenant community of the church if the person is found guilty and imprisoned. It is important to remember that God's discipline is not designed to bring about justice or punishment since Christ our Redeemer took our punishment. Christ vindicated God's holiness on the cross and He will serve as the righteous judge at the end of time.

2. **Based on the actions taken by the unrepentant person.** Even if those under warning have taken steps that seem irreversible (e.g., moved in with a lover, moved out of town, made declarations about ending all ties, cutting off all contact, threatening the church with a lawsuit, etc.) the elders should still offer a waiting period to allow God to work through His Spirit and people.

3. **Based on the wavering responses of the unrepentant person.** If those placed under warning have struggled between submission and rebellion throughout the various interactions and redemptive efforts, then a waiting period should be offered to allow sufficient time for the church to pray for and pursue them after they are informed.

Appendix 9.8

Withholding Communion

Versus

Open Communion

An issue related to open communion that church leaders often raise is "How can you withhold communion from those who are unrepentant while practicing an open communion table?" The term "open communion" describes when a local church allows anyone who professes faith in Christ and who examines themselves before the Lord to participate in the sacred meal, regardless of membership. The main concern is whether church leaders are being inconsistent when they keep a member from taking communion on the one hand but on the other hand, they are not making a concerted effort to know the spiritual condition of the non-members who participate in the sacred meal. Before addressing this concern, let's first take a look at the responsibilities of those taking communion then we will look at the responsibilities of the elders in overseeing their flock.

First, according to 1 Corinthians 11:27-32, no one should knowingly take communion in an unworthy manner whether they are a member, regular attendee or a visitor. Because every Christian is a part of the body of Christ, the universal church, every follower of Christ has the privilege of taking part in the sacred meal regardless of membership status. But with that privilege comes responsibility. Despite the universal invitation to all Christians to partake in the symbolic meal, every follower of Christ is accountable to God in how they approach the table. Even though the elders are not aware of the spiritual condition of every person who participates in the Lord's Supper, whether the church practices open or closed communion, God is aware of every person's heart and He is the one who judges and disciplines those who take the meal in an unworthy manner.

Second, elders are called to be proactive in protecting the flock from harm. Even when open communion is practiced, the elders have a responsibility to withhold communion from those members who are openly rebelling against God and who continually refuse to submit to Christ and His people. In such cases, withholding communion is not inconsistent with the practice of open communion because it represents the elders' efforts to protect those in rebellion from eating and drinking judgment upon themselves (1 Cor. 11:29). To put it simply, open communion should not absolve the elders of their responsibility to shepherd and protect the flock in this way.

The concern for inconsistency associated with withholding communion and open communion is addressed simply by the fact that the elders are only responsible for those under their care, not for non-members or members of other churches.

Appendix 9.9

Example Final Warning Letter[1]

Date

Name
Address
City, State Zip Code

Dear John,

We regret that you have not responded to our efforts to love you as
we have called you to turn back to Jesus Christ as your life, hope and
love. We are deeply saddened by your refusal to accept God's invitation to His infinite mercy. Since you have not responded to our initial
warning letter, we are sending you this final warning letter as a last
step before telling the church of your rebellion against God.

Please know that we are pursuing and confronting you out of our love
for you. You may not see it as such but we are fighting for you and not
against you. Just like you, we are all in desperate need of Christ and
His ongoing work of grace in our lives and would want you to do the
same for us if we were in your situation.

[History of Scriptural Violations]
Through a course of events culminating in January 2010, it was revealed you were guilty of adultery (Exod. 20:14; Matt. 19:18) and
you refused to turn back to Christ for truth and life (John 14:6;
cf. 2 Tim. 2:25-26). During this time, you have not cared for your
wife and children (1 Tim. 5:8; Eph. 5:22ff; 6:4; Deut. 6:5-9). You
withdrew from City Church community by not coming to Sunday Gathered (Heb. 10:24-25) and refused to listen and submit

---

[1]   This example letter should be used only as a guide as you prayerfully develop
the specific letter for your church. You want to make sure the wording, tone
and emphasis of your letter is consistent with your own church and specific
to the details of the situation being addressed.

to Christ as you refused to listen to members and church leadership as they repeatedly called you to turn back to your Redeemer (Matt. 18:15-17; Heb. 13:17). We as elders are accountable by God to care for you as a member of His body (Acts 20:28-31).

[History of Redemptive Attempts and Subsequent Responses]
You refused to listen to Kathy, along with Tom and Sharon, as they confronted you in love (Matt. 18:16) and refused to listen to Pastor Greg and other church leaders as they attempted to discuss with you how you can turn back to Christ and be restored within the City Church community. [Document significant sinful responses throughout the escalating church discipline process.] As a member of City Church, you covenanted to "follow the biblical procedures of church discipline and submit myself to discipline if the need should ever arise (Matt. 18:15-17; Gal. 6:1-5)."

[Explanation of Two Biblical Options]
Given your refusal to repent and submit to God, the elders present to you two biblical options: repent and work towards restoration with the church or refuse to repent and be removed from the covenant community of the church since we can no longer affirm your profession of faith in Christ (Matt. 18:17).

[Option 1—Repentance and Restoration]

[Repentance]
What does repentance look like for you at this point? First, we pray the Lord would grant you the grace to repent (2 Tim. 2:24-26), which will compel you to not live for yourself but instead, live for Christ (2 Cor. 5:14-15). You will seek to love your wife like Christ (cf. Eph. 5:25-29; 1 Pet. 3:7; Eph. 5:1-2) with humility and gentleness (cf. 1 Cor. 13:4-7) and to shepherd your children in the Lord (Eph. 6:4b). You will willingly submit yourself to the restoration process outlined by the church leadership. Please know you cannot do any of this apart from the grace of God. We want you to experience the deep and abiding love of Christ by trusting and obeying Him.

[Restoration]
A church leader will coordinate with the members in your community to love and restore you in the gospel and will lead the restoration process. As your church family, we promise to walk with you every step of the way as you work through the particular struggles that face you and your family. The Lord has truly blessed this community approach to restoration and transformation.

[Option 2—Refusal to Repent]

[Warning of Removal from Membership & Implications]
John, if you refuse to repent, seek restoration, and submit to Christ and His people for your care, we will carry out the most extreme discipline as outlined in Matthew 18:17—we will tell the church of the Scriptural commands you have blatantly violated and if you still refuse to listen even to the church, we will no longer be able to affirm your profession of faith in Christ.

[Actions Steps Taken Against the Offender]
What does it mean practically for us to treat you as an unbeliever? We will remove you from the community and care of God's people, the church. You will not be allowed to partake in communion. You will not be allowed in any City Church community groups or in any church social gatherings. The elders will no longer be responsible for your soul but we will prayerfully hand you over to your flesh, the world, and Satan (1 Cor. 5:5; 1 Tim. 1:20; 2 Tim. 2:25-26), so the Lord might grant repentance. All of these steps taken by the church are designed to be redemptive so that you might be brought back to Christ and your soul saved in the end (1 Cor. 5:5; 2 Tim. 2:25-26).

[Actions Steps Taken by the Church]
John, if you are removed from the church, we will ask the members of City Church to continue to pray for you so that you would turn back to Christ. We will instruct our members that they are not permitted to associate with you and pretend everything is okay or normal in the midst of your rebellious posture towards God and the church. We will inform our members that they are permitted to associate with you only for the purpose of engaging you with the gospel. We call our members to relate to you with humility and grace, in ways that both comforts and challenges you as they call you back to Christ by faith and repentance, all with the goal of redemption.

[Restoration Upon Repentance]
At some point in the future, if you express a desire to be restored to God and His church, as evidenced by confession of sin along with a renewed desire to trust and obey Christ, the elders will make steps to restore you back to church membership.

We want you to know that the enemy, the world and your flesh will shame you and tell you lies to get you to believe that what you have done can never be forgiven and that you can never be reconciled with God, your family and your brothers and sisters in Christ.

Look only to Christ and His finished work on the cross. There are no stains of sin too great for the cleansing blood of Christ.

We also want you to know that the elders and members of the church will commit to journey with you through the restoration process. We will treat you not as an outcast but as one of our own since we all need the deep and continual grace of the gospel.

[Deadline Date and Contact Person]
John, we encourage you to prayerfully consider the two biblical options we put before you. We pray you will respond to our plea for your repentance by turning to Christ as your only hope. If you desire to repent and take steps towards restoration in community under the oversight of the elders, please contact Pastor Greg as soon as possible to set up a meeting. If you do not contact Pastor Greg by this Sunday, May 12, 2010 by 5:00pm, we will understand that you refuse to abide to the conditions of this letter and the elders will then inform the church of your waywardness at our next Members' Meeting. If you still refuse to listen even to the church after a period of time, we will then remove you from the covenant community of the church.

[Closing]
John, please know we love you and desire for you to experience the joy of your salvation in Christ. Seek the Lord for wisdom and grace. Seek Christ, for He is calling you to come to Him in the midst of your pain, you weariness, and your confusion (cf. Matt. 11:28-30).

Grace and Peace in Christ,

The Elders of City Church

APPENDIX 9.10

Why Tell the Church?

WHY SOME CHOOSE NOT TO TELL THE ENTIRE CHURCH

Church leaders who hesitate or decide not to tell the entire covenant community offer a variety of reasons for their decision. In most cases, these reasons are not rooted in fear or disobedience but are based on what they think is best for both those who have turned their backs on God and the entire church community. Church leaders have expressed the following reasons for not telling the entire church gathering:

1. **Minimize the communication circle.** Only the people who know those being warned need to know since they are most affected and are most able to help.

2. **Minimize the shame.** Those being warned and their family will experience more shame if more people than necessary know about the situation.

3. **Minimize the irrelevancy.** People who do not know those being warned do not have a need to know since they will not cross paths, will not have a chance to engage them redemptively and may not even care.

4. **Minimize liability.** The church runs the risk of a lawsuit if they publicly announce the names of those who are being warned and who are faced with being removed from the covenant community. Also, a church opens itself up to a lawsuit if it is not consistent in publicly announcing those who are joining their covenant community on the front end and those who face being removed on the back end.

Given these practical considerations, why does Jesus command that the church be told when a person refuses to submit to God and His people after numerous redemptive efforts?

WHY TELL THE CHURCH?

As we have come to understand God's story of redemption and how He grows and changes us through our suffering and sin, we are better able to understand why Jesus commands us to tell the entire church when one of His own goes astray. Our Redeemer does not want us to tell the church so that we might comply with a process-driven church discipline procedure but as a natural outworking of a family who is bound together by the love of Christ through the Spirit of Christ. Telling the entire church also provides an opportunity for the church to live out a significant gospel truth about the body of Christ:

> If one member suffers, all suffer together; if one member is honored, all rejoice together. (1 Cor. 12:26)

The purpose of telling the church is not expressly for public shame but to unleash the entire church to pray for and pursue those who are straying so that everyone involved would mature in the grace of Christ and God would be glorified. The following are additional reasons for telling the entire church:

1. Maximizes those praying and pursuing.
The prayer of a righteous person has great power (James 5:16). Imagine when an entire community is pleading with God on behalf of those who are wayward. One church pastor shared that after he informed the church about a member who refused to return to Christ despite being pursued persistently with the love of God, note cards and stamps were handed out so that people could write a personal appeal expressing their love and concern for the wayward man. Even though the man was deeply touched by the love expressed by his church family, he ultimately refused to listen to them as well and was removed from membership. Despite the man's lack of repentance, the church was deeply impacted by their experience of being a part of God's redemptive mission.

2. Maximizes opportunities to love.
God mobilizes His church in beautiful ways when they are informed and called to pray for and pursue those who have turned their backs on Christ. The Spirit of God compels His people to love others at all times and in any situation, especially during times of need.

Betty sat and listened as the elders shared about a woman who left her husband and children for another man. God really moved in Betty's heart as she reflected on this particular church discipline situation involving a sister in Christ whom she didn't know. Without telling anyone else, Betty committed to pray for this woman. Almost a year later, Betty was overjoyed as she sat in another members' meeting when she heard that this woman, who was removed from the church, came back and told the elders that she wanted to be restored to God and His church. Shortly after that meeting, Betty started making regular contact with the woman, taking her out for meals, inviting her over to the house to hang out, and engaging in gospel conversations. Little did Betty know that God used her intentional and prayerful efforts in a significant way to help the woman experience the gospel and the love of Christ. The elders did not even find out about Betty's loving ministry until later in the restoration process.

3. Maximizes visibility.

Those who are blinded and weakened by the deceitfulness and power of sin will often withdraw from others, create division within the church through slander and lies, and confuse other believers through their words and lifestyle. Therefore, the pastors need to alert those under their care so that the members can see if and when those under discipline are deceiving, dividing and confusing the church. Elders often get reports from church members as they notice misleading or divisive interactions between those under discipline and those in the church through the various social networks. Many times such reports come from those who are not in the immediate circles of the person who is under discipline. It is beautiful to watch how the Spirit of God alerts His people to any divisive or confusing activity that may emerge from within the community and they in turn inform the elders. The more people who know, the less sin can hide and continue its destructive work.

In addition to maximizing sin's visibility to those in the church, telling the church also maximizes sin's visibility to those who are straying. Knowing that they will be fully exposed to the church, those who refuse to turn back and submit to Christ might reflect on what they are risking if they continue on their deviant path. When such waywardness reaches this point, most people have already "counted the cost"[1] for their willful rebellion and have resolved to "go all the way" and forge a new life that they are choosing for themselves.

4. Maximizes teaching and equipping.

Most people in church today do not understand church discipline because it is a topic that is rarely taught and is an aspect of the church that is seldom

---

1 The costs they consider include losing their relationships with God, their family and their network of friends in the church community. More than likely, they are well on their way of convincing themselves of their changing identity, from the person they use to be to the person they see themselves becoming in their new life.

exercised. The people of God will grasp the redemptive and comprehensive work of God when their elders gather them with the specific purpose of:

a. Offering a biblical perspective on how God's discipline is exercised through His church.

b. Informing the church about the reality of sin and the consequences of hardened hearts of those in their own church.

c. Telling the church about the ways the gospel community has stepped in by faith to bear burdens and to pursue others with the gospel.

d. Helping the church feel the weightiness of sin and suffering. Such exposure to sin's consequences helps to sober and deter the people of God from a careless approach to sin.

e. Praying for those who have turned their backs on God, for their families who have been devastated and for the entire church family to cling to Christ as their only hope as they live in light of the cross on this side of heaven.

5. Maximizes growth.

God grows His bride through suffering. God uses suffering to re-direct our eyes away from our fantasy world where life revolves around us and back to reality where God is on a mission and He has called us to join Him through a radical life with Jesus. Through the course of suffering, God humbles us by showing us our weakness, our sinfulness and our desperate need for our Redeemer. God uses such gospel gatherings where the people of God are informed about the waywardness of His people as a tangible reality check of the spiritual battle that rages relentlessly and as a call to suit up with the armor of God and fight for the souls of one another. The church grows in faith and repentance as it functions according to God's design, as the bride bears the burdens of one another and so fulfills the law of Christ (cf. Gal. 6:2).

Appendix 9.11

Guidelines for Telling the Church

How Do You Tell the Church?

After prayerful consideration, if the elders decide to inform the church about those who have consistently refused Christ and His offer for grace and forgiveness, they will have to work through a number of logistical and pastoral details before they gather the covenant community together to address matters of God's discipline. The pastors will need to address two broad details in their planning: (1) when the church will gather and (2) how the church will be informed and instructed.

When will the church gather?

There are no hard and fast rules for when the church should be gathered to hear matters of discipline. Since church discipline is a matter for the church, not the world, the primary issue church leaders need to decide regarding when to meet is whether they want only church members in attendance. This point will determine when they will present disciplinary situations.

For most churches that were surveyed, unless there was an urgent matter that impacted the entire church, the pastoral situations were announced during regularly scheduled meeting times:

a. During a regularly scheduled Wednesday night prayer meeting.

b. During a regularly scheduled or specially called members' meeting.

c. During any given Sunday night service or during a regularly scheduled Sunday evening set aside for family business.

d. Once a month during alternating Sunday morning and evening services during communion. The first month was used to inform the church so that they might pray for and pursue those who were straying. The second month was used to announce the names of those who have been removed because of their refusal to respond after receiving a final warning. Again, leaders will need to decide if they will present the discipline matters to members and non-members or dismiss all non-members before they proceed with the meeting.

e. Anytime via the on-line members' community. A handful of churches surveyed reported that they inform all of their members through various electronic technologies and church-based social networks. Church leaders need to research the legal liabilities associated with using electronic means to communicate matters of church discipline, especially given the issues of confidentiality.

There are some advantages of telling the church in this way: (1) ensures every member can read about the details of the discipline and not rely on hearing the information second-hand, which might increase the chance of gossip, (2) discipline situations can be communicated immediately versus having to wait for the next scheduled gathering time, and (3) members' meetings or other gatherings do not become associated with church discipline.

There are some disadvantages of telling the church in this way: (1) you cannot duplicate the experience of gathering together as a covenant community, including feeling the overall tone of the discipline, sensing the leading of the Spirit, hearing various expressions of emotions ripple across the auditorium, seeing the non-verbal responses of those witnessing the disciplinary process, and praying with brothers and sisters after being informed, (2) members might miss this unique but essential aspect of community life and (3) the confidential information can be forwarded to anyone with ease. Especially in the age of social networking, those who are being disciplined and those who desire to undermine the church can post derogatory blogs with the electronically-sent discipline information to the world in a manner of minutes. Granted, anyone can post the same blog by scanning a hard copy of any discipline document, but copying and pasting electronic communication only requires the click of a mouse. Ironically, the on-line means of communication, which is supposed to increase effectiveness and perhaps efficiency, can result in more work and chaos for the church in the long run.

Once the church has been informed, some churches follow-up with family members and their respective gospel community with a letter containing the essential elements of what was shared in the church gathering and in the final warning letter sent to the unrepentant person.

How can the church be informed and instructed?

Once the church leaders have decided when and how they will gather the church, the elders will need to plan out the logistics for the gospel gathering where matters of discipline will be addressed. The following aspects for the gathering need to be determined:

1. **Shepherding the church.**
Pastors shepherd through their teaching, leading and caring for the people of God. Here are some specific ways the elders can shepherd the church during this gathering:

   a. *Teaching.* It is essential that the elders offer a brief teaching on church discipline, ensuring that they paint a clear picture of God's redemptive work through gospel relationships, community and the larger church gathering. The elders' teaching needs to anticipate lack of understanding, confusion and even opposition from the members as they sit, reflect upon and experience the public discipline process as the body of Christ. The people of God need to walk away knowing that even though everyone is capable of the sins being addressed, they do not have to live in constant fear of being publicly disciplined because of their everyday struggle with sin if they live a life of ongoing faith and repentance.

   b. *Leading.* For each situation the elders need to carefully and pastorally outline the confirmed Scriptural violations involved and the individuals' ongoing refusal to submit to Christ and His people. The people need to understand that church discipline is not a power play by the elders, where the elders take action against people who fail to yield to their authority, but a redemptive response commanded by Christ in His Word to deal with those who have turned their backs on the living God.

   c. *Caring.* For each situation the elders should present a chronology of the sinful struggles of those who are rebelling against God and of the redemptive pursuit by the church. They should also summarize the intentional efforts of gospel community to help those in need. The people need to see the importance and the beauty of fighting for the souls of one another with the gospel in the relentless spiritual battle that exists between the kingdom of God and the kingdom of evil.

2. **Informing the church.**
The elders will share the names of those who have continually refused to listen to God and His people so that the church will know whom to pray for and pursue. The reality of sin and its consequences sets in deeper when people hear the names of those being disciplined. However, there are times in which the elders may decide not to release the names of those straying from God:

    a.   *Risk of life.* There might be times in which those in rebellion may be suicidal and the shame of public exposure may prompt them to injure or kill themselves.

    b.   *Inconsistent membership process.* If the church does not have a defined membership process where new members are announced on the front end and members are removed and announced on the back end, the church should not announce names since they run the risk of legal action. In such cases, the church leaders need to make the necessary changes to create a consistent membership process so that the church can be informed of such situations in the future as needed.

    c.   *Family concerns.* In some cases, there may be some circumstances where public exposure of a parent may have detrimental impact on the family members, especially children.

3. **Instructing the church.**
The elders will also instruct the church about their "next steps" as the body of Christ should the person repent or should the person continue in sin.

    a.   "Next steps" with repentance and faith. Despite their unbelief and rebellion up to this point, God can bring those who have turned their back on Him to repentance. The elders should outline how the church will respond if those who are being given the final warning should repent.

    b.   "Next steps" with refusal and unbelief. Given the reality of intense spiritual battles, most people do not turn at this point in the struggle. So the elders need to instruct the church of their responsibilities during the final warning period and subsequent removal if those who have been warned refuse to repent and believe. The elders need to remember that most of the church has never been in this situation before and they need to know how they should respond so that their efforts are consistent with God's redemptive work.

    c.   God's consistent call to return. The bride of Christ needs to be reminded over and over again that God continually calls her to return since we, the bride, are prone to wander. The grace of God and the beauty of the gospel are found in God's call to repentance through faith, promising that He will offer abundant compassion and forgiveness to His people through the enduring and redeeming blood of Christ.

4. Mobilizing the church.

The elders should call the church to pray for and pursue those who have turned their backs on God. God works above and beyond what we can ever ask or think (Eph. 3:20) so the pastors need to give the body of Christ a vision of how such redemptive efforts are part of God's redeeming work, even if they do not know or come across those being disciplined. There are amazing stories about how God orchestrates encounters between those under discipline and church members in the most unlikely places or circumstances.

5. Waiting on the Lord.

No one knows God's sovereign will but the elders should call the church to pray and wait with anticipation, knowing that God will accomplish His purposes according to His way and timing. Our God is faithful in the midst of our faithlessness (2 Tim. 2:13). God's justice and holiness will always prevail regardless of the outcome. The elders should also encourage the church to pray for mercy so that the covenant community would experience the privilege of seeing those who are removed be restored. Such restoration enables the church to witness the power of the gospel as God does His transforming work. But if God chooses not to restore them within the waiting period or in a lifetime, God is still faithful and His love is still powerful as He continues His beautiful work of redemption in the rest of the church.

Appendix 9.12

Example Manuscript for Telling the Church[1]

Brief Teaching on Church Discipline

Introduction:

Before we begin this portion of the members' meeting, let us go to the Lord in prayer—to ask for mercy, wisdom, and love ...

God's Story of Redemption

Throughout God's story of redemption we see a cycle we know all too well:

(1) the people rebel, (2) God disciplines His people, (3) the people cry for mercy and (4) God delivers them. Over and over again, we see God deal patiently and graciously with His stubborn and rebellious people so that they might return to Him, receive His compassion and forgiveness and experience His redeeming love. This was true for the Israelites. The same is true for you and me.

God relentlessly disciplines us as His children in our rebellion so that we share in His holiness and love through Christ:

> ... do not make light of the Lord's discipline, and do not lose heart when he rebukes you, because the Lord disciplines those he loves, and he punishes everyone he accepts as a son ... Our fathers disciplined us for a little while as they thought best; but God disciplines us for our good, that we may share in his holiness. No discipline seems pleasant at the time, but painful.

---

1   This example manuscript should be used only as a guide as you prayerfully develop the specific manuscript for your church. You want to make sure the wording, tone and emphasis of your manuscript is consistent with your own church and specific to the details of the situation being addressed.

Later on, however, it produces a harvest of righteousness and peace for those who have been trained by it. (Heb. 12:5-6, 10-11, NIV).

We also see in God's story that He doesn't remove His care from us when He disciplines us; rather He shows His care for us through His discipline. God never gives up on His people.

INFORM AND REMOVE FROM COVENANT COMMUNITY

But the Scriptures are clear that if there are those who persistently turn their backs on God and refuse to listen to Him and His people after numerous attempts and relentless pursuit, the church needs to be informed:

If he refuses to listen to them, tell it to the church; and if he refuses to listen even to the church, treat him as you would a pagan or a tax collector. (Matt. 18:17, NIV)

WHY MUST THE CHURCH BE INFORMED?

1. So that you as the church can be mobilized to pray for and pursue those who have totally rejected God through their lives.

2. So that you and I as the church can be reminded of the deceitfulness and danger of sin.

WHAT DOES IT MEAN TO TREAT SOMEONE AS "A GENTILE AND A TAX COLLECTOR?"

Simply put, to treat someone who once professed faith in Christ as a "Gentile and tax collector" is to no longer affirm them as a follower of Christ and to remove them from the covenant community established by the blood of Christ.

WHAT DOES IT MEAN TO REMOVE SOMEONE FROM THE COVENANT COMMUNITY OF THE CHURCH?

Remove from Covenant Community = Remove Community and Care

When people refuse to trust and obey Christ, they deny Christ as Lord and Savior. Imagine a member of the body of Christ rejecting Christ Himself. As a result, the church can no longer affirm their faith in Christ and we must remove them from the covenant community of Christ.

● Such removal reflects what they have already declared to Christ and His people—they desire to remove themselves from the community and care of God and His people.

- In a shocking and sobering way, the removal also symbolizes "handing them over to Satan." They have already joined the ranks of Satan by refusing to submit to God and His people. This truth is seen in 2 Timothy 2 as it addresses how we are to minister to those who oppose the truth:

  ... hope that God will grant them repentance leading them to a knowledge of the truth, and that they will come to their senses and escape from the trap of the devil, who has taken them captive to do his will. (2 Tim. 2:24-26, NIV)

- But don't miss this point ... God commands His church to remove those who refuse to turn back to Christ and to hand them over to Satan for a very personal and particular purpose—to redeem them by His love:

  When you are assembled in the name of our Lord Jesus ... hand this man over to Satan, so that the sinful nature may be destroyed and his spirit saved on the day of the Lord. (1 Cor. 5:4-5, NIV)

Transition: Given this brief overview of why and how God disciplines us, I will present a church discipline case on behalf of the elders ...

2. CHURCH DISCIPLINE CASE
In the case brought before you tonight, the person involved has refused to listen to the call to return to Christ and the biblical warnings of church leaders and members after multiple attempts. The elders have completed their investigation and it is with much sorrow, the elders bring before you, as the members of City Church, the case of John Smith.

  If he refuses to listen to them, tell it to the church; and if he refuses to listen even to the church, treat him as you would a pagan or a tax collector. (Matt. 18:17, NIV)

Case—In January 2010, church leaders were informed of John Smith's unrepentant adultery (Exod. 20:14; Matt. 5:27-30). After five months of being pursued and loved by his wife Kathy and his City Church family, and after several attempts and warnings from ministry leaders and elders, John still refused to listen to and submit to Christ and chose to abandon his wife and children (1 Tim. 5:8).

So as elders, we are informing you, as the church, about John's adultery and abandonment and his refusal to repent and submit to Christ:

First, Love John by Praying for and Pursuing Him
Prayer is one of the primary ways we can fight for each other's souls and trust in God.

God wants to unleash His power through the prayers of His people.

Second, Love Kathy by Praying for and Supporting Her

By God's grace, Tom and Sharon Davis' small group and other women from this church have been loving and supporting Kathy through all of this.

But as a church we tend to give more time and attention to the ones who have turned their backs on God than on the ones who remain. Let's learn from our mistakes and care for Kathy in such a way she experiences the love of Christ through the body of Christ through prayer and practical ways.

However, if John does not turn back to Christ and contact the elders by June 16, 2010 (4 weeks), then the elders will remove him from City Church's covenant community. Pray for John, for the Lord to grant repentance,

3. QUESTIONS AND WARNING

- **Questions:** We realize this is a lot to take in this evening ... if you have any further questions about God's discipline or what took place tonight, please talk to an elder.

- **Gossip:** We also want to warn you against any gossip, based on what we will discuss tonight—this is a family matter and should not be discussed with anyone outside the church.

- **Be Sobered:** On one hand, we encourage you to be sobered and sorrowful over the reality and consequences of sin.

- **Be Overwhelmed:** On the other hand we also want you to be deeply encouraged and overwhelmed by the power and love of your God, a God who loves you so much that He disciplines you in your rebellion so that you can enjoy His faithful and redeeming love and as a result, glorify God.

4. MOVEMENT IN PRAYER

Let's take five minutes and break up into groups of 3-5 people to pray for John and Kathy and their community. Pray for our entire church family— for the Lord to grant us faith and repentance, humility and love. I will close the time in prayer.

Close in Prayer ...

APPENDIX 9.13

Reminders for Community during the Discipline Process

GOSPEL COMMUNITY GUIDELINES

By the time the elders inform the church about the intentional rebellion of those straying from God, the men and women who have been directly involved have already experienced countless hours of fearful and anxious moments, emotional phone calls and meetings, gospel-filled conversations, inopportune interruptions and faithful prayers. Everyone is tired. If the particular struggle of the friend or family member is not stressful enough, everyone who has been bearing burdens within their community still has to manage the demands and stresses in their own lives. Nevertheless, Christ enables perseverance, strength and hope, especially in His radical mission of redemption.

As with anything that requires endurance, you need to remain focused and remember that God is accomplishing His transforming work in every person in the community, that the enemy is attempting to twist and defile every redemptive thought and activity and that the community needs to care for everyone, not just the ones who experienced the initial sin and suffering.

1. Remember God is Redeeming All of His People.

God exposes our hearts especially during times of frustration and difficulties. When we forget that God is also disciplining us as we bear burdens of others, we can become impatient since things are not happening in our timeframe or according to our plan. God wants us to grow in long suffering. When we focus on the sins of others and not our own, we can become haughty and self-righteous. God wants to grow us in humility. When we grumble about the difficulties of ministry and we argue that we didn't sign up for such headache and heartache, we can become apathetic and want to give up. God wants us to remember the selfless and sacrificial work of Christ on the cross on our behalf. If we fail to remember God's redemptive work in our own lives, we will fail to serve as a means of God's redemptive work in other peoples' lives.

2.   Remember the Devil is After Everyone.

In a similar but contrary way in which the Lord works, the devil wants us to use the efforts of the community to sabotage the gospel through undermining God and His people. Again, it is helpful to remember that whenever you experience any form of distraction through spending inordinate time on tangential issues that fails to get to the cross or get anxious about what may or may not happen in the future, you are being sidetracked and sin may remain hidden. Whenever you find yourself judging others—those you are trying to help, others in your group, or church leaders who are giving oversight—and you begin to blame, take sides, or avoid each other, you are being divided and sin begins to rule. Whenever you find yourself confused, full of doubt, and wanting to give up, you are being deceived and the sinful thoughts and feelings will determine what you see as truth and life. When the devil's strategies are effective, God and His gospel will be undermined and God's people will be derailed in their mission.

3.   Remember to Care for Everyone.

Invariably, those in community will need to be shepherded as they bear the burdens of others around them. Gospel ministry is never meant to be a one-way transaction but a mutual relationship where everyone is giving and receiving.

   a.   Care for yourself.

     Because the spiritual battle requires supernatural weapons supplied only by the Spirit of God,[1] we will burn out if we try to minister in the flesh, even with the best intentions. God wants us to rely upon Him moment by moment by clinging to Christ as we abide in Him, drinking the living waters and eating the bread of life. We can't care for others when we have nothing to give.

   b.   Care for the wounded.

     Because every battle has casualties, you need to tend to the wounded. The casualties generally come about either through enemy attacks targeting one's finances, health, marriage, children, work, or extended family or through the misdirected attacks from friendly forces. Such injuries can be explained by life in a fallen world, our own sinfulness and the constant attacks of the devil. The enemy

---

1   2 Cor. 10:3-5; Eph. 6:10-20.

wants the bride to fight against one another rather than fight for one another. For this and other reasons Jesus commands over and over again, "Love as I have loved you and forgive as I have forgiven you."[2]

c. *Care as God cares.*

Because of our own sin of partiality, we can care more about some than others and we can give preference to those who seem more lovely or influential.[3] Jesus tells us that even the Gentiles love those who love them back. By God's providential wisdom, you may end up caring for or being cared for by the most unlikely person in your community as the people of God come together and engage in gospel ministry to bear the burdens of others. It is beautiful to watch when God's people care for one another without preference—it is a living display of the gospel.

---

2 Eph. 4:31-32; 5:1-2; John 13:34-35; 15:12-17; Matt. 5:43-48; 6:14-15; 18:21-35; 1 John 4:7-21.

3 cf. James 2:1-9; 1 Cor. 12:14-26.

Appendix 9.14

Failing to Shepherd through Pastoral Issues

Ministry is tough. Church leaders often grow weary as they deal with suffering and sin on an ongoing basis. A serious side effect of shepherding fatigue is to pull back from leading and caring for those under care.

Failing to Follow-up and Warn.

The demands of ministry are overwhelming, demanding and relentless. Most pastors strive to be faithful in their God-given responsibilities but there are times in which shepherding issues will not be addressed as needed due to a pastor's overloaded schedule, forgetfulness, fear of not knowing how to deal with a given situation, a dislike of conflict, procrastination, and even "compassion fatigue."[1] However, God makes it clear what He expects from those He places in leadership and He holds them accountable for their pastoral responsibilities.[2] By God's grace, pastors can look to and follow Jesus, their Great Shepherd, as He empowers them by His Spirit to accomplish His will regarding His church.

But God offers a stern warning to those who neglect their shepherding responsibilities. In the same way in which a shepherd who fails to warn and protect his sheep from impending danger is held responsible for the blood of his flock, God warns the watchmen of His people that if they fail to warn the people of their wicked ways, they will be held responsible for the harm they may experience.[3] Given the incessant demands of ministry,

---

1 Compassion fatigue is a term that describes when those who serve others on a regular basis become weary and burned out; consequently, they do not respond to presenting needs despite having a heart of compassion.

2 Ezek. 34; Heb. 13:17.

3 cf. Ezek. 3:18-20; 33:5-7.

church leaders need to look for and equip ministry leaders so that they can help bear the burdens of caring for the bride of Christ.

FAILING TO SHEPHERD THE GOSPEL COMMUNITY.

Even if pastors step into a shepherding situation they can misstep in offering the best care by not shepherding the gospel community involved.

1.   Equipping gospel communities.

One of the best ways to shepherd gospel communities is to show them how the gospel applies to suffering and sin. This particular task cannot be accomplished in a training weekend but requires ongoing preaching and teaching on the gospel life coupled with on-the-ground shepherding where you as a leader can show them how to navigate through the difficulties of life with the gospel. Once you show them through your example, then you need to supervise them until they have a basic understanding and practice of how to minister the gospel in personal and specific ways.[4]

2.   Coordinate and communicate with gospel communities.

In addition to equipping the gospel communities, the pastor overseeing a given shepherding situation needs to coordinate and stay in regular communication with the small group leaders and anyone else involved. Realistically, this is when the on-the-ground training will begin and continue for those in community. Furthermore, before the elders tell the church about the unrepentant person(s) in any given community, one or more elders may need to go to the small group to inform and answer any questions. Since those in the group probably have not been personally involved in this type of situation before, group members may have a number of questions, fears, and doubts that will need to be addressed.

3.   Watch for spiritual warfare within gospel communities.

The church leaders also need to watch for ways in which the enemy may be establishing footholds within the church in spite of good equipping and coordination. Such collateral damage that spins off from the sinful struggles of those rebelling against God can start because of people losing sight of the gospel as they deal with the situation, not agreeing with the leaders' direction or manner in which the situation is being handled, or succumbing to the divisive and destructive influence of the rebellious one(s). The devil scrambles his forces whenever the church steps up by faith to fight for the souls of one another for the glory of God.

---

4   Refer back to "A Three-Prong Approach to Equipping" in Appendix 8 to review the essential components of effective leadership development.

Appendix 9.15

Elders Gathering to Consult and Lead

Dealing With Shepherding Fatigue

1. **Look to the Real Savior.**
Especially after leading through a pastoral situation that results in removal, church leaders can wrestle with their own calling and effectiveness. Leaders can also become weary of the relentless demands of ministry as they experience the chronic brokenness of suffering and sin and deal with difficult situations that seem to result in more heartache than hope. Remember that there is only one Savior but He gives us the privilege of participating in His mission of redemption and so that we can see the power of the gospel to save and change people.

2. **Shepherd God's People.**
Leaders may want to pull away from the intense and ugly aspects of the ground war ministry but it is crucial that they stay the course. God matures His leaders pastorally as they work with others through the difficult struggles of life. God will also grow them personally as they learn more and more about the power and persistence of His love in their own lives as they see their own sin in the lives of others. Remember your calling as a shepherd of God's people.

Part of effective shepherding is to consult and coordinate with your fellow elders and other church leaders. Any one leader will not have the experience required to lead without help from others. Even if a given leader has significant shepherding wisdom, he is prone to have blind spots due to his own sin, overload, or simply not considering a certain biblical or practical perspective. Leaders need to not only consult with one another but also come together to make decisions and lead as a unified team.

But as with every aspect of life and ministry, you need to be intentional about getting with other leaders and chiseling out sufficient time to discuss and pray through the various shepherding issues.

1. **Consulting as Elders.**
In God's wisdom, He called not just one leader but a plurality of elders to oversee each local church.[1] The collective wisdom of elders minimizes overlooking important details and dynamics that could make the difference in how a shepherding situation is handled.

   a. *Organizing the elders.*
   Regarding how the elders are deployed when it comes to church discipline, each church will have to determine what is the best organization for their context. Some churches include all elders in discipline discussions while others establish a designated discipline committee. Other churches will have less formal approaches where the elder assigned to the community addressing the discipline consults with other elders in their shepherding realm while at other churches, the elder or staff leader consults with an executive group of elders who deal with church-wide and legal issues.

   b. *Scheduling a meeting time.*
   Again there are a number of ways in which meeting times are scheduled to discuss new or ongoing discipline cases. Some churches address shepherding situations at weekly or bi-weekly elders meetings but there may be times given the urgency of the situation that an impromptu meeting may need to be called so that the elders can address the situation immediately.

   c. *Reviewing cases.*
   The church leader who is overseeing the presenting shepherding situations should summarize the pertinent details so that the elders can quickly understand and assess the case. It is ideal for the summary to be submitted to the elders for review prior to the meeting but in most cases the briefing takes place during the meeting. The following information should be provided as a minimum:

   i. *What is going on?* A brief overview of the situation.

   ii. *When did this take place?* A chronology of events in timeline format to include location(s).

---

1   The following passages are generally cited when showing that a plurality of elders are assigned to any given church: Acts 14:23; 20:17, 28; 1 Tim. 5:17; Phil. 1:1; Titus 1:5; James 5:14-15; 1 Thess. 5:12; Heb. 13:17.

iii. *Who has been involved?* From the family, gospel community, leadership and anyone else.

iv. *What efforts have been made?* By the church leaders, family and community.

v. *What have been the responses?* By the unrepentant person, others involved in his sin, and his or her family?

vi. *What are the proposed next steps?* Based on all of the information.

vii. *Any questions or insight?* Elders may ask relevant questions, offer additional insights, and request additional information.

The elders will be given a verbal summary in most cases but there are some churches where a written summary is required. Regardless of the review format, the church leader who is overseeing the given pastoral situation must keep detailed notes and electronically file relevant emails and text messages so that he will have a paper trail that corresponds to the chronology of events.

2. Leading as Elders.

After reviewing all of the pertinent information in careful and prayerful discussions, the elders will need to make several decisions. Such decisions are essential in providing pastoral leadership in difficult situations. Here is a list of possible actions that the elders will need to consider in order to escalate the redemptive pursuit:

a. *Issue warnings (Chapter 9, Appendices 9.1-9.7, 10.1)*

b. *Remove from church gatherings (Chapter 10)*

c. *Remove from serving.*

d. *Withhold Communion (Chapter 9, Appendix 9.8)*

e. *Tell the church (Chapter 9, Appendices 9.10-9.12)*

APPENDIX 10.1

Possible Responses after a Warning

Here are some possible responses and issues you need to prayerfully consider:

1. **No Response.**
A failure to respond is a response in itself.

2. **Expressed Anger.**
Despite the fact that this response does not reflect a posture of humility and brokenness, it may show a willingness to talk things out, which may lead to a personal meeting. If subsequent conversations stay tilted toward anger and accusation with an unwillingness to submit to Christ and His Word, then the elders should lovingly stand firm in the gospel and issue another warning so that they might repent and receive the Lord's abundant compassion and pardon.

3. **Expressed Confusion and Doubt.**
Those who have turned their backs on God may wrestle with immense shame and guilt. They may believe the lie that God will never forgive them for their actions, so they either slip into hopeless inaction or resolute rebellion, thinking they have crossed the point of no return. In either case, the gospel speaks to every confused and doubtful thought and emotion that may arise.

4. **Expressed Repentance.**
As a result of the prayers of His people and their intentional redemptive interactions and through the work of the Holy Spirit, hardened hearts may

begin to soften. The elders will need to discern the nature of the expressed repentance.[1]

a. *Godly sorrow.* Sorrow that is from the Lord leads to repentance and a life consistent with the gospel. Those who are repentant should be able to articulate their sin against God and others and trust in Christ fully for hope and change. There should also be a desire to ask for and receive forgiveness from those they have wronged as well as a desire to reconcile relationships affected by their sin. It is important to recognize that those who express repentance at this point will gain more and more clarity as they begin to emerge out of the darkness of sin and their minds are increasingly renewed by the grace of God.

b. *Worldly sorrow.* Those who express remorse may do so out of their flesh rather than by faith. They may regret being caught, publicly exposed, and confronted with the consequences of their sins. They may indicate some willingness to change and submit to Christ and His Word but they may push back on those who are shepherding them and put conditions and limits on what they will and will not do. Over time, they will either move towards godly sorrow or grow embittered or apathetic to the redemptive shepherding process, at which point, they may revert back to their rebellious ways. If the latter response occurs, the elders should warn them once again to repent and return to Christ.

---

1   You will find a more detailed discussion of gospel repentance in Chapter 11.

Appendix 10.2

The Importance of Church Membership

Even though you will not find the term "membership" explicitly stated in the Scriptures, you will read about communities of believers who gather regularly for worship, teaching and caring for one another as they encourage, exhort and serve each other.[1]

If you step back and consider the aspects of the church associated with God's discipline you will see that some form of membership is essential—for the elders to oversee the people God has entrusted to them, for the people who God calls to love one another and for God's process of discipline through His church.

For God's Overseers

God appoints and holds elders accountable for shepherding His people (Acts 20:28; 1 Pet. 5:2-4). How can elders be held accountable for overseeing those under their care unless they know who is in their flock?[2] Additionally, how can elders be "examples to the flock" unless there is regular contact and relationship with those for whom they are responsible?[3] It seems that God's design for His church includes the implicit reality of a membership list or covenant so that God's appointed leaders can effectively shepherd His people.

---

1   To help you think further about the significance and implications of church membership see the following works: Mark Dever, *What Is A Healthy Church?* and *The Deliberate Church*; Jonathan Leeman, *The Church and the Surprising Offense of God's Love: Reintroducing the Doctrines of Church Membership and Discipline*.

2   Heb. 13:17; cf. Jer. 23:1-4; Ezek. 34:1-10; James 3:1

3   1 Pet. 5:3; cf. 1 Cor. 11:1; 2 Tim. 3:10-11

For God's People

God calls His people to lock arms to fight and care for one another in the midst of the battle of life on this side of heaven.[4] Brothers and sisters in Christ who have covenanted together within a local church know with whom they need to make disciples and bear burdens as they encourage and challenge one another with the gospel.[5] Those who have committed to the same church co-labor with one another as they engage in gospel mission while obeying and submitting to the leadership of their elders (cf. Heb. 3:17). Moreover, the overseers protect the purity of the church by affirming the profession of faith in their membership while the people benefit from the variety of relationships and gifts found within those who gather week after week, year after year. It seems that God designed His church with membership in mind for the care and growth of His people through enduring, responsible and committed relationships.

For God's Discipline

God disciplines His people so that they may share in His holiness (Heb. 12:3-11). God's instruction in 1 Corinthians 5 only makes sense within the realm of membership. How can you remove those rebelling against the Lord "from among you" (v. 2), deliver them over to Satan "when you are assembled" (vv. 4-5) and "not to associate" with such unrepentant ones (vv. 9-11) without a designated community of believers associated with membership?

Additionally in 2 Corinthians 2, membership is implied when it is stated that "the majority" punished those who refused to repent (v. 6), and is also implied when the church is called to forgive and love those who have been disciplined (vv. 7-11). It seems that God designed the church to carry out His discipline through a gathering of believers who have covenanted together for the cause of Christ.

---

4   See Appendix 6.1 for extensive overview of God's "one another commands."

5   Matt. 28:18-20; Gal. 6:1-2; Heb. 3:12-14; 10:23-25; 1 Tim. 5:1-16

APPENDIX 10.3

The Significance of Removal for Everyone

Removing someone who persists in rebellion is always a significant and challenging occurrence in the life of any church. It is critical that church leaders look around for the continuing effects of removal that will ripple throughout the community.

SIGNIFICANCE FOR CHURCH LEADERS

Church leaders need to recognize that when they inform the church of those who are relentlessly rebelling against God and when they remove them from covenant community, not only are they following God's will but they are also participating in His redemptive mission. As under-shepherds of the flock, pastors need to remember they are called to follow the leadership of Jesus, the Great Shepherd, who knows all too well the battles that rage not only in the souls of His people but also in the heavenly realms "against the rulers, against the authorities, against the cosmic powers over this present darkness, against the spiritual forces of evil" (Eph. 6:12). Martin Luther, the Protestant reformer, speaks to the necessity of God's discipline carried out by His church:

> For the dear Man, the faithful Bishop of our souls, Jesus Christ, is well aware that His beloved Christians are frail, that the devil, the flesh, and the world would tempt them unceasingly and in many ways, and that at times they would fall into sin. Therefore, He has given us this remedy, the key which binds, so that we might not remain too confident in our sins, arrogant, barbarous, and without God, and the key which looses, that we should not despair in our sins.[1]

---

1   Cited in Mohler, SBJT, 23, Martin Luther, "The Keys," in *Luther's Works* (American Edition), ed. Conrad Bergendoff, gen. ed. Helmut T. Lehmann, Vol. 40 (Philadelphia: Fortress, 1958) p. 373.

Pastors need to remember that such disciplinary action taken in response to ongoing rebellion is part of God's loving and redemptive pursuit. When overseers of God's bride fail to initiate and follow through with one of God's ordained means to "remedy" the soul disorders of His people, they fail to do what is best for those who are unrepentant, thereby cooperating with the schemes of the enemy and becoming guilty of treason against their Savior King.

SIGNIFICANCE FOR GOSPEL COMMUNITY

The men and women who have been involved throughout the weeks and months of heartache have seen the ugliness and the destructiveness of sin up close and in personal ways. In most cases, the men and women who have journeyed with those directly impacted by the ongoing rebellion of the wayward ones have also seen the ongoing redemptive efforts of the gospel community and leadership. Consequently, they can more easily understand the need to remove the community and care from those who have turned their backs on God. However, they and others may still struggle with discipline that seems contrary to the grace of the gospel. Marlin Jeschke, a pastor who has written on this very issue, speaks to this gospel paradox of God's discipline:

> Thus excommunication, rightly practiced, never cuts men off from grace. On the contrary, its function is to prevent persons from anesthetizing themselves against grace. Excommunication is the form under which the church continues to make grace available to the impenitent.[2]

We too readily make grace all about ourselves. We typically praise God for His grace when circumstances conform to our desires and when we receive more than we deserve. But we tend not to see that grace is all about God and His glory. Seldom do we see God's grace when we suffer under His discipline as He humbles us and exposes the wickedness in our hearts. God's grace reigns as it disrupts and causes a redemptive discomfort when God needs to shatter our adulterous hearts. How can such disciplinary action be seen as God's grace? Apart from God's powerful grace, we would be left to our own sinful desires and stubborn hearts. But by God's redeeming grace, He breaks our rebellious hearts so that we can once again enjoy the full joy and everlasting pleasure found in our intimate yet submissive relationship with our Redeemer.

The people of God need to trust in His ways rather than what seems right in our own eyes. The gospel community needs to remember that

---

2   Jeschke. *Discpling the Brother*, p. 105.

those who are unrepentant receive God's discipline because they have chosen to live as enemies of God and His church.

SIGNIFICANCE FOR THE UNREPENTANT ONE

Those removed from the covenant community of the church might see any disciplinary action taken against them as ridiculous, unloving, self-serving, and contrary to the gospel. Paradoxically, the men and women removed under discipline express relief and grief simultaneously. They experience relief because the removal ends the constant pursuit from those in the church and represents the beginning of a "new chapter" in life. They experience grief because they realize all that has gone wrong, all that is being lost, and all that has to be addressed if there is any hope of reconciliation.

More than likely those who refuse to listen and submit to God do not see themselves behaving like the stubborn children of Israel who set out to return to Egypt without asking for the Lord's direction, "to take refuge in the protection of Pharaoh and to seek shelter in the shadow of Egypt" (Isa. 30:2). They would not say that:

> ... they are a rebellious people, lying children, children unwilling to hear the instruction of the LORD; who say to the seers, 'Do not see,' and to the prophets, "Do not prophesy to us what is right; speak to us smooth things, prophesy illusions, leave the way, turn aside from the path, let us hear no more about the Holy One of Israel." (Isa. 30:9-11)

But despite their blindness and wayward desires, God wants them to believe and experience His steadfast love through His unrelenting grace and redemptive pursuit:

> Therefore the LORD waits to be gracious to you, and therefore he exalts himself to show mercy to you. For the LORD is a God of justice; blessed are all those who wait for him. For a people shall dwell in Zion, in Jerusalem; you shall weep no more. He will surely be gracious to you at the sound of your cry. As soon as he hears it, he answers you. (Isa. 30:18-19).

God never loses sight of His mission even when we are blinded by our sinfulness. Not only does He want those whom He disciplines to hear His continual call to return and receive His abundant compassion and forgiveness, but He also wants to remind His people that they are on a journey towards Zion, where there will be no more suffering and shame, where they will dwell forever in the presence of His glorious grace. For those removed who may not be Christian, Christ is offering them the same good news of the gospel so that they too can journey with Him for all eternity.

SIGNIFICANCE FOR FAMILY MEMBERS

For family members, the removal of a loved one from the church can represent the climax of a painful journey marked by great heartache coupled with shattered hopes and dreams. Grief and mourning have ebbed and flowed during the countless times they have prayed for and pleaded with the one being removed, but to no avail. Those closest to the one removed may also struggle in a variety of ways—doubts mixed with regret—"Could I have done anything different ... or "if only ..."; shame and embarrassment—"What will people think of me/us?" or despair—"What do I do now?" "Will everyone avoid me, too?" If there ever is a time for the enemy to establish another foothold, it is now.

The family needs the love and support from their gospel community more than ever after the removal of their loved one. They need brothers and sisters in Christ to remind them that God never grows weary and gives power to the faint (Isa. 40:28-29), God is with them in the midst of their suffering (Ps. 23:4) and Jesus and His Spirit are interceding for them with groans too deep for words (Rom. 8:26, 34). They need to be reminded that bitterness and unforgiveness will harden their hearts, blind them to God's redemptive work and keep them from seeking reconciliation should God bring their loved one back to Christ. They may also need help in practical ways—e.g. household chores, home maintenance, financial matters, parenting help and school and after-school activities. The church needs to remember that for the family members of those removed, life will not return to "normal" in the days, weeks and months that follow.

APPENDIX 10.4

Instructing the Church
how to relate to those removed

Church leaders need to teach the body of Christ about God's discipline and their responsibility as the church. The church needs to understand the big picture of how God redeems His rebellious people through His discipline. They need to understand their role during the redemptive pursuit, particularly in the aftermath of removal. If they fail to understand each of these points, they can inadvertently or purposefully undermine the redemptive process and the leadership of the church, create division and minimize the seriousness of the situation—both the sinfulness of rebelling against God and the severity of being removed from the body of Christ. Remember that God's people cannot effectively engage in His mission if they lack understanding.

To keep from neglecting shepherding responsibilities in the aftermath of removal, church leaders need to develop a plan of care for all involved. In addition to the steps discussed throughout this chapter, here are some summarizing guidelines to consider:

● **Address Any and All Questions and Fears.**
The elders and other ministry leaders should make the time to answer questions and address fears that may arise in the aftermath of the removal. The church can be confused especially in cases where the person who was removed was known throughout the church. Concerns like, "I don't understand why he had to be removed" and fears like, "If it happened to her, it can happen to me as well" have to be addressed. The flesh, the world and Satan can establish a foothold when such questions and fears are not addressed, and as a result, paranoia and division may emerge. Leaders also

need to be on the lookout for members threatening others with church discipline due to their lack of biblical understanding. Remember that God's people need to be shepherded and led.

- **Explain the difference and similarities between dealing with those removed and dealing with those who are unbelievers.**

Is there a difference between how you should treat one who has been removed from membership and a person who has never professed faith in Christ? Yes and no. *Yes*, in that we should take care to avoid and not associate with the one removed from fellowship in the ways already described; whereas, we should not avoid our unbelieving neighbors. Those removed from the covenant community have dishonored God and the church, and their attitude and actions may have confused, even divided the family of God. *No*, in that we should love and pursue those removed from the church in the same way we would with those who have never professed faith in Christ. But know that with those who have been removed, you will be able to use gospel truths with more freedom and weight given their past profession of faith. Such truths can fan the flames of the Spirit within them or help them see that they never truly trusted and submitted to Christ, thus prompting them to seek Christ for salvation.[1]

- **Encourage Persistent Prayer.**

The church leaders should encourage the church to never stop praying for those who have been removed. Persistent prayers will be the primary means of the church's persistent pursuit. This is easier said than done. Some churches will keep the names of those removed on a weekly prayer list to serve as a reminder while those closest to those removed will be more conscious of the ongoing need to pray for them. Remember that the removal is a means for future redemption and does not signify the end of our relationship with them.

- **Interact Redemptively, Not Socially.**

The Scriptures are clear that God calls the church to avoid and not associate with those who refuse to listen and submit to Him. But what does this really look like in everyday life? On one hand, the family of God cannot pretend everything is fine, but on the other hand, such avoidance should not take on a posture of self-righteousness, nor should it be seen as a form of blacklist or punishment, or be used as a means of coercion or manipulation. Instead, such disassociation is meant to simultaneously declare that the person is not right with God and that God and His people are calling

---

1   Edwards, p. 119. Richard Sibbes also writes, "It should encourage us to duty that Christ will not quench the smoking flax, but blow on it till it flames" p. 50.

the person back through faith and repentance. Pastor Steve Viars offers a helpful example of how he relates to those removed from the church:

> We cannot go out to dinner, we cannot go out to the store without running into someone that's been disciplined by this church. That's the value of an ongoing pastoral ministry. Again, we would treat them just like we would an unbeliever. We're going to befriend them. We're not going to walk down the other aisle in the grocery store. We're going to greet them. We're going to love on them. But if that conversation goes beyond a sentence or two my arm is going to be around that person and I'm going to be telling them we love them and are praying for their repentance and we would be so glad to receive them back into our membership and treat them like a person who knows Christ as soon as they repent. I have those kinds of conversations all the time and we train our church members to do the exact same thing so if they continue to be friends with the person who's been disciplined, and many times they do, part of that friendship is regular encouragements to repent.[2]

It is important to remember that there is no "script" that you should or should not say. Some may approach an encounter with those who have been removed with a self-righteousness attitude while others may lean towards fear and avoidance. Instead, allow the Spirit of God and His love to work in and through you. We need to remember that we all are in desperate need for the grace of the gospel. We also need to remember to view the encounter as a redemptive opportunity to reflect the glory and grace of the gospel. Use the description of love in 1 Corinthians 13:4-7 to be your guide in how you and those in your community should interact with those who have been excluded from the church:

a. *Love is patient and kind*—be kind and patient even when they are not.

b. *Love does not envy or boast*—do not envy their situation or boast in your situation even when they do.

c. *Love is not arrogant or rude*—do not be self-righteous or condemning even when they are.

d. *Love does not insist on its own way*—seek their best interest in spite of your discomfort and their selfishness.

e. *Love is not irritable or resentful*—do not be bitter or resentful towards them even if they are.

f. *Love does not rejoice at wrongdoing, but rejoices with the truth*—do not rejoice in their discipline. Rejoice when there is evidence of God's grace.

---

2   Pastor Steve Viars, Faith Baptist Church, Lafayette, IN, during the Church Discipline Interview.

g. *Love bears all things, believes all things, hopes all things, endures all things*—Always believe that God and His gospel are more powerful than their sin and show this in your attitude and actions towards them.

● **Encourage family members**.
Even though the covenant relationships associated with the church are severed, the natural relationships of the family—between spouses and between parent and child—still exist and should still be honored.[3]

a. *Be a light.* Family members have the most interaction with those disciplined if they still live in the same house. Whether they live in the same house or not, family members should reflect Christ when they relate to those who have rejected Christ. God instructs a wife whose husband is disobedient to the Word of God to place her hope in Christ and live out the gospel before her husband so that she may be a redemptive influence on her rebellious spouse.[4] God knows and addresses the sinful realities of marriages.

b. *Care for the children.* Children will struggle when a father or mother is disciplined as a result of refusing to submit to God and listen to His church. More than anything they will grieve the loss of a parent who may have abandoned them, grow bitter at a parent's betrayal or behavior and may develop shame in response to the family situation. The church and the offended parent should spend much time with the children, allowing them opportunities to ask questions, to express their broken hearts, to work through their confusion and to learn how God cares for them in the midst of their suffering. Pray that the children come to know Christ in deeply personal ways through their trials.

c. *Honor parents.* These same children need to be reminded that God calls them to honor and respect their parents in all circumstances. Being hurt does not give them permission to be disrespectful and act out against their parents. God can use the redemptive love and forgiveness of a child to bring conviction and clarity to a wayward parent.

● **Offer guidance for work-related interactions**.
Some men and women in the church may work with or have a developed business relationship with those removed from the church.

---

3   Edwards, Jonathan. *The Works of Jonathan Edwards*, Volume Two. "Sermon V. The Nature and End of Excommunication," p. 120.

4   cf. 1 Pet. 3:1-6.

a. *Work, not socialize.* Work has to go on as usual. If you have to work with or for the person who was removed for disciplinary reasons, you will need to address the unique situation directly. Best case, both of you will agree not to say anything about the church which could serve to damage the testimony and image of Christ's bride in the eyes of the world. Worst case, the one disciplined will take out his frustrations with the church on you and will either keep it between the two of you or will make slanderous remarks about you and the church in front of others at the workplace. Either way, much prayer and grace is needed.

b. *Decide prayerfully.* If you have a business relationship with the one removed, you will need to prayerfully decide whether you want to continue the business arrangement as it currently stands. You will have more freedom if you are a business owner since you have direct responsibility for the welfare of your company regarding your decisions. However, if you are an employee with a company, you may not have any choice but to maintain the business arrangement. Again much prayer and grace is needed.

- **Help in time of need (relational, financial).**
However, keep in mind that you should still extend help so as to protect those removed through extreme times of sickness and issues of safety, as well as food and clothing. You pray that God will use such times to humble them and to show them their desperate need for Christ. Such mercy during times of need reflects the kindness of our redeeming God and can soften hardened hearts and lead to repentance. One word of caution. Be wise when offering aid so you do not help them continue in their sinful lifestyle.

- **Believe that exclusion is necessary.**
Some would argue that the church welcomes any unbeliever to the Sunday services and community events hosted by the church, so why would they exclude anyone from fellowship? As you think about this argument, you should consider several important points.

a. *Exclusion is for those in the church.* Unlike unbelievers, those removed from the church through God's discipline were part of the church and claimed to be a believer yet refused to submit to God and His people.

b. *Exclusion is God's discipline.* God commands such exclusion to help them experience biblical shame associated with sin and the consequences of their rebellion. They cannot enjoy and benefit from the community and care of God's people as they did before they rejected God.

c. *Exclusion protects the church.* Their presence can confuse the body, especially when their conversations with those in the church may be used to gain sympathy or to deceive others. Ministry leaders need to consider the nature of the offense, the potential for divisive influence within the community, and the potential danger posed by the offender when deciding if those removed need to be totally excluded from church gatherings.

d. *Exclusion is redemptive.* You must remember that God commands the church to remove and exclude those who are unrepentant for one purpose: their redemption.[5]

---

5   2 Thess. 3:14; 1 Cor. 5:9-13; 2 Cor. 6:14-17; Titus 3:10.

Appendix 11.1

Legalistic versus Gospel Repentance

As you move toward repentance and restoration with a wayward sheep, it is important to remember what a gospel-shaped view of repentance looks like. Despite the fact that repentance is an ancient and well-worn path, the legalist in all of us can demand or look for the wrong things in repentance.[1] As with all things in life, we cannot rightly understand repentance apart from the gospel message and mission. Here are some helpful distinctions between legalistic and gospel repentance:

1. Repentance *focuses on relationship.* Legalistic repentance focuses on the behavior while gospel repentance focuses on the offense against God (cf. Ps. 51:4).

2. Repentance *flows from God.* Legalistic repentance flows from worldly sorrow that flows from man's shameful or guilt-ridden will, resulting in despair and death, while gospel repentance flows from godly sorrow according to God's redemptive will, resulting in hope and life (cf. 2 Cor. 7:9-10).

3. Repentance *steps out by faith.* Legalistic repentance hesitates out of fear of judgment while gospel repentance steps out by faith believing that there is no condemnation for those who are in Christ (cf. Rom. 8:1).

4. Repentance *seeks Christ.* Legalistic repentance seeks to be made right through ongoing and various means of self-atonement (eg.

---

[1] This section highlighting the differences between legalistic and gospel repentance is prompted by Tim Keller's work on religious versus gospel repentance in his work, *All of Life is Repentance.*

self-condemnation, extreme efforts to keep the law, relentless restitution, etc.) while gospel repentance seeks atonement and forgiveness through the finished work of Christ alone while still taking responsibility to right the wrongs as much as possible (cf. 1 John 1:9; Phil. 2:12-13).

5. Repentance is *honest and humble*. Legalistic repentance might be honest but proud, or humble but dishonest, while gospel repentance discloses everything without defensiveness and leads the person to submit to whatever the gospel calls for so that one can be made right with God and others.

6. Repentance *focuses on redemption*. Legalistic repentance is seen as negative and as something we avoid while gospel repentance is seen as positive and as something we pursue (cf. Heb. 12:7-10). Here is a quick test. Whenever you hear someone's repentance do you focus more on the confessed sin than on the work of God that brought the person to repentance? If you focus more on the sin and what they need to do to avoid sinning in the future, then you may emphasize the person's performance rather than Christ's perfect and finished "performance" on the cross.

7. Repentance *results in gospel fruit*. Legalistic repentance results in little change and little relational intimacy. Why? Because legalistic repentance leads to increasing legalistic efforts to improve performance with limited help. Gospel repentance results in heart change and intimacy with Christ. Why? Because gospel repentance leads to increasing freedom to trust and draw near to the perfect Redeemer with the unlimited help of the Holy Spirit (cf. Ps. 130).

If we fail to understand repentance in light of the gospel, we will not only deepen the legalistic roots within the church but we can also hinder the redemptive work of God's discipline through His people.

APPENDIX 11.2

Example Restoration Plan After Removal[1]

INTRODUCTION[2]

We rejoice in God's powerful and loving mercy in bringing you to repentance. We prayed that we would have the privilege of seeing God restore you to Himself and His people through the redemptive efforts of His church. Before we look at the specifics of your restoration plan, we need to step back and be reminded of God's ever-faithful work of restoration.

GOSPEL RESTORATION

Throughout the Scriptures, God brings His wayward people back to Himself so that He might restore their relationship with Him. Everything about the gospel life is supernatural and is enabled by the Spirit of God—from our awareness, confession, and repentance of sin to our forgiveness and reconciliation with God. Such gospel practices require faith and result in redemptive change for all involved.

In His redemptive story, God primarily pursues and restores His wayward people so that He might restore His relationship with them. In other words, restoration is all about relationship. Not just a relationship

---

1   This example plan should be used only as a guide as you prayerfully develop the specific plan for your church. You want to make sure the wording, tone and emphasis of your plan is consistent with your own church and specific to the details of the situation being addressed.

2   The first three and a half pages of this plan serve as a necessary foundation for the restoration plan. You can reduce this introductory material but consider that those being restored will need a biblical perspective to understand the details associated with the restoration process.

in concept but a relationship where His love and faithfulness meet our sinfulness, and where His righteousness and peace kiss and overwhelm our rebellious hearts (cf. Ps. 85:10-11).

Not only does God restore His relationship with us but He also showers us with His blessings. Because of His steadfast love and mercy (Ps. 51:1) God restores us so that we might rejoice in Him (Ps. 85:6), dwell with Him in His glory (Ps. 85:9), be immersed in peace found only in Him (Isa. 57:19), and be captivated by the joy that comes with His salvation (Ps. 51:12). He also restores us so that our hearts and souls will love and obey Him (Deut. 30:1-6). In other words, God restores us primarily for His glory, but also for our good so we might experience every blessing associated with the supernatural reality of being in relationship with the one true living God. He not only loves us but He delights in us as His children (Zeph. 3:17).

Even though God has given us a clear picture of how He restores His people throughout redemptive history, He also provides specific and concrete instructions in the letters given to the New Testament churches. God makes sure that we connect the dots between the eternal realities of redemption and the temporal realities of suffering and sin within the church so that we can serve as ministers of reconciliation.

> If anyone has caused grief, he has not so much grieved me as he has grieved all of you, to some extent—not to put it too severely. The punishment inflicted on him by the majority is sufficient for him. **Now instead, you ought to forgive and comfort him**, so that he will not be overwhelmed by excessive sorrow. I urge you, therefore, to **reaffirm your love for him**. ... in order that Satan might not outwit us. For we are not unaware of his schemes. (2 Cor. 2:5-11, NIV)

God calls us to forgive, love and reconcile with others by the power and grace of His Spirit, just as He does with us, so that we might reflect Him and His gospel message, and as a result, bring glory to Him. God also knows that Satan can gain a foothold within the church if there is an unwillingness to forgive and a spirit of harshness (2 Cor. 5:11).

WHY USE A RESTORATION PLAN?

A restoration plan is not meant to be "a set of hoops" that you have to jump through to earn forgiveness or a time of testing so that you prove your repentance. Rather this plan is meant to serve as a guide for all of us as we journey together. A restoration plan also serves to care for the ones who were directly impacted by your waywardness, minimizes confusion and frustration for you, and informs and instructs the church how they can best love you.

By the grace of God and by faith, you have come back and expressed a desire to be made right with God and others. We celebrate that! But as the psalmist described himself while in the depths of his rebellion, "I was senseless and ignorant; I was a brute beast before you" (Ps. 73:22, NIV). In some situations, God can bring about immediate clarity and wisdom but in most cases there may still be blindness due to the disorienting haze of sin. Even though, by His grace, you see your overriding need for your Redeemer, you need time to journey with brothers and sisters in Christ as God untwists your confused thinking, sheds light on your sinfulness and rekindles your affections for Christ. This journey takes time but it is all part of the path of repentance.

A Growing Repentance

This notion of ongoing and increasing repentance does not apply only to you but to each one of us. Let's see if you can relate to the following dynamic. As God brings more and more clarity and conviction of your sinfulness, you are able to confess more fully. As you develop a growing understanding of your sinfulness, you will become more desperate for Christ and His finished and gracious work on the cross. As you grow in your personal understanding of the cross of Christ, you will experience and be compelled more and more by His love. As you grow in believing God's love for you, you will turn to Him more fully and more frequently in the midst of your ongoing struggles and temptations. With each cycle, your repentance grows deeper, more frequent, and comes with greater fervor.

Our ongoing growth in repentance flows from our growing understanding of God's mercy. Believing more and more that God laid every bit of our wickedness onto His Son who nailed it to the cross and covered it with His blood makes the reality of turning back to Christ in repentance more and more attractive. Even more, although God knows the depths of our sin, He does not reveal the full weight and wickedness of our sins all at once, for if He did, we would be utterly overwhelmed. God reveals our sinfulness incrementally, showing us more of our wickedness while showing us more of His love. This increasing exposure of our sin and His love leads to increasing repentance. It seems most merciful that our Redeemer will not reveal the fullness of our sins until He reveals the fullness of His glory, when we are finally immersed and secured in His glorious grace as we dwell together for all eternity as His consummated bride.

Gospel Fruit Associated with Repentance

God graciously brings about our repentance by the power of His Spirit.[3] Because His Spirit works continually in us, we can expect to see gospel

---

3   cf. 2 Cor. 7:9-10; James 4:7-10; Joel 2:12-13

fruit associated with our intimate relationship with Christ (John 15:1-17; Gal. 5:22-23). Consequently, every one of us as God's children should have a desire and willingness to:

- Submit to and obey Christ and His Word with increasing humility, gentleness, patience, and diligence to preserve the unity and peace of the church.[4]

- Confess general and specific sins committed against God and others while developing a growing sense of God's mercy and our wickedness.[5]

- Seek forgiveness and reconciliation with those impacted by our sinful decisions and actions.[6]

- Submit to and follow the elders' leadership in and through the life of the church.[7]

Your restoration is not based on doing everything perfectly. God knows that we all struggle to live in obedience by faith. But He has given us His Spirit so that we might see and believe His goodness and love as expressed through His Word, even through His commandments. His Spirit also enables us to see, confess and repent of our rebellion against Him.

Please know that the things listed above are expected of every follower of Christ so we are not asking of you anything different from what God asks of all of His people. Therefore, should you develop a relentless hardness of heart expressed by apathy, arrogance or willful disobedience without repentance, know that your restoration will be delayed. Again, we are committed to fight for you and with you as we all press on in the fight of faith.

OUTLINE AND DETAILS

John, the following is a proposed outline of your restoration process approved by the elders. We will not impose a timetable on your restoration but anticipate the process will take some time due to the severity and duration of your sin against God, your wife and family, and your church family. The elders worked with Kathy in developing some of the details associated with the plan.

- *Sunday Gathered and City Church Events*—We encourage you to attend any of the Sunday gathered services with your family. You are also

---

4   Eph. 4:1-3; Col. 3:1-17; 1 Pet. 1:2, 13-16

5   Ps. 32; Prov. 28:13; 1 John 1:9

6   Matt. 5:23-24; Mark 11:25; Rom. 12:17

7   Heb. 13:17

encouraged to attend any City Church events such as the Medical clinic, Fall Festival, etc.

- *Communion*—Because you were removed from membership through church discipline, we ask that you do not take communion at this point in your restoration process. We are eager to see the fruit of repentance and restoration in your life as we journey in community with you, just as we would with a new believer.

- *Communication and Interaction with Kathy*—You are free to communicate with Kathy so that you can work towards reconciliation. Those overseeing your restoration will be in regular contact with Kathy to ensure she is comfortable with your interactions during the restoration process.

- *Small Group*—You are free to re-enter Tom and Sharon's small group. They look forward to journeying with you as a gospel community so that everyone can experience God's redemption. They will walk together with you to live out the gospel focusing primarily on your relationship with God and secondarily on your relationship with others—friends and family as appropriate.

- *City Church Members*—The church leaders will communicate your desire for reconciliation at our next member's meeting, and share some of the details of your reconciliation process. This won't be full restoration, but the first communication is to ensure that there isn't confusion regarding your presence in the gathering and wider community, enabling the body to pray for you and cheer on your restoration.

- *Service*—You will be allowed to serve in Mercy Mondays if you choose and if you do, a City Church member will accompany you as you serve our neighbors in the surrounding community.

- *Counseling and Redemption Group*—In order to work through your struggles with suffering and sin, we ask that you enter into weekly gospel counseling through City Church Counseling and to participate in the next Redemption Group. If you choose to seek help from an outside resource, we ask you provide a written consent so that a church leader can be periodically updated by the outside resource.

- *Work and Restitution*—You will be expected to work full-time during this restoration process to provide for yourself so that you will experience a critical aspect of biblical manhood. You will also need to meet with a financial counselor to work out a budget and debt-reduction plan.

- *Review and Enforce*—We want to ensure you understand and submit to every aspect of this restoration plan approved by the elders. If you fail to complete this restorative process you will not be restored as a member. Depending on the reasons for not completing this process, you may not be permitted to take part in any aspect of City Church. This restoration plan is subject to adjustment as the church leaders see necessary.

- *Complete and Celebrate*—If and when you complete this restoration process, we will announce your restoration to fellowship in a member's meeting so that we can rejoice and celebrate God's powerful and beautiful redemption.

I have read, understand, and agree to all of the terms of this restoration plan, by the grace and mercy of God.

Printed Name	Signature	Date
Printed Name	Signature	Date
Elder Printed Name	Elder Signature	Date

APPENDIX 11.3

Establishing a Redemptive Community

BACKGROUND

There are times when it is not appropriate for those who are being restored to be placed in a regular small group given their ongoing struggle with sin and unbelief and so it would be helpful to have a special small group set up for them. It is not uncommon for those who have turned their backs on God for some length of time not to see the realities of their sin and how they have hurt those around them even though they expressed repentance. Depending on the depth and duration of their waywardness, they may be on the path of repentance for months before they can fully see their sin and their need for Christ. The elders will need to decide whether the person's involvement in a regular community group will cause confusion and division due to their spiritual instability.

GROUP MEMBER SELECTION CRITERIA

- Those selected should have a clear understanding of the gospel for their own lives and be intentional about helping others to live out the gospel, as demonstrated in community. They should demonstrate the ability to comfort and confront others with gospel truths in love as they address issues of unbelief and lies with each other.

- Those selected should have a clear understanding of the messiness of redemption since there will be many struggles of sin and suffering throughout the process.

- Those selected need to have a clear understanding of biblical man-hood (or womanhood) and relationships since many issues related to manhood (or womanhood) will need to be untwisted and redeemed within the context of relationships.

- Those selected should commit to this redemptive community for at least six months.

GROUP SIZE

- The group leader needs to ensure there are enough people involved so that no one person is carrying the ministry load and the group is able to handle the various needs of the restoration process.

- The group should consist of a minimum of 4-5 people, to include the one being restored. This size group ensures that the burdens and responsibilities associated with the restoration can be distributed among a number of people and also allows for a variety of interests and gifts within the group.

ROLES AND RESPONSIBILITIES

- Each person should commit to pray consistently for one another, especially for the one being restored—specifically the person's relationship with God and his growth in the gospel through ongoing faith and repentance.

- Each person should commit to spend regular time with the one being restored on a weekly basis outside of the group time, seeking to enjoy some aspect of the gospel life with the person, such as work, worship, Bible study, prayer, and interacting with gospel intentionality.

- If the one being restored is living at a rescue mission or a rehab facility, visit the person in accordance with the prescribed visitation hours.

- This intentional redemptive community should be in place formally until the one being restored is approved to join a regular small group.

GROUP LEADER'S RESPONSIBILITIES

- The group leader should take into account each person's gifts and talents and coordinate their efforts to offer the one being restored constant and well-balanced redemptive community.

- The group leader should keep the elder overseeing the restoration process informed of any significant developments, to include times of great blessings and struggles.

- The group leader should keep abreast of each of the group members serving in this restorative process so that he is aware of the quality and consistency of care being offered, as well as checking on each group member's well-being.

- The group leader should have a copy of the official restoration plan agreed to and signed by the one being restored and the City Church elders.

OTHER ASPECTS OF THE RESTORATION PROCESS

- If the one being restored is participating in a rescue mission program or in a rehab center, take the time to learn about the participant's requirements to serve and contribute to the specific community. You can learn about such requirements by talking to the program director and by reading the associated materials.

- The elder overseeing the restoration process, or one appointed by the elder, should meet with the one being restored on a regular basis for gospel care and counseling.

- Those directly involved in the redemptive community will be briefed on the restoration plan that was agreed to and signed by the one being restored and the church elders.

APPENDIX 11.4

Example Manuscript for a Restoration Celebration[1]

BRIEF TEACHING ON GOD'S DISCIPLINE THROUGH THE CHURCH
Before we talk about discipline, let me review God's story of redemption so that we can be reminded of a bigger story being played out in our everyday lives ...

- *Creation*—God began human history by creating heaven and earth, including the first man and woman. But it didn't take long before ...

- *Fall*—Adam and Eve rejected God's Word and believed the lies of the enemy. Every person since then has an inborn rebellion against God.

- *Redemption*—God knew we were helpless and incurable in our sin condition so He sent Jesus as our Redeemer, to rescue us from our slavery to sin and to reconcile us with our God through His finished work on the cross.

  - It is important to remember that God is redeeming us through every detail and difficulty of our life stories as we journey towards home.

  - God is also redeeming us as we live life together as the family of God, as we help one another to live out the gospel.

---

1   This example manuscript should be used only as a guide as you prayerfully develop the specific manuscript for your church. You want to make sure the wording, tone and emphasis of your manuscript is consistent with your own church and specific to the details of the situation being addressed.

- *Consummation*—But the cross is not the end of the story.

  - At the end of time, God will consummate the marriage between Jesus Christ and His bride, the church, and He will dwell with us and we will dwell with Him in perfect, intimate union:

    Then I saw a new heaven and a new earth, for the first heaven and the first earth had passed away, and there was no longer any sea. I saw the Holy City, the new Jerusalem, coming down out of heaven from God, prepared as a bride beautifully dressed for her husband. And I heard a loud voice from the throne saying, "Now the dwelling of God is with men, and he will live with them. They will be his people, and God himself will be with them and be their God. He will wipe every tear from their eyes. There will be no more death or mourning or crying or pain, for the old order of things has passed away." He who was seated on the throne said, "I am making everything new!" (Rev. 21:1-5, NIV)

GOD'S STORY OF REDEMPTION SERVES AS THE CONTEXT TO UNDERSTAND HIS DISCIPLINE.

- Because of our ongoing struggle with sin, we demand our own way and want God's story to revolve around us. We want to be the hero of our story and we want God to play His part according to our script.

- But the great news of the gospel is that our deepest and most persistent sins can't even separate those who are in Christ from the love of God.

  Who shall separate us from the love of Christ? Shall trouble or hardship or persecution or famine or nakedness or danger or sword? ... No, in all these things we are more than conquerors through him who loved us. For I am convinced that neither death nor life, neither angels nor demons, neither the present nor the future, nor any powers, neither height nor depth, nor anything else in all creation, will be able to separate us from the love of God that is in Christ Jesus our Lord. (Rom. 8:35, 37-39, NIV)

  - But our holy God loves us too much to allow our ongoing rebellion to go unchecked. God disciplines us because He wants us to experience lasting joy and perfect love found only in our relationship with Jesus.

    ... do not make light of the Lord's discipline, and do not lose heart when he rebukes you, because the Lord disciplines those he loves, and he punishes everyone he accepts as a son... Our fathers disciplined us for a little while as they thought best; but God disciplines us for our good, that we may share in his holiness. No discipline seems pleasant at the time, but painful. Later on, however, it produces a harvest of righteousness and peace for those who have been trained by it. (Heb. 12:5-6, 10-11, NIV)

How Does God Discipline Us? Through His Word and People.

- Has God ever convicted and challenged you as you <u>read</u> or <u>listen</u> to His Word?

    For the word of God is living and active. Sharper than any double-edged sword, it penetrates even to dividing soul and spirit, joints and marrow; it judges the thoughts and attitudes of the heart. (Heb. 4:12, NIV)

- God also disciplines us through His people in gospel community. This is why He gave us the "one another commands."

    See to it, brothers, that none of you has a sinful, unbelieving heart that turns away from the living God. But encourage one another daily, as long as it is called Today, so that none of you may be hardened by sin's deceitfulness. (Heb. 3:12-13, NIV)

Unfortunately ...

There are times in which God's people continue to rebel against Him despite repeated efforts to **pursue** them and **persuade** them to return to Christ to receive abundant compassion and pardon.

In these situations, God commands the church to treat such rebels as those who do not believe in God:

    ... if he refuses to listen even to the church, treat him as you would a pagan or a tax collector. (Matt. 18:17b, NIV)

What does it look like for the church to treat someone as "a pagan and a tax-collector?"

- The apostle Paul gives the church some guidance in these situations:

    When you are assembled in the name of our Lord Jesus and I am with you in spirit, and the power of our Lord Jesus is present, **hand this man over to Satan ... you must not associate** with anyone who calls himself a brother but is sexually immoral or greedy, an idolater or a slanderer, a drunkard or a swindler. **With such a man do not even eat... Expel** the wicked man from among you. (1 Cor. 5:4-5, 11, 13, NIV)

- Throughout history, the church has treated those who refuse to submit to God as a "Gentile and tax-collector" by removing them from the covenant community of the church.

Removal from Covenant Community = Removal from Community and Care

- But let's think about this removal. When the church removes those who refuse to listen to and submit to God and His people, the removal reflects what they themselves have already declared against Christ and His people—they desire to live apart from the community and care of God and His people.

- This also holds true when the church is directed to "hand them over to Satan." They have already joined his ranks by refusing to submit to God and His people. God clearly teaches in James:

   You adulterous people, don't you know that friendship with the world is hatred toward God? Anyone who chooses to be a friend of the world becomes an enemy of God. (James 4:4, NIV)

- But don't miss this point ... God commands His church to remove those who have turned their backs on Him so that He might redeem them in their rebellion through His discipline:

   When you are assembled in the name of our Lord Jesus ... **hand this man over to Satan**, so that the sinful nature may be destroyed and his spirit saved on the day of the Lord. (1 Cor. 5:4-5, NIV)

QUESTIONS AND WARNING

- We realize this is a lot to take in this evening ... if you have any further questions about God's discipline, please talk to an elder afterwards. We want to make sure that you understand the mercy and love expressed by God's discipline.

- We also want to warn you against any gossip, based on what we will discuss tonight.

- On one hand, we encourage you to be sobered and sorrowful over the reality of suffering and the consequences of sin.

- On the other hand we also want you to be deeply encouraged and overwhelmed by the power and love of your God, a God who loves you so much that He disciplines you in your rebellion so that you can enjoy His faithful and redeeming love and as a result, glorify God.

TRANSITION ...

- In 2009, City Church removed eight people from the covenant community of the church. It was a painful season for us as a church, but God grew us as we submitted to His leadership because we were convinced that God's redemptive discipline reflects His love.

- Since then, the elders have been asking God to bring them and others back to Christ so that we as the church could see and experience the full cycle of God's redemptive work.

- Since 2009, one woman who was removed in March 2009 was restored earlier this year by God's grace.

- Tonight, we have the privilege to celebrate God's redeeming work as He restores John Smith back to the body of Christ.

- God is answering our prayers! So let's keep praying for those you know who have been removed from City Church's covenant community.

INVITE UP THE MEN FROM REDEMPTIVE COMMUNITY ON STAGE

LET ME SHARE A BRIEF OVERVIEW OF GOD'S REDEEMING WORK WITH JOHN ...

- **In June 2010**, John Smith was removed because of his unrepentant adultery, one month after the church was informed and John was given his final warning.

- **In October 2010**, four months after being removed, God's powerful and persistent love enabled John to begin his journey of repentance as he approached the elders and asked to be restored to God and to City Church.

- **In October 2010**, John agreed to a restoration plan that included a redemptive community of men—Tom Davis, Brian Smalley, George Connelly and Pastor Greg—who have been meeting weekly with John on Sunday afternoons, encouraging and challenging one another with the gospel.

- John has also received much love and support from his wife Kathy and his children.

- **Back in May 2010**—Larry Perkins, a City Church member, sat and listened to how God was disciplining John through the church. The Lord compelled Larry to pray for John as he sat and listened to Pastor Greg encourage the church to pursue and pray for John before he was finally removed. Since October 2010, Larry established intentional times of eating and working with John so that he could encourage John with the gospel.

- **What is so beautiful** is that the elders were not even aware of how God was using Larry to redeem John until recently.

- During this restoration process that began in October 2010, John recognized and took responsibility for his past sinfulness, confessed and asked for forgiveness from God and those he hurt and sought reconciliation on the basis of the grace and righteousness of Christ.

JOHN SMITH'S RESTORATION:
City Church family, are you ready to celebrate?

- John, the elders have prayerfully overseen your journey of faith and repentance as others in your gospel community have encouraged and challenged you with the gospel. We can affirm your profession of faith in Jesus Christ and your desire to trust and obey Him. Does this mean you will never struggle with unbelief and rebel against God? Not at all. You, as well as all of us, will continue to struggle to live by faith on this side of heaven. But because you are in Christ, by the powerful and gracious work of His Spirit, you will continue to turn back to Him in repentance for life and love.

- We celebrate your renewed relationship with Christ and we welcome you back to City Church's covenant community.

- To symbolize this moment, we will ask you to sign the Membership Covenant. The covenant highlights your responsibilities to City Church and our responsibilities to you.

JOHN SIGNS CHURCH COVENANT

- John, as a member in right standing, you may also partake in communion and enter back into the City Church community without any restrictions.

- One of my high points of John's restoration process was when he read a portion of his journal entry written while he was staying with his brother in Chicago. We asked John to share his journal reflection and prayer with you so that you might get a glimpse of God's powerful and merciful work in bringing him to repentance.

JOHN READS JOURNAL REFLECTION AND PRAYER (DIRECT OTHER MEN TO RETURN TO THEIR SEATS)

TRANSITION TO COMMUNION:
We are going to close our time by remembering the finished and complete work of Christ on the cross through communion. It will be a beautiful time of sharing the symbolic meal together as a family, as one body, the bride of Christ.

Allow the Spirit of God to help you examine your hearts, your relationship with God and your relationships with others and confess any sins God may reveal and turn to Him for mercy and grace so that you do not eat and drink judgment upon yourself.

- I pray we will all have a renewed understanding of our desperate need for Christ and the transforming work of the Holy Spirit so that we might live by faith in Christ.

ON THE NIGHT HE WAS BETRAYED...

- He took bread and when He had given thanks, He broke it and said, "This is my body which is for you. Do this in remembrance of me."

- In the same way, He took the cup, after supper saying, "This cup is the new covenant in my blood. Do this, as often as you drink it, in remembrance of me."

We will serve communion first to John and the men who have been in his life, then you can make your way to the stations around the auditorium.

CLOSE WITH A SONG OF CELEBRATION

APPENDIX 12

Minimizing your legal liability

Church leaders need to be wise as they engage in gospel ministry, recognizing the law of the land and being aware of details and practices that minimize legal liability. The following guidelines will help you to review your current policies and practices. It is always wise to have a trusted lawyer, who understands the nature and mission of the church, to review any relevant documents that may be referenced during church discipline.

1. Ensure church covenant, church by-laws, and disciplinary guidelines address key issues:

    a. A member waives the right to withdraw membership unilaterally (otherwise the accused can avoid discipline by slipping out the back door).

    b. Church discipline will be carried out even after an unrepentant person withdraws from involvement with the church. You may consider adding the following statements to your church by-laws:

    "If a member withdraws from membership while the subject of a pending disciplinary action according to Matthew 18:15-17, such withdrawal shall not cancel the Elders' authority to complete the appropriate disciplinary action."

2. Ensure regular attendees are made aware of church discipline guidelines through the church's by-laws, membership class material, and church covenant. You may consider adding the following statements to the following documents and sections:

a. Church By-Laws, Section on Church Discipline:

"The methods described here also cover any and all disputes or claims arising from or related to church membership covenant, doctrine, policy, practice, counseling, and discipline, including claims based on civil statute or for personal injury. By joining this church, all members agree that these methods shall provide the sole remedy for any dispute arising against the church and its agents, and they waive their right to file any legal action against the church in a civil court or agency."

b. Church Covenant:
Church Leaders covenant to the following ...

"We covenant to exercise church discipline when necessary (Matt. 18:15-20; 1 Cor. 5; Gal. 6:1-2)."

Church Members covenant to the following ...

"I covenant to follow the biblical procedures of church discipline and submit myself to discipline as I strive to live out the gospel in community (Matt. 18:15-20; Gal. 6:1-5). If I withdraw from membership while the subject of pending disciplinary action according to Matthew 18:15-17, I expressly consent and submit to the elders' continuing authority to complete the disciplinary process set forth in our church by-laws."

c. Membership Agreement Form—"By signing this form, I indicate my agreement with the church by-laws, doctrinal statement, and covenant, and agree to live, teach, and provide counsel in accordance with and not contrary to these documents. My responsibility will be to notify the church elders if at anytime I can no longer commit to these documents, or if I have any questions, comments, or concerns regarding [name of church]."

d. If the elders are aware of the offender going to another church, they are obliged to inform the new church of the offender's status. You may consider adding the following statements to your church by-laws:

"If a member withdraws from membership while the subject of a pending disciplinary action according to Matthew 18:15-17 and begins attending another church, the Elders are obliged to inform the new church of the offender's status."

e. The elders have delegated authority to oversee the discipline process, to include investigating the situation once they are informed, leading in the redemptive process, and informing the church of the name of the offender, the general nature of the offense, and the action steps to be taken by all members.

3. Ensure the following practices are implemented and followed:

   a. Have a consistent membership process—from announcing new members, members who move and those who are removed for discipline reasons.

   b. Summarize church discipline policies through membership classes, membership interviews, and the church covenant.

   c. Teach regularly on church discipline.

   d. Equip your gospel communities to engage in everyday mission with one another.

4. Ensure church discipline is carried out in a redemptive, biblically faithful manner:

   a. Follow church discipline guidelines consistently.

   b. Always act in a loving, patient, and redemptive manner.

   c. Never show favoritism.

   d. Always speak the truth.

   e. Communicate only with people who have a legitimate right to know.

   f. Substantiate any unproven allegation before taking public action.

   g. Base decisions on clearly articulated biblical grounds.

   h. Always keep restoration as the ultimate goal.

   i. Consider precautions when informing the church:

      i. Carry out church discipline issues within a gathering of your covenant community, with members only.

      ii. Remind members not to gossip or talk to anyone about what is shared in a members' meeting regarding church discipline since this deals with family business.

      iii. Videotape or audiotape the scripted presentation to protect against possible defamation charges.

Acknowledgments

Now more than ever I am embracing the significance and beauty of God's bride, the church. Apart from God and his people, this book would not be remotely possible. God continues to show me the importance of being committed to a covenant community known as the local church. God has been helping me to understand his church not conceptually, as the subject matter of a book or as the means through which God's discipline is accomplished, but as the living and breathing testimony of God's profound and powerful gospel.

As with any endeavor, God has used specific people to bear burdens and to encourage me during the various phases of this work. First, I am indebted to the pastors and members at Sojourn Community Church, as we have journeyed together, understanding and experiencing God's redeeming work through his living Word and people. We repeatedly acknowledge that God is doing an amazing work in spite of our inadequacies. God has been growing us through the challenges of everyday gospel ministry as He overwhelms us by the immense suffering and sin of life and by his relentless and transforming grace. Sojourn has supported me in numerous ways throughout the months of writing, in particular through prayer and encouragement, along with the time and space to read, reflect and write.

Knowing that my experience with church discipline was limited to Sojourn, I knew I needed to broaden and deepen my pastoral experience on this aspect of the church. I had the privilege of surveying ten groups of churches from different denominations and networks through a one and a half hour telephone interview involving two to four pastors, all who had experience in shepherding God's people through church discipline. Special thanks to the following pastors who shared their hearts with a spirit of humility and grace: (Sovereign Grace) Andy Farmer, Covenant Fellowship, PA; Corby Megorden, Covenant Life, MD; Mark Lauterbach, Grace Church. CA; Vince Hinders, Sovereign Grace Church, VA; (Texas Group) Lee Lewis, Village Church; Jerry Clark, Denton Bible Church; Patrick Peyton, Stonegate; (Southern Baptist Group) Jonathan Leeman, Capitol Hill Baptist Church, Wash. D.C.; Andy Davis, First Baptist Church, Durham, NC; (Presbyterian Group) Marion Clark, 10th Presbyterian, PA; Scotty Smith, Christ Community Church, TN; (Midwest Group) Rick Donald, Harvest Bible Chapel, IL; Todd Augustine, College Church, IL; Joe Bartemus, College Park Church, IN; (Acts29 Group 1) James Noriega, Mars Hill, WA; Bob Thune, Coram Deo, NE; John Ryan, Summit Community Church, MO; (Acts29 Group 2) Kevin Galloway, Countryside Church, IN; Phil Taylor, Terra Nova, NY; Joel Lindsey, Journey Church, MO; (Missional Community Group) Abe Mysenburg, Soma, WA; Michael Tinker and Jonny Woodrow, The Crowded House Network, England; (Biblical Counseling Group) Steve Viars, Faith Baptist, IN; Dan Dumas, Grace Community Church, CA; (Scotland Group) Derek Lamont, St Columba's Free Church of Scotland; Calum MacInnes, retired pastor of a APC Church in Inverness; David Court, New Restalrig Church of Scotland, Edinburgh. I was deeply encouraged by these pastors since they represented a growing number of churches that are faithfully carrying out God's discipline through the church.

Editing is a grueling process but much love and thanks goes to Carol Steinbach, Luke Daugherty and John van Eyk for their careful and gracious work as they made the experience a true blessing. Endless thanks goes to Ryan Brandt who helped with critical research and Crystal Sridhar for formatting and printing the multitude of rough drafts so that my "reading team" could weigh in and offer their helpful feedback—Greg Allison, Rusty McKie, James Santos, Mike Wilkerson, Andy Farmer, Bobby Gilles and Ben Lawson.

Thanks also to Willie MacKenzie and Christian Focus for catching the vision and offering an opportunity to create this work.

Much gratitude is owed to those who journeyed with Karen and me in community over the long months of writing— Mike and Cindy Hynes, Brandon and Laurie Hochhalter, Tim and Gretchen Dillman and John and Ginny Tackett. The conversations, meals, prayers, encouragements and space to create were invaluable.

I am thankful for regular family gatherings with our children Ryan, Whitney and Ashley and Jesse along with our grandson Asher. Times around the dining room table always provided comic relief and served as a reminder that life is more than work.

Words cannot express my love for Karen, my earthly bride of nearly three decades. She has journeyed with me for most of my life and reflects our Redeemer through the way she faithfully loves me in spite of knowing me. She is my biggest "cheer-leader" and "prayer warrior" as God's gift to me. I praise God that He has given us the privilege of experiencing his redemptive work as "one flesh."

I will greatly rejoice in the LORD;
my soul shall exult in my God,
for he has clothed me with the garments of salvation;
he has covered me with the robe of righteousness,
as a bridegroom decks himself like a priest with a beautiful headdress,
and as a bride adorns herself with her jewels.

For as the earth brings forth its sprouts,
and as a garden causes what is sown in it to sprout up,
so the Lord GOD *will cause righteousness and praise*
to sprout up before all the nations.

(Isa. 61:10-11)

BIBLIOGRAPHY

Adams, Jay E. *Handbook of Church Discipline*. Grand Rapids, Michigan: Zondervan, 1986.

Bargerhuff, Eric. *Love That Rescues: God's Fatherly Love in the Practice of Church Discipline*. Eugene, OR: Wipf & Stock, 2010.

Baxter, Richard. *The Reformed Pastor*. Carlisle, PA: The Banner of Truth, 1989.

Baxter, Richard. "Directions for Hating Sin." http://www.puritan-sermons.com/

Blomberg, Craig L. *Matthew*. The New American Commentary, Vol. 22. Nashville, TN: Broadman Press, 1992.

Boice, James Montgomery. *The Gospel of Matthew: The Triumph of the King*, vol. 2. Grand Rapids, Michigan: Baker Books, 2001.

Bruner, F.D. *Matthew: A Commentary*. Grand Rapids, MI: Eerdmans, 2007.

Calvin, John. *Commentary on the Harmony of the Evangelists, Matthew Mark, and Luke*, vol. 1. Grand Rapids, Michigan: Baker Books, 2009.

_____ *1 & 2 Timothy & Titus*. Wheaton, IL: Crossway, 1988.

_____ *Commentary on the Book of the Prophet Isaiah*, vol. 3. Grand Rapids, MI: Baker Books, 1996.

_____ *Institutes of the Christian Religion*, Book 1, Philadelphia, PA: The Westminster Press, 1960.

Davies, W.D., and Dale C. Allison Jr. *The Gospel According to Matthew*. In *A Critical and Exegetical Commentary*. Edinburgh: T&T Clark, 1991.

Dever, Mark. *What Is A Healthy Church?* Wheaton, IL: Crossway, 2007.

_____ and Paul Alexander. *The Deliberate Church: Building Your Ministry on the Gospel*. Wheaton, IL: Crossway, 2005.

Edwards, Jonathan. *The Works of Jonathan Edwards*, Volume Two. "Sermon V. The Nature and End of Excommunication," Carlisle, PA: The Banner of Truth, 1995.

Fee, Gordon. *1 and 2 Timothy, Titus, New International Biblical Commentary*. Peabody, MA: Hendrickson Publishers, 1988.

France, RT. *The Gospel According to Matthew*. Leicester, England: Inter-Varsity Press, 1985.

Green, Michael. *The Message of Matthew: The Kingdom of Heaven*. Leicester, England: Inter-Varsity Press, 2001.

Grudem, Wayne. *Systematic Theology: An Introduction to Biblical Doctrine*. Grand Rapids, MI: Zondervan Publishing House, 1994

Hauerwas, Stanley. *Matthew*. Grand Rapids, Michigan: Brazos Press, 2006.

Hughes, Philip E. *Paul's Second Epistle to the Corinthians*. Grand Rapids, MI: Eerdmans, 1962.

Jeschke, Marlin. *Discipling the Brother: Congregational Discipline According to the Gospel*. Scottsdale, PA: Herald Press, 1972.

Lauterbach, Mark. *Transforming Community: The Practice of the Gospel in Church Discipline*. Carol Stream, IL: Christian Focus Publications, 2003.

Leeman, Jonathan. *Church Discipline: How the Church Protects the Name of Jesus*. Wheaton, IL: Crossway, 2012.

_____ *The Church and the Surprising Offense of God's Love: Reintroducing the Doctrines of Church Membership and Discipline*. Wheaton, IL: Crossway, 2010.

MacArthur, John. *The New Testament Commentary: Matthew 16-23*. Chicago, IL: Moody, 1988.

Morris, Leon. *The Gospel According to Matthew*. Leicester, England: Inter-Varsity Press, 1992.

Mounce, Robert H. *Matthew*. San Francisco: Harper and Row Publishers, 1985.

Richardson, Wyman. *Walking Together: A Congregational Reflection on Biblical Church Discipline*. Eugene, OR: Wipf & Stock, 2007.

Ryle, J.C. *Matthew: Expository Thoughts on the Gospels*. Wheaton, IL: Crossway, 1993.

Sande, Ken. *The Peacemaker*, Grand Rapids, MI: Baker, 2004.

_____ and Ken Johnson. *Resolving Everyday Conflict*. Grand Rapids, MI: Baker, 2011.

Sibbes, R. *The Bruised Reed*. Carlisle, PA: The Banner of Truth, 1998.

Spurgeon, Charles. "Prodigal Love for a Prodigal Son," Sermon, March 29, 1891, Metropolitan Tabernacle, Newington, *Spurgeon's Expository Encyclopedia*. Grand Rapids, MI: Baker, 1996.

_____ *The Treasury of David*, Vol. 1, Hendrickson Publishers, 1988.

_____ *The King Has Come*. Old Tappan, NJ: Fleming H. Revell Company, 1987.

Strauch, Alexander. *If You Bite & Devour One Another: Biblical Principles for Handling*. Colorado Springs, CO: Lewis and Roth Publishers, 2011.

SUBJECT INDEX

Scripture Index

THE
TRANSFORMING COMMUNITY
THE PRACTISE OF THE GOSPEL IN CHURCH DISCIPLINE
MARK LAUTERBACH

ISBN 978-1-85792-875-4

The Transforming Community

The Practise of the Gospel in Church Discipline

Mark Lauterbach

Jesus, in his ministry, received the empty, the broken, the lost and the diseased. Mark Lauterbach shows how compassion, mediated through a functioning body of believers, provides the answers to human waywardness and maintains the integrity of the church.

Although this is a book about church discipline, it is really about a spirit-empowered community. Mark uses real situations from his experience to help us turn principles into practice.

> ...a biblically sensitive and pastorally wise book on a subject many people would just as soon forget about: accountability among Christians. True church discipline is not about reinforcing legalisms but rather nurturing believers with a covenanted community of faith.
>
> Timothy George
> Dean of Beeson Divinity School, Samford University, Birmingham, AL

Mark Lauterbach was called to ministry while a student at Princeton University. He has served as a pastor for 31 years and now is the primary preaching elder at Grace Church in San Diego. He is married to Rondi (33 years), and they have three children and three grandchildren.

Tim Cooper and Kelvin Gardiner

PASTORING
the PASTOR

Emails of a Journey through Ministry

"Convicting, compelling and ultimately uplifting"
Colin S. Smith

ISBN 978-1-84550-784-8

Pastoring the Pastor

Emails of a Journey through Ministry

TIM COOPER AND KELVIN GARDINER

Daniel Donford is a new pastor: excited, filled with bright dreams, anticipating a big future for him and his new church, Broadfield Community Church. However opposition and obstacles lie just ahead, and both may end his journey into pastoral ministry before it has really begun. But Dan has an Uncle Eldon, if anyone can see Dan through his trials and disasters, Eldon can. The wisdom he offers, via a series of emails, might just be enough to see Dan transformed into the mature, selfless, loving pastor God wants him to be.

> Convicting, compelling and ultimately uplifting; this insightful probing of the realities of pastoral ministry will make you smile, lead you to pray, and encourage you to persevere.
>
> Colin S. Smith
> Senior Pastor, The Orchard Evangelical Free Church, Arlington, Illinois & President of Unlocking the Bible

Tim Cooper lives with his wife Kate and their four sons in Dunedin, New Zealand. He is Senior Lecturer in the History of Christianity in the Department of Theology and Religion at the University of Otago. Before taking up this post he was the pastor of LifeSwitch, a church in the Hutt Valley on the outskirts of Wellington, New Zealand's capital city.

Kelvin Gardiner has pastored churches in New Zealand, the Philippines and the US. For ten years he led a ministry leadership organization overseeing one hundred US churches and providing pastoral support for overseas mission teams. He and his wife Jill currently offer pastoral care for mission agencies in Asia and Europe.

"This book is a goldmine for anyone involved in helping hurting people."
Edward Donnelly

Helpful Truth in Past Places

The Puritan Practice of Biblical Counseling

Mark Deckard

John Flavel
Jeremiah Burroughs
John Owen
John Bunyan
Jonathan Edwards
William Bridge
Thomas Brooks

ISBN 978-1-84550-545-5

Helpful Truth in Past Places

The Puritan Practice of Biblical Counseling

MARK A. DECKARD

Helpful Truth in Past Places examines the teachings of leading Puritan writers-theologians who were masters at understanding the nature of human beings and applying Scripture in practical ways to help people with their struggles and problems. Looking to Scripture as the final authority, the Puritans grounded their own counselling practices in a proper view of the sovereignty of God and the underlying heart issues of people. By understanding why people struggle and the provision God makes for our struggles, counsellors today will be better equipped to guide those they counsel toward God-appointed solutions.

> This book is a goldmine for anyone involved in helping hurting people. Mark Deckard takes seven Puritan classics and shows how pastor-preachers wrote them to provide biblical counsel which was profound and balanced, realistic and tender. The principles he extracts are as relevant for the 21st century as when they were first expounded. In these pages is something far better than a 'system' or set of counseling techniques. We are invited instead to gain wisdom - a deeper understanding of people & of how God's grace can change and strengthen them through 'the sufferings of this present time'. That the author stimulates us to read the Puritans with new eyes is a bonus. The final chapter is a marvellously useful summary of how and where to find contemporary counsel from the riches of the past.
>
> Edward Donnelly
> Principal of Reformed Theological College,
> Belfast, Northern Ireland

Dr. Mark Deckard serves as Director of Biblical Counseling Training, a ministry of Christian Counseling Associates. He has been involved in leadership and administrative roles with CCA and with the Prison Ministry in York.

Christian Focus Publications

Our mission statement –

STAYING FAITHFUL
In dependence upon God we seek to impact the world through literature faithful to His infallible Word, the Bible. Our aim is to ensure that the Lord Jesus Christ is presented as the only hope to obtain forgiveness of sin, live a useful life and look forward to heaven with Him.

Our Books are published in four imprints:

CHRISTIAN FOCUS

popular works including biographies, commentaries, basic doctrine and Christian living.

CHRISTIAN HERITAGE

books representing some of the best material from the rich heritage of the church.

MENTOR

books written at a level suitable for Bible College and seminary students, pastors, and other serious readers. The imprint includes commentaries, doctrinal studies, examination of current issues and church history.

CF4·K

children's books for quality Bible teaching and for all age groups: Sunday school curriculum, puzzle and activity books; personal and family devotional titles, biographies and inspirational stories – Because you are never too young to know Jesus!

Christian Focus Publications Ltd,
Geanies House, Fearn, Ross-shire,
IV20 1TW, Scotland, United Kingdom.
www.christianfocus.com